relationship between what have come to be seen as our clashing Red and Blue cultures." —Harvey A. Silverglate, cofounder and director of the Foundation for Individual Rights in Education and coauthor of *The Shadow University: The Betrayal of Liberty on America's Campuses*

"Naomi Schaefer Riley's investigation into whether a common faith can bridge the racial gaps on a college campus yields fascinating results. Her account of the missionary generation's attitudes on race is just one of a number of features that make this balanced, well-researched book a must-read for anyone interested in America's cultural and political future."
—Abigail Thernstrom, member of the U.S. Commission on Civil Rights and author of *No Excuses: Closing the Racial Gap in Learning*

"Naomi Schaefer Riley has written a thoughtful, well-reported account of the way in which the nation's private religious schools are coming to terms with issues of the day—and issues of religion. She counters many secular stereotypes that religious schools—Jewish, Mormon, or Evangelical Christian—are populated by intellectual dodos and that they are indifferent to the concerns of modern culture. On the other hand, she shows that very few of the religious schools in the U.S. are likely to inculcate strictly sectarian values, and that, where they try hard to, the results are mixed. This book is a welcome addition to the debate over the contribution of religiously based schools to education in America."
—David Aikman, author of *Great Souls: Six Who Changed a Century* and *A Man of Faith: The Spiritual Journey of George W. Bush*

"This book offers a clear, well-researched, sympathetic, but also searching account of colleges and universities that define themselves as religious. It is, to my knowledge, the best balanced, most analytical, and most thought-provoking book of its kind."
—Mark A. Noll, McManis Professor of Christian Thought at Wheaton College and author of *America's God: From Jonathan Edwards to Abraham Lincoln*

"Naomi Schaefer Riley's *God on the Quad* is a fascinating exploration of twenty religious colleges. Riley's fine reporting skills and eye for detail make the case studies come alive. Comparing evangelical, Catholic, Bud-

"A fascinating journey through an America that few of us have been paying attention to: the country of the deeply religious, primarily Christian, young in the various colleges devoted to educating them, while keeping them safe from the spiritual corrosions of America's youth culture. Told gently but searchingly, this story is not only interesting in itself but one that anyone who cares about the future health of this society cannot afford to let slip by."   —Midge Decter, author *of Liberal Parents, Radical Children* and
        Rumsfeld: A Personal Portrait

"In the world of American higher education, 'diversity' is always embraced in theory, but frequently disdained in practice. There is no better illustration of that fact than the ill-informed and incurious suspicion of the nation's religious colleges emanating from the ranks of the 'educated.' For those in the grip of such entirely preventable ignorance, this splendid book is the perfect antidote. Anyone who still believes that America's religious colleges are crudely anti-intellectual backwaters will be profitably shocked by the reality described in Naomi Schaefer Riley's lucid and meticulously researched account, which vividly evokes the rich and varied texture of life in these unique institutions. And anyone who still believes that religious colleges must abandon or dilute their religious mission in order to make a real contribution to American society will discover that something closer to the opposite is true."
        —Wilfred McClay, author of *The Masterless:*
        Self and Society in Modern America

"Naomi Schaefer Riley's *God on the Quad* is an important and refreshing new look at the vitality of a younger generation of well-educated religious people who want to make a difference in the deeply divided and conflicted America they are inheriting."   —Alphonse Vinh, National Public Radio

"Naomi Schaefer Riley's remarkably intelligent, fair-minded, incisive, fascinating, and penetrating foray into the world of religious institutions of higher learning illuminates as well some of the causes and consequences of the hostility shown toward religious students on our secular campuses. Anyone seeking to understand how the religious and the secular must, and can, co-exist and even nurture each other in a free and tolerant society must read this book. It casts in an entirely new—and sensible—light the dhist, and Jewish approaches to religious higher education, she takes the reader inside campus subcultures outside the higher-education mainstream. *God on the Quad* includes treatments of institutions that rarely open their doors to researchers. The chapter on Bob Jones University is itself worth the price of admission. Riley's blend of critical journalism and humane empathy makes *God on the Quad* a pleasure to read."

—John Schmalzbauer, author of *People of Faith: Religious Conviction in American Journalism and Higher Education*

"As the cultural conflicts rage in the U.S., there is no more important battleground than our university campuses. Naomi Schaefer Riley gives a balanced examination of various religious universities that are achieving great success and bright, religiously committed graduates who will have a deep impact on America's future. This book will surprise and perhaps trouble you."

—Fr. C. J. McCloskey, research fellow at the Faith and Reason Institute, Washington, D.C., and former Catholic chaplain at Princeton University

"The intellectual life and dynamism of religious colleges would surprise many who tend not to take them seriously. A bad mistake. In *God on the Quad,* Naomi Schaefer Riley offers a compelling account of their high quality and intense vitality. Far from the bigoted enclaves of the imagination of our intellectuals and media, these colleges are training students in intellectual and personal discipline, dedication to the claims of an ethnically diverse and rapidly changing society, and, above all, how to live your faith in the world. Their goal could not be less narrow or sectarian. To the contrary, they are purposefully training the leaders of the future—people with a commitment to public service and to shaping our world. The graduates of religious colleges are entirely capable and splendidly prepared to meet these goals and more. To underestimate their influence on our future would be a serious error. And those who share their goals and admire their vision will find in *God on the Quad* a wealth of heartwarming information—and, especially, an exciting vision of possibilities for the future of our society. A joy to read, this book is also an arresting picture of a new generation that is poised to change the face of our culture and public life." —Elizabeth Fox-Genovese, professor of history at Emory University

"This is an exciting book, and it appears at an exciting time—as college administrators, policymakers, journalists, and, most important, students themselves are coming to realize that the education offered by America's seven hundred religiously affiliated colleges and universities is some of the best in the country. On her travels, Naomi Schaefer Riley interviewed administrators, faculty, and most of all, the students, who, contrary to our facile assumptions about overprotective parents, in nearly all cases have freely chosen to attend sectarian schools, sometimes turning down offers from Harvard or Princeton. She discovers plenty of tensions as students struggle with bans on alcohol or premarital sex and the colleges struggle to define their religious identity in a militantly secular culture. What distinguishes these colleges and their students is their seriousness—about faith, intellectual engagement, and their own destinies—and that's what keeps away the sense of emptiness that pervades college life elsewhere."

—Charlotte Allen, author of *The Human Christ:*
The Search for the Historical Jesus

"How can one journalist capture so well the essence of various religious worldviews and their complex applications within higher education? My understanding of the history, traditions, current issues, and possible futures of each religious tradition's engagement with learning and culture was gratefully expanded. Everyone interested in protecting the diversity and exploring the common cause of these seven hundred or more institutions will be enthralled by this book."
—Robert C. Andringa, president of the Council for Christian Colleges & Universities

"Moving from Mormon, fundamentalist, conservative and liberal Catholic, Jewish, Baptist, and evangelical educational institutions, Naomi Schaefer Riley's wide-ranging book is evenhanded, perceptive, and oftentimes surprisingly revealing. She examines the roles of women, race relations, student life, and various approaches to integrating faith and intellectual life. She is an astute observer who captures well the complex and multidimensional aspects of each tradition. Everyone working in religiously oriented higher education—and even those outside it—will want to read this volume and come to grips with the challenges—and the opportunities—that Riley highlights in this timely book."

—Michael Cromartie, editor of *A Public Faith:*
Evangelicals and Civic Engagement

GOD ON THE QUAD

GOD ON THE QUAD

How Religious Colleges and the Missionary
Generation Are Changing America

Naomi Schaefer Riley

ST. MARTIN'S PRESS ⚠ NEW YORK

Portions of Chapter 7 reprinted from *The Public Interest,* No. 152 (Summer 2003), pp. 81–99, © 2003 by National Affairs, Inc.

www.stmartins.com

ISBN 0-312-33045-6
EAN 978-0312-33045-3

First Edition: January 2005

10 9 8 7 6 5 4 3 2 1

To Jason L. Riley

Contents

Acknowledgments

A person doesn't go from writing 800-word newspaper articles to a 300-page book without a lot of help.

First, I'd like to thank the faculty and administrators at all of the colleges and universities I visited. Without their patience and willingness to answer innumerable questions about their faith, their backgrounds, and their teaching, I would still be floundering to figure out the basics. I would especially like to thank Carri Jenkins, Thomas Susanka, Bernard Dobranski, Baxter Ennis, Devorah Ehrlich, Bernard Lander, Phil deHaan, Shirley Mullen, Alfred Balitzer, and Michael Beaty.

As for the students, I can only say that their kindness in welcoming me into their homes and their lives made the research for this book an experience I will continue to treasure long after *God on the Quad* is on the remainder shelves. In particular, I'd like to thank Zee Cramer, Jenny Ebbeling, and Christopher McGowan, exemplars of the missionary generation who have gone beyond the call of duty in continuing to speak with me long after I departed their respective campuses.

This book would not have been possible without the financial support of the Phillips Foundation. The help and advice of John Farley, as well as the other Phillips fellows, has proved invaluable. I'd like to thank the Templeton Foundation for not holding my youth and inexperience against me, and Arthur Schwartz, who has continued to be a great source of advice and support throughout. The Randolph Foundation has been instrumental in allowing me to pursue this research to the greatest extent and to devote my full attention to *God on the Quad* for well over two years. The support of the John M. Olin Foundation is also greatly appreciated.

Statistics provided by the Council for Christian Colleges and Universities, the UCLA Higher Education Research Institute, and the Higher Education Directory have been very useful, and I'd like to thank the various people at those organizations who have helped me, including Ron Mahurin, William Korn, and Mark Schreiber.

The Ethics and Public Policy Center has been my home away from home for the last few years. And I'm grateful to Adam Keiper for keeping up my Web site, and Christine Rosen for her advice and humor.

I have had a number of advisors for this project, but one in particular was willing to take on that role formally—Terry Teachout. The most important ideas in this book were formed as a result of his probing questions. Alan Wolfe has also offered much more help than any young author could hope for.

There are several editors who started me on this path, but the first and best is Erich Eichman. He suggested I write about faith six years ago, and since then his editing has continued to make me sound like a better version of myself. I am very grateful to Karl Zinsmeister, who humored my first whim to report on religious colleges when I wasn't old enough to rent a car, and who, upon my return, suggested this book topic. I'd like to also thank Jenny Schuessler, who helped me figure out how to write about this topic for a general audience.

I'm thankful to my late and great professor, Richard Marius, for his inspiration; Willy Jay for telling me to quit using the first person, among other useful pieces of advice; Christine Whelan for helping me focus and occasionally distracting me during long hours at the New York Public Library; and Lisa Findlay for her reassurance that it would all turn out okay. I'd also like to thank Kathryn Lopez and Alicia Chesser for answering my constant barrage of religion questions.

My agent, Teresa Hartnett, has worked tirelessly on my behalf. Her excitement about this project has not let up from the fateful moment we met in a bar in New York City downtown. Joseph Cleemann, my editor at St. Martin's Press, has given this book all of his care and consideration, and his challenges to me have made it better than I'd ever hoped.

The seeds of this book were probably sown when I was two years old and, I'm told, my parents started researching my college options. It would be hard to imagine two people who care about education and understand its transformative effects more than David and Roberta Schaefer. For the consideration they have given to their children's education, as well as that of their students, and the thousands of other young people whose lives they've affected, I'd like to thank them. It would be hard to overestimate the effect on this book of the years of discussions that I have had with my parents and my sister. For that, and for their love, I am deeply grateful.

This book is dedicated to my husband, Jason, who welcomed me home from each trip, listened to all my stories, and helped me think more deeply and critically about this and every topic. His strength and his love are a guiding force.

INTRODUCTION

In February 1988, with his novel *The Bonfire of the Vanities* on the best-seller list, social satirist Tom Wolfe gave a Class Day address at Harvard in which he described ours as the era of the "fifth freedom"—freedom from religion. "After you've had every other freedom—the four that Roosevelt enunciated," Wolfe observed in an interview with *Time* a few months later, "the last hobble on your freedom is religion. We saw it in the '60s in the hippie movement, when tens of thousands of young people quite purposely emancipated themselves from ordinary rules."

Today, the legacy of that emancipation is most viscerally felt in the nation's universities. College faculties, which are now demographically dominated by baby boomers, continue their generation's endeavor to "liberate" others from the strictures of orthodox religion and traditional morality. Students who do arrive on campus their freshman year with some traditional religious identity quickly find themselves a beleaguered minority both in the classroom, where their beliefs are derided as contrary to the principles of tolerance and "diversity" (since they are not accepting of every lifestyle and don't believe that every viewpoint deserves equal consideration), and in their extracurricular lives, where their sensibilities are consistently offended by what they regard as the amoral behavior of their peers and its tacit approval by college officials.

In April 2001, for example, the student judiciary at Tufts University voted to withdraw recognition from the Tufts Christian Fellowship for refusing to let a "practicing" lesbian run for one of the group's offices, holding that the exclusion violated the school's nondiscrimination policy. Similar controversies have since arisen for Christian groups at more than a dozen schools, including Williams and Middlebury colleges and Ball State University. In 1995, a Muslim student group at the University of North Carolina at Chapel Hill was denied recognition because it would not allow non-Muslims to hold office. In 2003, a Christian women's residence at Purdue University was told it could not consider gender in choosing its membership or it would risk losing recognition as a campus group and its building.[1]

In other respects as well, religious students regularly confront a hostile environment on today's college campuses. A Harvard student running for president of the undergraduate council a few years ago was vilified by the campus newspaper for his religious beliefs. He never mentioned them on the campaign trail, but a young woman on the election commission, unbeknownst to him, had e-mailed some friends asking them to pray for the candidate. That was enough for the editorial board of the Harvard *Crimson* to warn that the candidate's "ties to religious groups have raised concerns among many students." In an earlier, more widely publicized case, a group of Orthodox Jewish students at Yale sought to live off campus because the coed dormitories forced them routinely to encounter half-naked members of the opposite sex in the hallways. The students were denounced for being "judgmental" about their classmates' behavior, and told that if they did leave campus, they would still have to pay the seven thousand dollar dorm fee. As a Yale spokesman explained, coed dorms are just one "aspect of the Yale educational experience."

While some students are able to find religious fulfillment in off-campus churches and other religious organizations, both formal religious practice and adherence to traditional moral codes drop off among undergraduates. Among the relatively few students who are actually involved in faith groups on campus, many describe themselves as "spiritual, not religious." A recent book entitled *Religion on Campus* offers a clear picture of what this means. At a weekly meeting of the Wesley Foundation (a United Methodist group) on a large western university's campus, for instance, the leaders asked, "How can we keep the spark of God burning inside us this week?" The responses included, "I'm a vegetarian, and that's religious to me," "Smile," and "Take time to be quiet and alone." Another student who is active in the (Catholic) Newman Center, calls herself a "spiritual junkie," citing as an example her experience of turning out the lights in the room with a male friend and listening to the Indigo Girls.

Feel-good spirituality turns out to be a sorry substitute for the real thing. Academic insiders and outsiders alike have often described a certain malaise among today's college students. For example, a 2002 *New York Times* story

---

[1] For more examples of the type of problems that traditionally religious students have experienced at secular colleges, please see the Web site of the Foundation for Individual Rights in Education: www.thefire.org.

profiled Jeffrey Lorch, a sophomore at Columbia, whom the reporter found typical of the more than 2,600 students who had sought help at Columbia's counseling center the previous year. Jeffrey apparently has no real problems, but it takes him three quadruple espressos and an unknown quantity of Prozac to get through the day. Looking at his college experience, Jeffrey notes, "There have been times when I've felt like every conversation [I've had at school] was a sham."

"Souls without longing." That's what Robert Bartlett, a professor of political science at Emory University, calls the dozens, if not hundreds, of Jeffreys he has encountered in the classroom. In a striking essay in *The Public Interest,* Bartlett argues that this malaise is evident in the "narrowness of students' frame of reference or field of vision; in the pettiness of their daily concerns; in the tepid character of their admiration and contempt, their likes and dislikes; in the mediocrity of their ambitions. . . . The world could be their oyster, but they tend to stare back at it, pearls and all—and yawn."

Bartlett argues that one "cause of students' ennui is the absence of religion in their lives," a problem articulated by the seventeenth-century theologian and scientist Blaise Pascal. As Bartlett summarizes Pascal's view, "Without knowledge of or concern for God, human beings vacillate between fits of diversion, which keep them from thinking of their fundamental condition, and enervating boredom which reminds them of it."

But to say these students are "without longing" is to miss the point. Obviously they long for something. Otherwise, why all the caffeine, alcohol, and psychotropic medications? Indeed, a recent UCLA survey on spirituality in higher education found 75 percent of undergraduates were "searching for meaning or purpose in life," while 78 percent discuss religion and spirituality with their friends.

Of course, alcohol, caffeine, and late-night bull sessions are long-standing aspects of American college life. What has changed, however, is that the spiritual longings of these students are less likely than their predecessors to be fulfilled in today's universities.[2] Only 8 percent of the students in the same survey reported that their professors frequently encourage classroom discussion of religious or spiritual matters or provide opportunities to discuss the purpose or meaning of life. Most faculty, of course, would not be surprised by those numbers. They would say that it is not part of their job

---

[2] A hundred years ago, for instance, most of the nation's most prominent universities were religious themselves, and so discussions of religion in class and chapel attendance were a staple of university education.

description to host such discussions, and, given the current legal climate in which educational institutions—both public and private—are brought to court for allegedly using public money to advance religious causes, many professors would rightly worry that talking about God in class, not necessarily promoting a religious worldview, would provoke loud complaints from some corners, if not lawsuits.

Sociologists and pundits from David Brooks and Gertrude Himmelfarb on the right to E. J. Dionne and Michael Lind on the left agree that, more than ever before, Americans are living in a nation divided between a religious and a secular culture. In addition to the generational divide, there is also a geographical one. Those who consider traditional religion a small and sometimes backward part of American life, best confined to the private sphere, are part of Blue America, while those who find faith governs their attitudes and behavior both publicly and privately are part of Red America. What started out as a political formulation—the states colored red on television newsroom maps, inland and largely more rural areas, voted for Bush in the 2000 presidential election, while the blue-colored states, more urban and coastal, went for Gore—is also a cultural one, with religious practice being the most reliable indicator of which side of the divide people fall on.

The crudest formulation of the difference came from political strategist Paul Begala, who infamously wrote:

> *Tens of millions of good people in Middle America voted Republican. But if you look closely at the map, you see a more complex picture. You see the state where James Byrd was lynch-dragged behind a pickup truck until his body came apart—it's red. You see the state where Matthew Shepard was crucified on a split-rail fence for the crime of being gay—it's red. You see the state where right-wing extremists blew up a federal office building and murdered scores of federal employees. The state where an Army private who was thought to be gay was bludgeoned to death with a baseball bat, and the state where neo-Nazi skinheads murdered two African-Americans because of their skin color, and the state where Bob Jones University spews its anti-Catholic bigotry: they're all red, too.*

Red America sympathizers fired back, referring to the Blue side as "the Porn Belt"—that part of the country in which sex videos constitute the largest share of the home-video market. Mark Steyn, writing in *National Review,* described Blue America as constituting people who had been rushed through the immigration process without sufficient background checks, along with "Al Sharpton's entourage, gay scoutmasters, partial-birth abortion fetishists, [and] Hollywood airheads."

Four years later, that divide has not changed. According to a recent poll by the Pew Research Center for the People and the Press, voters who frequently attend religious services favor President Bush by a margin of 63 percent to 37 percent, while those who never attend lean Democratic by 62 percent to 38 percent. And the fires are continually being reignited. Evolutionary biologist Richard Dawkins and philosopher Daniel Dennett, in an attempt to give non-believers a sort of rallying cry, recently urged that atheists henceforth be referred to as "brights." Dawkins coyly leaves it to others to find a name for religious people.

Most representatives of Blue America, though, are not interested in the goings-on in Red America—they refer to that area between the coasts as "flyover country"—but a group of Red Americans is determined to change the culture of Blue America from the inside out.

Call them the "missionary generation." The 1.3 million graduates of the nation's more than seven hundred religious colleges are quite distinctive from their secular counterparts. And the stronger the religious affiliation of the school, the more distinctive they are. The young men and women attending the twenty religious colleges I visited in 2001 and 2002 are red through and through. (Though the schools are sometimes located in blue states, the majority of their students hail from red states and their attitude toward faith is all red-state.) They reject the spiritually empty education of secular schools. They refuse to accept the sophisticated ennui of their contemporaries. They snub the "spiritual but not religious" answers to life's most difficult questions. They rebuff the intellectual relativism of professors and the moral relativism of their peers. They refuse to accept their "fifth freedom."

In practical terms, these students challenge what has become, since the sixties, the typical model of college-student behavior. They don't spend their college years experimenting with sex or drugs. They marry early and plan ahead for family life. Indeed, they oppose sex outside of marriage and homosexual relationships. Most dress modestly and don't drink, use drugs, or smoke. They study hard, leaving little time for sitting in or walking out. Most vote, and a good number join the army. They are also becoming lawyers, doctors, politicians, college professors, businessmen, psychologists, accountants, and philanthropists in the cultural and political centers of the country. While they would disagree among themselves about what it means to be a religious person, it is assumed that trying to live by a set of rules, generally ones laid down in scripture, is the prerequisite for a healthy, productive, and moral life.

Administrators and faculty of many seriously religious colleges of all different denominations believe they can produce young professionals who will transform the broader secular culture from within. If they're right, the implications are enormous. Advocates of religious higher education argue: CEOs won't need to scramble to send their employees to business ethics classes when they can hire college graduates who already know them; the armed forces may find it less difficult to recruit from the educated classes than they have in fifty years; faith in our elected leaders may override the cynical attitudes that have characterized American politics for the last half century; instead of appointing special committees, hospitals may be able to hire entire staffs of doctors with backgrounds in bioethics; and secular universities may be overrun by professors studying the interaction of religion with philosophy, science, mathematics, or literature. Is this vision of the future realistic? Can these young men and women become pioneers, bringing an ethical perspective back into their professions, their schools, their communities, and their government institutions?

The initial signs of this cultural shift are everywhere. A Brigham Young graduate was just elected governor of Massachusetts, one of the most liberal states in the Union. Indeed, the number of BYU grads living in New England went from 100 to 3,000 in the last ten years. House Speaker Dennis Hastert, an alumnus of the evangelical Wheaton College, has become one of the most effective occupants of that position in recent years, according to a recent profile in the *New Yorker*. Wheaton also ranks eleventh in the nation in the percentage of graduates who go on to receive PhDs. It was two women who had attended the Baptist Baylor University who were captured by the Taliban while they were doing missionary work in Afghanistan. Yeshiva University, which is ranked by *U.S. News & World Report* as one of the top fifty research universities in America, recently graduated its first Rhodes Scholar. The Ave Maria School of Law just had a higher percentage of its graduates pass the bar than any school in Michigan. Although Ave Maria, a conservative Catholic school, is too new to have received full accreditation from the American Bar Association, its students (whose average LSATs would make it the twenty-fifth ranked law school in the country) are being sought after by leading law firms, justice department offices, prosecutors, and federal judges. Probably less surprisingly, more students at Bob Jones University dropped out to join the army after September 11 than did students at Harvard.

Religious higher education is on the rise in America. The numbers back up the anecdotal evidence here: Colleges and universities with strong faith identities, which enforce strict rules on alcohol, relations with the opposite sex, and attendance at religious services, and offer classes from a religious perspective, are becoming more popular, even while their academic standards have risen. For instance, enrollment at the over one hundred member institutions of the Council for Christian Colleges & Universities (four-year liberal arts colleges committed to teaching Christian doctrine, hiring only professors who share the faith, and providing a Christian atmosphere outside the classroom) jumped a remarkable 60 percent between 1990 and 2002, while the number of students at public and private schools barely fluctuated. As a percentage of total enrollment in institutions of higher education, the number of students at colleges with religious affiliations has not changed much over the last twenty years (8.34 percent in 1984 and 8.07 percent today), but schools with the strongest religious identities have been steadily gaining.

While evangelical schools like the members of the CCCU are at the heart of this new strength in religious higher education, they are hardly alone. Schools affiliated with the Church of Jesus Christ of Latter Day Saints have been expanding, in part because of the fast-growing Mormon population. Not only has BYU added an Idaho campus to its Utah and Hawaii ones, but a new Mormon college (not officially affiliated with the church) was recently established in Virginia. It has grown to a student body of five hundred in six years and is already looking to expand its campus. Populations at Catholic colleges and universities have seen a dramatic rise as well. Applications to Notre Dame, for example, have risen steadily in the last decade—a rise of 23 percent last year broke the 1994 record of 20 percent. And numerous smaller Catholic schools have opened across the country to cater to a more strictly religious population. In California, Thomas Aquinas College, a small Catholic "Great Books" school at the forefront of this movement, is operating at capacity, and its administrators are considering opening another branch on the East Coast. Yeshiva University, the country's flagship Orthodox Jewish college, has many more qualified applicants than it can take, and the more recently established Touro College has stepped in to cater to more traditionally Orthodox students. The trend toward religious higher education extends from the fundamentalist Bob Jones University to the newly established Buddhist college, Soka University.

These developments, of course, did not occur in a vacuum. The number of students attending nondenominational Christian elementary and high schools (usually evangelical) and Jewish day schools has climbed significantly in the last decade. Homeschooling, meanwhile, has experienced a much more dramatic rise in popularity, growing annually at a rate of 15 to 20 percent, to approximately 1.5 million families, according to the Census Bureau. A nationwide survey by the National Center for Education Statistics reports that 38 percent of homeschooling parents cite religion as the main reason for their decision.

Looking at the larger context, the growth in religious education is not surprising. During the 1990s, the churches that grew the fastest demanded the highest commitment from their members, including regular attendance at worship services, strict behavioral codes, tithing, and public confessions of faith. While mainline Protestant churches continued to lose members, the Mormon Church, for instance, grew by about 19 percent, and the evangelical Churches of Christ and the Roman Catholic Church recorded increases of 18.6 and 16.2 percent respectively. Over the last twenty-five years, Gallup polls have consistently shown that American teens are slightly more likely to attend worship services than adults. Much of the energy driving the current "great awakening" in organized religion is coming from the most traditional corners, and young people are the ones demanding stricter rules and more tradition.

Both a Gallup poll and a University of Pennsylvania study recently noted a positive correlation between teen church attendance and parents' level of education. Richard Gelles, coauthor of the Penn survey, noted: "Karl Marx would say religion was the way lower classes delude themselves into thinking that life is fair. Marx was wrong. Faith is embraced as part of a commitment to traditional values—hard work, education, religion." Plenty of Americans assume that education is some kind of substitute for religion—that only people ignorant of modern science or philosophy would believe in God as the creator or rely on him for moral guidance. But the facts do not bear that assumption out.

The attitude that faith and intellect are incompatible has a long history in America. In 1932, a few years after the Scopes trial, Philip E. Wentworth, then a recent Harvard graduate, wrote an article for the *Atlantic Monthly* entitled "What College Did to My Religion." Having grown up in a strict Presbyterian household in the midwest, Wentworth was discouraged from attending Harvard by his local pastor, who feared he would lose his faith, and told instead to try a denominational college nearby. Sure enough, Wentworth writes of his career at Harvard (with the zeal of a convert to secularism), "In the course of time the impact of new knowledge and especially knowledge of science and the scientific method wrought great havoc with my original ideas. All things, it seemed, were subject to the laws of nature. This concept supplied my mind with a wholly new pattern into which my religious beliefs refused to fit. In such an orderly universe, there seemed to be no place for a wonder-working God."

The stinging reply to Wentworth came three months later in an article in the same magazine by Columbia religion professor Bernard Iddings Bell. "[Mr. Wentworth] seems to be reasonably intelligent, not at all incapable of understanding religion. The trouble is that he apparently has no knowledge of what religion is. He has outgrown a crude and semi-magical concept of God, such as a child may properly hold, with no realization that grown men mean by religion something both more delicate and more complex." Bell goes on to blame Harvard for the deficiency.

Seventy years later, Josh Jalinski, a senior at a public school in New Jersey, was faced with the same choice as Phillip Wentworth. Having excelled in his academic and extracurricular pursuits, Josh was admitted to Harvard. But Josh, an evangelical Christian, keeping in mind his ambitions to go to seminary, get a PhD in history, and then to become mayor of Asbury Park, work as a minister there, and start his own Christian school, chose to attend Bob Jones University instead. It's unlikely that Josh or his fellow religious college students will experience the sort of spiritual crisis that Wentworth did. Strongly religious colleges aim to give their students (perhaps now more than in the 1930s) the tools to succeed in the secular world and the strength to do so without compromising their faith.

Though it is important to understand the mission that religious colleges see for themselves, my ultimate concerns in this book are not the same as those of the members of the religious communities that sponsor them. I am not simply trying to determine whether religious colleges and universities will keep their distinctive identity over time, or whether they will be successful in propagating their particular faith.

The most important question about the recent growth of religious higher education for observers of American civic and political life is whether this movement tends to make religious communities more insular; whether this missionary generation, as its leaders hope, will transform the broader, secular culture from within; or whether those hopes are bound to be dashed by the influence of secularism on these young men and women. While I can offer no definitive answer to this question, I hope to illuminate it in this book by providing extensive profiles of six of the most significant schools I visited, and then, in subsequent chapters, considering some of the most salient issues affecting the identity of religious colleges and the interactions of their graduates with the outside world.

I must readily acknowledge that the schools I visited were chosen somewhat haphazardly. First, the schools I discuss constitute a tiny fraction of the religiously affiliated colleges out there, and for each school I stopped at, I heard about another four or five that I should also have visited. I tried to visit schools of a variety of denominations, but the number of each kind of school does not correspond with the population they represent. In some cases, I visited a few from one religious group to see if my observations were true across institutional lines. For the most part, I focused on undergraduate programs, but there are a few graduate schools I visited as well, which I think display characteristics similar to the colleges. I picked some well-known schools of which many readers are likely already to have at least some impressions, and others that are quite obscure to the general public.

I tried to spend time mostly at schools that have strong religious affiliations, but that judgment is inevitably subjective. As indicators of the strength of a school's religious affiliation I considered such factors as whether the majority of a school's students were religious, whether professors had to sign a statement of faith, whether they had to be of the same denomination as the school, whether the school had mandatory chapel attendance, and how strict the behavior codes were. The schools described here nonetheless represent various levels of religiosity; in a couple of cases, the schools turned out to be hardly religious at all.

On the basis of interviews I conducted with students, administrators, faculty, and alumni at each school, this book addresses four sets of questions:

1. *Why have students chosen the school?* Answers to this question were often far-ranging, and included factors such as the students' family life, their religious practices growing up, and what kind of primary and secondary schools they had attended, as well as their families' financial situations. Of course, their academic performance in high school was also an issue. I tried to interview some students at each school who had transferred there from secular colleges, since they were in a position to

provide useful comparative judgments. I also asked students what their friends and family at home thought of their decision to attend that school.

2. *How is the curriculum different from that of secular schools?* In my interviews with professors and administrators, I asked how the mission of each school is evident in its curriculum. I sat in on both secular and religious classes to assess the academic caliber of students and professors. I tried to determine how much religion entered into secular classes, and how much freedom of debate there was in religious classes. I also examined how each school dealt with the issue of academic freedom for both students and professors.

3. *What is the life outside the classroom like?* This was the most enjoyable part of the project. I spent time visiting dorms, hanging out with students on weekends, approaching them in student centers or on quads. I spoke to students both individually and in groups, to see how they interacted with each other. I asked about dating and drinking and dress codes. Having made inquiries about the official rules, I tried to learn from students about the extent to which they were actually followed. I asked about recent controversies: Which students or faculty had been dismissed, and why? I sat in on meetings of clubs, from Bible study groups to newspaper editorial meetings. I attended musical performances and intramural games. I asked about race relations on campus. I tried to interview students who were religious minorities at the school to find out how they felt about their status there. I went to religious services with students, both on campus and off.

4. *How will these colleges affect students' post-graduation choices?* Finally, I wanted to know what students planned to do after they graduated. Of course, most couldn't tell me exactly how their choices would have been different if they had attended a secular school, but I asked them to explain what parts of their religious education had significantly shaped their plans. I asked them to speculate about whether their religious beliefs would affect the way they practiced their various professions. I asked about whether they intended to have families, and when. I asked both women and men their thoughts on balancing family and career. I asked them where they wanted to live—in what area of the country, and in what type of community. Did they need to be sur-

rounded by coreligionists or were they satisfied being in a minority? What did they think of the secular world? Did they intend to proselytize? If so, how would they do it? And generally, I asked how they envisioned their future roles in the community and in the country.

Readers of *God on the Quad*, I should note, will not find interviews with graduates of these schools who have since left the faith or decided that their education was a failure. It is not because such people aren't out there—they are, and they're easy to find; just type "Bob Jones" or "ex-Mormon" into Google—but rather because such graduates are unlikely to have an effect on the culture that is different from graduates of secular schools. Moreover, I assume that readers of this book can come up on their own with dozens of reasons why they would not want to attend a school like Bob Jones University or Brigham Young (though the freshman retention rates at these schools are very similar to those of secular schools at the same academic level). My interviews with the members of these religious college communities will, I hope, provide answers as to why young men and women *do* choose to attend these schools and what they are learning that is different.

I began the first formal interviews for this book on September 10, 2001. The next day, two thousand miles from home, I sat on the edge of my hotel bed, looking out over the strip malls to the treeless mountains beyond, wondering more than anything else about how to get home. Home for me is Blue America. I have lived in four states, all in the northeast. I attended two secular colleges and grew up with a sense that religion, while socially beneficial (in that it provided people with a moral compass they might not otherwise have), was not true. In other words, I had already expected to feel distinctly out of place on these campuses. And the events of that Tuesday morning only intensified the feeling.

Over the next week, the students at Brigham Young tried to welcome me into their lives. While national tragedies tend to bring out the best in many people, the first representatives of the "missionary generation" I encountered could not have made a greater impression upon me. Their kindness and compassion, their civic-mindedness, their understanding and interest in national and international affairs, the quiet comfort they were able to find in their faith, and their ability to relate to this stranger in their midst gave me cause for optimism.

At the end of his Class Day address, Tom Wolfe worried that the "religious self-discipline that ran through the American people from one side to the other" and held this country together through the nineteenth and twentieth centuries has now disappeared. Wolfe predicted that the twenty-first century would be a period of "revaluation," in which we will have to "create an entirely new ethical and moral framework." Searching for a person who "has a higher synthesis on the order of Rousseau or Jefferson that will light up the sky and lead mankind into a new era," Wolfe asked his audience, "Where else should we find such a person but at Harvard?" Where else, indeed?

CHAPTER ONE

AN OASIS IN THE DESERT:
THE APPEAL OF BRIGHAM YOUNG UNIVERSITY

Zee Cramer looks at her boyfriend, Adam, from across the long, barren living room—only two chairs, a couch, a coffee table, and a mini-stereo resting on some milk crates stand between them. Suppressing giggles, Zee and Adam each assume a squatting position. And then, with a couple of friends looking on, the two start lumbering toward each other. One frog leg and then the other with their rear ends almost brushing the ground. They move faster as they get closer, but not so quickly that they lose their balance. Finally, Zee and Adam reach each other, both red from the laughter. They lean in, grab each other's calves, and squeeze affectionately. This elaborate mating ritual, Zee tells me, was dreamed up to accommodate one of her former roommates who became offended when she saw Adam touching Zee's thigh. The girl's rule—that "all leg-touching must be below the knee"—may seem a little extreme, but at Brigham Young University, it's not so far from the norm.

Zee "is on the BYU list of top twenty-five girls to marry," according to her ex-boyfriend, Greg Erekson. And it's easy to see why. Zee is a lovely five foot ten or so, slender, with brown hair that drops past her long neck to just below her shoulders. Though she gave up her dance major a few years ago, the training is evident even in the way she sits. In her vowels, you can detect the remnant of a South African accent—she spent the first ten years of her life there.

I meet Zee on a Saturday night at her house, which she shares with nine other girls. Six live in the main part and the others share the basement. It's not a fancy place. It could use a paint job and the grass out front is far from green (not surprisingly, since BYU is in the middle of the Utah desert). Most of BYU's 35,000 students live off campus in similar arrangements.

I chat with Adam while Zee is getting ready. Blond and thin, Adam looks nothing if not comfortable in his preppy uniform of khaki shorts and two well-worn T-shirts, layered one on top of the other. His combination of black socks and soccer sneakers oddly seem not simply acceptable, but trendy.

Like his beat-up brown Saab, which we take to dinner. "Thai, Chinese, Indian, Vietnamese, Tibetan?" they ask if I have a preference. The town has more ethnic restaurants than I would have expected in Utah; they do a booming business off students who return from their two-year missions in foreign countries and crave the foods they left behind. We settle on Indian.

Zee and Adam order appetizers, entrées, and dessert. Either they think I'm picking up the tab or they have more disposable income than most of the college students I know. The latter is certainly possible: BYU is funded almost entirely by tithes from the Mormon Church, so tuition is only about $3,150 per year for students in the Church, and only about 30 percent more for non-Church members. (By comparison, two of the private universities listed closest to BYU in the *U.S. News & World Report* 2004 ranking—Boston University and Southern Methodist University—charge $28,906 and $23,588 respectively.)

Tuition rates were not a big issue for Adam, who grew up in the well-to-do New York suburb of Norwalk, Connecticut. When I ask him how he came to Provo, he starts at the very beginning. Adam was raised Catholic. His father doesn't practice, but he and his two brothers accompanied their mother to church regularly when they were growing up. He never really "felt connected to God" through the Catholic Church, but having maintained some belief in a divine being, Adam immediately began looking for another faith when he started his freshman year at the University of Denver. After attending a number of different churches, synagogues, and temples, he settled on the Church of Jesus Christ of Latter Day Saints. Only there, he tells me, did he find the "connection" he wanted. But then, instead of continuing his education in Denver, he was moved to go on a mission.

Having spent two years knocking on doors to spread the Mormon gospel in Korea, Adam knew he couldn't go back to his former school; he wanted to attend Brigham Young. His parents, Adam explains, were hardly thrilled with his conversion to Mormonism or with his decision to attend BYU, but he thinks "they are dealing better with it now, since they see how much it has done for my life." On a trip east to meet his family, Zee recalls, they ran into an old coach of Adam's. The man couldn't believe how Adam looked— "clean-cut and well-dressed." It's a little hard to imagine that Adam was ever a mess, but his new faith and his new school seem to have given him direction. He used to describe himself as an "artsy type" who painted; now he majors in industrial arts and wants to get a job at a major company designing the shapes of products—"maybe cars," he offers.

Even though Mormonism has made him a little more staid, at heart Adam is a guy who grew up near New York City and finds the entertainment offerings in Provo to be lacking. Knowing that their faith prohibits (among other things) drinking, smoking, and seeing any movie with an R rating, I ask what they usually do on Saturday nights. Zee says the parties and the dancing, though not "the usual bump and grind," are fun. Noticing my skepticism perhaps, she jokes that Mormon gatherings tend more often than not to involve board games, Kool-Aid, and ice cream. The last two, she acknowledges, are the staples. Though the school has a very athletic (and outdoorsy) population, students at BYU consume sweets at an alarming rate, often keeping bags of mini candy bars in their backpacks.

As much as Adam enjoys junk food and board games, he says he has more fun when he heads home. His most recent trip included going with some high school buddies to see Madonna in concert at Madison Square Garden. They originally bought "nosebleed" seats, he recounts, but were thrilled when a woman—seeing that they were looking through their binoculars before the show even started—concluded that they must be really big fans and gave them seats on the floor. Though Adam thinks seeing Madonna is an experience you must have "to be part of this generation," Zee doesn't listen to her music. Some of the songs are okay, she acknowledges, "but I gave up a long time ago trying to find the ones that weren't offensive." Zee is pretty picky about movies, too. In the last few months, she has walked out in the middle of *Rush Hour 2* and *The Fast and the Furious,* both rated PG-13. "If I wouldn't watch it in the temple, why would I watch it in a public place with all of these people sitting around me?" Adam, who is three years younger than Zee, quickly agrees. He says he likes the way she puts things.

Zee has had a few years to sort out these questions. When she was twenty-one, she says she went through a "crisis of faith."

"I was sick of the Mormon thing and I just went searching. I wondered if I believed in this stuff just because I had learned it from such a young age." But she later decided that wasn't the case. Her youngest sister (Zee is the fourth of five siblings) is what Mormons call "inactive." Zee says she is bothered not because her sister has strayed from the faith, but because she seems "unhappy" as a result.

"She could have been a good singer," Zee laments, "but now she smokes."

Whatever the decisions of her peers, the woman sitting before me seems content with her faith. She talks about how "comforting" it is "to hear things and know that they are absolutely true, and I can rely on them no matter what." Looking back on her experience as a missionary for eighteen months in Washington state, Zee describes the thrill that people get from learning of the Mormon faith for the first time. "There are prophets of old, and there are prophets today. And people hear this and they can't believe it. But when they hear it, it rings true, and they respond." One of Zee's friends, Lisa, uses similar language to describe the happiness she derives from Mormonism. In the inscription to a *Book of Mormon* she gives me, Lisa writes, "I have read this book, and by doing so, I know that it is true, and that it is of God. The things contained in this book bring the greatest joy and peace that you can ever have in life."

As devoted as Zee can be to her faith, she does have a sense of humor about it. She told me she once saw an episode of *South Park* (the only one she has ever watched) that depicted a group of people who had just arrived in hell. A few of them kept raising their hands, telling the devil that there had been a mistake: they had been very good Christians and belonged in heaven. Finally, the devil tells them to gather around him so he can reveal the reason for their eternal damnation: "Okay, here's the deal," he says. "The Mormons were right."

Zee is perfectly hysterical by the time she explains the scene that follows, in which the devil, walking through heaven on his way to a meeting with God, finds himself surrounded by small, irritating Mormons trying to persuade him to join in a game of Scrabble. They also insist on telling the devil all the things in life (and afterlife) they are grateful for. Zee pauses to see if I get the joke, and I do, but only because earlier in the day I made a visit to Temple Square in Salt Lake City, the Mormon equivalent of the Vatican, where the missionaries (mostly from foreign countries) pepper their architectural descriptions and history lessons with sentiments of thankfulness. One of my tour guides was "grateful for prayer" because it helped her get through the time away from her family. The other was grateful that God had reserved a special place for her in heaven. Childlike and earnest in their navy blue jumpers, both were "grateful" that, as the Mormon faith promises, they would live on in heaven with their families, eternally.

After dinner, as I drive back to the hotel, my mind returns to this conversation. I know that Zee and Adam were both missionaries themselves in the not too distant past, but did they ever have to sound like the girls at Temple Square?

Sunday morning prayers—the sacrament meeting, as it is called—begin at eleven A.M., but when I arrive at Zee's house at quarter till, things are in disarray. The start time apparently isn't late enough for Minji Cho, Zee's freshman roommate. Though the other girls have all jumped up and down on her bed, she doesn't budge. Not hung over, of course, Minji stayed up all night chatting online. We leave a few minutes before eleven without her.

Turnout each Sunday is around 90 percent—not surprising, since in order to enroll at BYU every fall, students must receive a stamp of approval from their local bishops, based partially on their level of attendance at the sacrament meeting. Mormons do not go to their temples for regular services on Sundays (just for ceremonies like marriages and baptisms); they are divided geographically into wards of 150 or 200 people, like voting precincts, which can gather anywhere. At BYU, the student wards meet in classrooms and auditoriums on campus. "It's amazing," one of the school's development officers explains to me, "the way Sunday, BYU transforms itself into a giant church."

We take seats in the third of what look to be about twenty rows. There is no altar per se, just a raised platform in the front of the room, with a few chairs, a podium, and an old upright piano. The students mill around for a few minutes and then Bishop Bailey, a rotund, middle-aged man with silvery hair, steps up to the podium to make some introductory announcements. In the LDS Church, the bishop is a layman, who is "called" by the Church to serve in the role for three to five years. Some of the bishops at BYU are professors or administrators, and others—like Bailey, a lawyer—are local professionals.

The opening hymn is a spirited one, led by a heavily made-up young woman named Melody. She is wearing a long, silk, flowered skirt and a mauve silk blouse, both tight enough to be revealing, putting Melody in violation of BYU's campus dress code. For the sake of modesty, students are prohibited from wearing shorts or skirts that end above their knees, shirts that are sleeveless, or clothing that is "faddish" or "form-fitting." Steve Baker, director of BYU's honor code office, acknowledges that there are students who do not abide by the school's "dressing and grooming" rules. "It's not followed absolutely strictly, but that's not the intent." The idea, Baker emphasizes, is to set a standard, and, "if you look around, [the students] do stick to it pretty darn well."

After the hymn, Bishop Bailey thanks Melody and then moves on to ward business—assigning a "calling" to some of the students in the ward. Usually lasting one semester, a calling can range from teaching Sunday school, to visiting the elderly, to leading the prayer committee. The bishop is supposed to seek divine guidance in deciding who is assigned to which task, no matter how small or mundane. A few days prior to the sacrament meeting, individual students meet with the bishop to discuss their interests and their other time commitments, after which they are nominally given a choice regarding whether to accept the calling or not. Lisa, who receives a calling today, says she has never heard of anybody refusing one.

The number of hours students spend on their callings varies. Andrea Ludlow, the opinion editor of the school's newspaper, tells me that this semester she is the first councilor of the relief society (the women's section of the ward), a ten to twelve hour a week commitment. "No matter how much it takes," Andrea tells me, "you always find the time."

This attitude certainly extends to students' academic pursuits. Damon Linker, a former professor of political science at the school, tells me he immediately noticed a difference in the attitudes of the kids at BYU compared with students elsewhere. "They are bright-eyed, waiting to pounce to get the highest grade." They have a "tremendous respect for authority, which means you don't have the problem you do at other universities where you give a low grade and they threaten to sue you." Instead, he recalls, "The students would come up and say, 'I'm so sorry I disappointed you.'"

Linker's observations held true for the several classes I attended. Students in Zee's environmental history class, for example, had done their reading thoroughly and were paying close attention through a lecture by a not particularly charismatic teacher. Similarly, a class on Church history elicited twenty minutes' worth of questions from students in the auditorium though it was supposed to be a lecture.

Alan Wilkins, the vice president for academic affairs, attributes this enthusiasm not just to the atmosphere the school provides, but also to the kind of the students who choose BYU in the first place. Despite its state-university size population, BYU is a pretty selective institution. With 100,000 Mormon high school graduates each year, BYU can get students with an average ACT score of 27, an SAT score of 1100 or so, and an average GPA of 3.7. About a hundred National Merit Scholars enter in each class and about half of the freshmen have graduated in the top 10 percent of their high school class.

Moreover, Wilkins notes, "National surveys say that our students spend more time preparing for class and [paradoxically] feel less prepared for class than students at other schools." Wilkins finds this easy to explain: "Our students are hungry. They're anxious. They are kids who come and hustle. They have fun, but they are not spending as much time in parties." BYU students have "a seriousness of purpose," directly related, Wilkins believes, to their religious beliefs.

"The glory of God is intelligence," explains Wilkins, when I ask how students' faith relates to their secular academic pursuits. It's a statement I hear repeated throughout my week at BYU. Learning anything, from calculus to sociology, is considered a religious pursuit at the school. To drive home this point, Wilkins cites studies of Mormons that were done in the seventies and eighties which—though he acknowledges it may seem "counterintuitive"—showed respondents with higher levels of education felt a stronger commitment to the Church.

Partly to maintain this connection between religious dedication and academic seriousness, BYU ensures that an overwhelming percentage of its faculty is Mormon. That's possible because the Mormons produce a very high number of PhDs per capita, and because the school uses aggressive recruiting techniques—administrators and faculty keep a close eye on Mormons coming up through the academic ranks. In addition, like the students, the faculty is self-selecting. Since all professors, regardless of whether they are Mormon, must sign on to the school's honor code—which includes swearing off alcohol, caffeine, premarital sex, and smoking—many non-Mormons don't bother to apply. With the ones who do, like Linker (who is Catholic), the school is completely up front about its aims. Not only did the department chair explain the honor code during his first phone conversation, including the fact that he would have to shave any facial hair, but Linker also says they were "very explicit that there was almost no chance of this turning into a tenured position."

The faculty as a whole, says Jim Gordon, a professor at BYU's law school, has actually become more religious in recent years. According to Gordon, in the mid nineties, the administration became concerned that a handful of the Mormon faculty appeared to have lapsed in their religious commitment. And so in addition to the requirement that they adhere to the school's honor code, all Mormon faculty must now receive a yearly recommendation from their local bishop, like the students, certifying that they are attending their ward meetings regularly and paying tithes. At that time, Gordon explains, "People who were not active in the Church either reactivated or said 'I don't want to be here anymore,' and left."

The administration has also taken a closer look at faculty's intellectual adherence to Church doctrine. About ten years ago, English professor Gail Turley Houston found herself in hot water after suggesting that Mormons should pray to Mother in Heaven as well as Father in Heaven. Since the Mormon Church does maintain that God (a male) is married, her statements did not seem particularly outlandish to some professors I spoke with, but the result was that Houston was denied tenure. The American Association of University Professors (AAUP) subsequently censured the school for violating Houston's academic freedom. Gordon, who composed the university's response to the AAUP, tells me, "Students and faculty ought to be able to ask questions. They should not be trammeled or constrained by religious views." But, he argues, "there is another kind of academic freedom: Institutional academic freedom is necessary for an organization to define itself."

BYU attempts to shape not just the publications and research of faculty members, but more significantly, their statements in the classroom. When Linker was teaching Aristophanes' *The Clouds,* he tells me, one of his students complained to the department chair that the assigned reading contained a vulgar scene, and that Linker actually brought up the questionable passage (in which a character is masturbating) in class. Though Linker believes his colleague understood the intellectual justification for the discussion, he was asked not to teach the play again. According to Linker's account, "He said 'it would be better if you don't,' and he told me that 'the standard has to be set at the most sensitive Mormon.'" Linker interpreted this to mean "the most sheltered, most closed-minded Mormon from rural Utah, who has never met a non-Mormon in his life."

Interestingly, Linker says that the divide between Utahn and non-Utahn Mormons is the key to understanding most conflicts at the school. The former (who make up 30 percent of the school's population) have, of course, typically grown up around less religious diversity and—as a result, Linker believes—less social and intellectual diversity than their non-Utahn counterparts. He notes that the seminars he taught on "the 'God is dead' crowd"— Hegel, Kant, et al.—were almost uniformly populated by non-Utahn Mormons. These students, says Linker, "felt freer to talk to me about the school's atmosphere because I was not a Mormon. They would complain, 'This place is so stuffy, no one teaches anything that challenges you.'" Even though Linker maintains that he "toed the line on everything, I was seen as the person who would tell you things you would never hear. Without saying Nietzsche is right, I would get them to understand how someone would think the things he did." Linker left BYU after two years.

Just as the faith provides the foundation for academics at BYU, it also drives life outside the classroom. After the initial service each Sunday, the ward breaks up into the men's group and the women's group for Bible study. Since it is the beginning of the year when I visit, the bishop substitutes the lesson time with a coed orientation. As we walk into the auditorium, students pass out sheet music for "Getting to Know You." When Bishop Bailey announces that the first item on the agenda is a sing-along, there are a lot of giggles in the audience, and a certain number of sighs—"This does not usually happen," Zee assures me—but almost all of the 190 students sing. Then, proceeding with the orientation, each member of the ward is asked to come up to the microphone to give the following information about himself: name, major, year, hometown, the location of your mission if you have been on one, one word that describes you, and one goal for the semester.

The scene for the next two hours resembles a combination bachelor auction–beauty pageant. Students quickly skip over their major, to announce that their one word is "available" or that their goal for the semester is "to date the cute girl sitting on the piano bench." Some try to emphasize their desirable characteristics. "My roommates say I'm like a mom." "I think I'm angelic." Melody tells the audience: "My friends said I should use three words to describe myself: Dee. Lish. Ous." Bishop Bailey, sitting behind the podium, looks taken aback by the exaggerated hip movement accompanying her answer. Zee seems a little surprised herself, but even among the students at Brigham Young, she tells me, she observes "a range of behavior."

Standing in line for cheese and crackers after the meeting, a short, plain-looking young woman approaches Zee. She explains to Zee and me that she graduated in the spring but hasn't moved away yet, in part because Provo is a great place for her to date. Zee inquires about the miniature silver ring hanging on her necklace. "Oh, my roommate just got married and it's this tradition in Mexico to have a charm in the middle of the cake." Her roommate gave her the charm, she tells us, in the hope it would help her get engaged soon. "Of course, I'm not even dating anyone now." In fact, as the crowd around me nibbles on cookies and punch, I slowly become aware that every conversation in the room is about marriage.

One of Zee's roommates tells me that the focus on marriage at BYU is not nearly as bad as at the nearby Mormon junior college, Ricks,[3] where the unofficial motto is "Ring before spring or your money back." But some students think the situation is better at Ricks. Like BYU, the male-female ratio at Ricks is roughly 1:1, but BYU's wards also include students from the predominantly female Utah Valley State College. So the perception at BYU is that there are many more available women than men on campus.

---

[3] Ricks College has since become a part of BYU Idaho.

All of Zee's friends ask about Adam, who used to be a part of Zee's ward, but moved into a different one this year. They heard rumors of Zee and Adam's engagement. Wondering how incompetent a reporter I am, that I've spent seven hours with this woman, studying every detail of her life, and didn't manage to figure out she was engaged, I subtly glance down at Zee's ring finger. It's bare. Perhaps noting my look of confusion, Zee later explains to me that she can't decide what to do about Adam. He has proposed three times during the last couple of years, but she continued putting him off. Over the summer, she dated other men, most of them in the ward (which has created some awkward situations). But then a few weeks ago, Adam proposed again. This time, she accepted the ring, but recently she has decided she's not comfortable with it.

Zee's indecision seems unexceptional at BYU. Many students I spoke with have been engaged more than once, and one guy in Zee's ward was divorced. Students seem to rush into engagement, with courtships that can last as little as a week or, more usually, a month or two. "There was a girl in the newsroom last year," Andrea Ludlow recounts critically, "[who] met a guy on Saturday, and was engaged by the following Saturday. The engagement lasted a month and then they broke it off." A member of BYU's student government tells me about a friend who dated for nine days before getting engaged, and another friend who is getting divorced next month. The student center has a bulletin board dotted with index cards, selling wedding rings and engagement rings. Prices are crossed out all the way down the cards. "$75 OBO," reads one bottom line. Zee supposes that some of her friends who are having marital problems rushed through their courtships and engagements because they were eager to have sex.

Premarital sex (including during the engagement period) is forbidden not only by the LDS Church but also by BYU's honor code. But since with the exception of some freshmen, most BYU students live in off-campus housing, it is hard for an outsider to imagine how rules governing relations between the sexes would be enforced. Students do have a curfew of eleven P.M. on weekdays and one A.M. on weekends, but the administration does not perform random checks at students' homes. Rather, support of the honor code is so universal that students will typically approach their roommates if they disapprove of their behavior, or, in some cases, report them, either to the ward bishop or to the administration. Minji tells me that her friend's roommate threatened to report her friend if she didn't remove a poster of k. d. lang from her room, simply because the singer is a lesbian.

But Zee's housemates may demonstrate a higher level of tolerance for certain behaviors. For instance, though students may not have members of the opposite sex in their bedrooms, that clearly went on in Zee's house. The girls who live in the basement, for instance, recall a recent incident in which one of their roommates' boyfriends came out of her bedroom looking disheveled. After letting a few minutes elapse, the girl followed, apparently hoping her roommates wouldn't notice. "I can't believe she thought she could fool us," one of them giggles. But they tell me they had little interest in reporting the infraction. They also imply that they suspected nothing more than some dramatic necking was going on behind the door. Indeed, one way to discern that BYU students generally follow the honor code when it comes to sex is by listening to the way they talk about less "serious" activities. When a former boyfriend of Zee's claimed, for instance, that she had been his "first good kiss," she blushed deeply and changed the topic immediately.

But more serious infractions are not greeted with amusement by anyone. For instance, unmarried men and women are strictly forbidden from living together, even as friends; so when BYU student Julie Stoffer joined the cast of MTV's show *The Real World* during the summer of 2000, and lived for a few months on national TV with members of the opposite sex, BYU suspended her. Homosexual behavior is also not tolerated, and two gay students were recently kicked out of BYU when their respective roommates reported their behavior.

Jim Gordon, who was the bishop of a student ward for a few years, acknowledges, "I have had experience with people whose lifestyles were not really compatible with BYU's honor code, usually in the area of sexual relations." Ralph Hancock, a professor of political science and former ward bishop, tells me that once or twice he did not recommended students for readmission at the end of the year. He recalls one young man who was not particularly committed to the university or to the Church, but he still wanted to take advantage of the low-cost education. Hancock didn't think it was appropriate to allow him to continue at BYU.

Indeed, the bishops constitute the first line of defense in BYU's disciplinary process, and most problems are resolved by them before they are brought to the administration's attention. If matters do reach a more serious point, students are given every opportunity to repent and improve their ways. The result does not seem to be a game of "gotcha" in which students are kicked out often.

Indeed, BYU is nothing if not transparent about its rules, a list of which appears on the school's Web site. When they apply, students must not only sign a statement to the effect that they will adhere to the honor code, but they must also submit an essay about what it means to them. Baker believes that "students have an understanding of what life will be like here" in part because "they have been raised in a similar environment at home." And it seems to be working. BYU's freshman retention rate stands at 92 percent.

Even the students who are not Mormon (1 percent of the school's population) generally come from a similarly traditional culture. Foreign students like Su Jung, a slight young woman from Beijing, and her husband, David Dai, a graduate student originally from Shanghai, tell me that the school's atmosphere really appealed to them. "Rules are part of our life [in China]," he explains. "We are used to being disciplined. We are humble. It's part of the Confucian culture."

Of the non-Mormon students who come from within the U.S., many are part of strict religious groups. Though they often share Mormon sensibilities about sex and alcohol, and are even willing to submit to BYU's religious education requirements (14 credits worth of Mormon doctrine) in order to attend, cultural conflicts sometimes arise anyway. During my visit to campus, for instance, one of the school's Muslim students is found, in then-President Merrill J. Bateman's words, "glorying in what happened in New York. We just took him aside and said, 'That's not us. We don't do that. You need to be respectful of everyone.'" If he does not comply, Bateman tells me emphatically, he will not be allowed to remain at the school.

Though this behavior might have been tolerated at other schools—students at 146 colleges in 36 states held rallies opposing a U.S. military response in Afghanistan and hundreds of professors at public and private universities stated that they thought America got what it deserved[4]—anti-American sentiment is almost non-existent at BYU. On the morning of the attack, the usual Tuesday "devotional" service was attended by 20,000 students who showed up to recite the pledge of allegiance, recite a prayer, and listen to President Bateman speak. In the days that followed, many classes substituted "The Star-Spangled Banner" for their usual opening hymn. Enormous crowds gathered in the student center to watch CNN, American flags popped up everywhere, and many students wore their ROTC uniforms to class.

The patriotism at BYU, explains Damon Linker, derives directly from the Church and its teachings. "The U.S. exists [in the Mormon view] so

---

[4] For more information on the reaction on college campuses to the events of September 11, please see "Defending Civilization: How Our Universities Are Failing America and What Can Be Done About It," a report by the American Council of Trustees and Alumni, available on their Web site www.goacta.org.

that the Latter Day Saints can have safe haven in the world. The Mormons teach about the Founding through the lens of it being a divine act. In that sense, to be patriotic is to serve God." The conflation of religion and patriotism has important implications for political life at Brigham Young, even when there is no national crisis. For example, students vote in droves. Linker, who was teaching at BYU during the (relatively unexciting) '98 congressional elections, says that when he asked his introductory class who among them had been to the polls, "all one hundred twenty students raised their hands."

Mormons generally, and BYU students specifically, are overwhelmingly Republican, in part due to their religious beliefs about issues like abortion, sex education, and gambling (they are against all three). But Linker argues that "Mormons are not only socially conservative but deeply right-wing libertarian." For its first hundred years of existence, the LDS Church was in constant conflict with the federal government over territorial sovereignty. The resolution of that conflict in the late nineteenth century—when the Church outlawed polygamy and Congress granted statehood to Utah—resulted in a calmer relationship between Church and state. Still, the LDS Church has learned to appreciate "small government." Mormons' love of America really boils down to a love of the liberty it gives them, what Linker calls "the political structure that lets them be who they are."

Despite the high rates of voter participation, politics seems almost nonexistent at BYU. The Republican Club has about 300 or 400 members and the Democratic Club about 30 or 40. But when 95 percent of the campus is voting one way, there is little reason to campaign. Indeed, campaign signs are not even allowed on campus. But, politically speaking, what is most conspicuously absent at BYU are protests. Since the 1960s, sit-ins, teach-ins, and marches have been a rite of passage for students on the road through higher education. But during my time at BYU, I did not overhear so much as a mild complaint about administrative policies like the dress code, let alone more heated debate about issues driving college protests today—living wages for school employees and third-world sweatshop workers.

Even the Brigham Young University Service Agency (BYUSA), the school's student government, simply does not—as a matter of principle and policy—disagree with the administration. As the council tells it, they have a mission statement that echoes that of the university as a whole and that of the administration. More significantly, since the school's leadership is controlled directly by the Church (its leaders, including the Church's president and prophet, Gordon B. Hinckley, make up the board of trustees), as far as the students involved in BYUSA are concerned, the administration is being guided by a divine hand.

The situation at the *Daily Universe*, BYU's student newspaper, is largely the same. Andrea Ludlow, the petite energetic redhead who is the paper's opinion editor, recites the policy: "We can criticize BYU or the university's policies but not the Church." She confesses, though, that it is often difficult to distinguish. There is certainly a different role for a newspaper at a religious school, Andrea tells me, but the bottom line is that "there's a manager at every single newspaper and they will have their issues they won't let you print." At our paper, she says, "We're not going to quote someone who says President Hinckley is a whatever."

The kind of respect shown for the Church leadership is hardly restricted to members of the newspaper staff and the BYUSA. On Sunday evening, after a full day of religious activities, thousands of students go back to the Marriott Center to watch President Hinckley give a sermon on closed-circuit TV. Referred to as a "fireside," the address, specifically tailored to young adults, is delivered by a member of the Church leadership once a month. This week, Hinckley takes up some of the media coverage that Mormons are receiving in advance of the 2002 winter Olympics being held in Salt Lake City. "The problem with many of the newspaper columnists," he says, "is that their attitude is negative, always criticizing and seldom praising." He warns students against this sort of "cynical" behavior.

Though the speech itself seems unremarkable, the scene in audience is not. Listening to the fireside is in no way a curricular requirement, but almost all of the students in my section of the arena are taking notes. The men write on plain pads, and the women use colored pens in personalized journals, some hand-decorated with flowers and other pictures. Amazingly, I spot only one student dozing. In the car on the way home, Zee gushes about the fireside: Hinckley "does such a good job of not condescending to us." The whole talk, she says, "It just felt right." Her roommates agree.

As widespread as support of the Church and the school is, it is not universal. Minji did not like the fireside at all. Later, she tells me privately, "It was a little scary, the way everyone knows all the words to the hymn." She thinks for a minute, and adds, "It's a little too organized." The whole time, she tells me, some things her friends at home told her "were ringing in my ears," such as their claim that "Mormonism is a cult." This is Minji's first fireside, her first week at BYU, and perhaps most importantly, her first year as a convert to LDS.

Minji was raised Baptist by her mother and older sister, with whom she emigrated from Korea when she was ten. They disapprove of Minji's conversion, and they are angry about her decision to attend BYU, believing her career prospects will suffer as a result of her decision to turn down a scholarship to UC Davis. But after converting to Mormonism in December of her senior year of high school, Minji decided that if she was serious about her new faith, she couldn't be around the kind of temptation that comes with being a state university student. But that hasn't stopped her from dressing like one. At the fireside, for instance, she is wearing a short denim halter-top dress with an unzipped sweatshirt hanging off her shoulders. Her bare legs and denim sneakers are too casual for the occasion, and her straight hair, cut jagged around the face, with streaks of red throughout, makes her stand out in the clean-cut BYU population.

After the death of her best friend when she was fourteen, Minji's rebellion began. She likes to talk about that stage of her life—a lot. During a few conversations over the course of a week, she mentions her tremendous alcohol tolerance, her experience with strip poker, getting voted "horniest pervert" at her high school, her belief that nudity is a good thing, and going to wild parties at various colleges near her home in Oakland. Minji seems out to convince me, her roommates, and anyone else who will listen that she has "been there and done that," an effort not uncommon among college freshmen anywhere, but a little surprising at BYU. On the other hand, she is equally vocal about the fact that, thanks to the Church, she has been able to leave all of her self-destructive behavior behind.

Which is not to say she is altogether happy about her new life. She mocks a lot of Church doctrine, and particularly the girls who are a little too earnest about it. She doesn't believe much of the history of the Mormons, and she certainly "would never try to convert anyone." Minji also complains about the rules—like the fact that she can't eat out after the fireside because Mormons are not supposed to spend money on Sundays. She confesses to me that she is not looking forward to her ward calling because it will be hard to balance with her time-consuming computer-science major. Minji is even skeptical of the Mormon beliefs regarding relationships. She tells me she is dating a guy, but she has no intention of "getting serious," and doesn't really think much about marriage or family. Looking into Minji's future, it's likely that this more than her other objections to Mormonism will make her exceptional.

* * *

Despite all of the melodramatic scenes of broken engagements, brief courtships, and quick divorces, when I ask BYU students about their futures, all of them mention marriage and family as their most important—and immediate—goals. They speak about the issues with a certain amount of solemnity and practicality uncommon among their generation. There is no discussion, for instance, of waiting for a "soul-mate." Nor is the rush for marriage entirely or even mostly due to students' sexual urges. For the large majority of undergraduates who are not from Utah, and who plan on returning to communities where there is not a large Mormon population, their best chance to find a spouse who is an LDS member is at BYU, and by the time they graduate, 45 percent of the women and 55 percent of the men are married.

But this does not seem to interfere greatly with their academic goals and professional plans. During a gathering at Bishop Bailey's home and an ice-cream sundae party Zee brings me to, I try to survey the students about their career plans. One young woman who grew up in Utah told me she was teaching at a nearby elementary school and couldn't wait to relocate to upstate New York, where she would continue teaching but also write a book about "all of the stereotypes people associate with redheads." One of Adam's friends asks me all about where to live in Manhattan. He has an interview at Columbia's medical school the following week. A number of the student government leaders have done internships in Washington and are hoping to return there in some political capacity. Zee wants to go to graduate school, probably, but first would like to spend a couple of years working on documentaries about third-world countries. Zee's ex-boyfriend, Greg, wants to go teach in inner-city Los Angeles, where he did his mission. He also would like to get a PhD in teacher education and teach the history and philosophy of teaching. But he tells me, "My dream, my end, is to start up my own school, my own charter school."

Though they acknowledge some people might not understand their religion, BYU students don't expect to have problems finding work. Christi White, who spent last summer working for IBM in Burlington, Vermont, where a number of BYU grads have congregated, says that employers appreciated the mission experience that some students brought with them. Not only were return missionaries a bit older than most college graduates but they also have lived in other countries and speak foreign languages. Christi's experience interviewing for summer positions as well as for jobs after graduation made her think that, "Employers find BYU grads to be honest and hardworking. We go into the workforce not to just sit back and surf the Web even if no one is watching." David Dai, the Chinese graduate student who is not Mormon, believes recruiters are interested in him because of, not despite, his BYU connection. He thinks employers "come to BYU because we are more honest and more family oriented."

Indeed, the students I meet also have very definite ideas about how and where they want to raise their children, more so, I think, than their secular counterparts. Perhaps this is because family life is more imminent for them. Perhaps it is because of their religious beliefs: Mormons believe they will live on with their families eternally. But the students I interviewed do not see their goals for raising families as specific to their faith. As Andrea Uale tells me, Mormons want "what everyone wants. They want safety. They want their kids not to be part of gangs, not to be in jail. It all depends on good families and good schools."

Over a Thai dinner, Zee and her ex-boyfriend, Greg, talk to me about their plans for the future. He hasn't found the right woman yet but when he does, Greg tells me, he would like ten children, and like most other students I speak with, he expresses a desire to make sure "my kids are exposed to non-LDS children." Taking a handful of sticky rice, he explains, "When I was growing up, there was one family on the street who wasn't LDS. So we didn't play with the kids. It was like there was a rain cloud over their house. I want my kids to grow up in a neighborhood where people are people and beliefs are beliefs. Not in this ultra-Mormon place where it becomes cultural."

Zee readily agrees. Oddly, she remembers her family being disappointed when they moved from Las Vegas to Salt Lake City. Compared with the Mormons of Las Vegas, Zee claims, no one in Utah was trying very hard to live a Mormon life—they thought living with other Mormons was enough. Greg believes that living in a large Mormon-only community, even one like BYU, "You can lose a lot of the constant pursuit of ideas and you settle for just being in a place."

In fact, as much as the students I spoke with enjoyed their time at Brigham Young, like Greg and Zee, they couldn't see staying in such an overwhelmingly Mormon atmosphere for a longer term. Andrea Uale observes, "BYU is kind of like an oasis. You come and you drink up and you love it and love it, and then you pursue other aspirations." But this analogy seems only half right. BYU may be like an oasis but, for the most part, the students don't seem to view the rest of the world as a desert.

Zee, for her part, is back with Adam now, and eagerly anticipates life with him outside of BYU. "When you go out of this community," she explains, "you have this new strength and you can give it to other people." The following Thursday, as I say good-bye to Zee, she tells me she can't wait to come visit me next summer in New York City.

CHAPTER TWO

THE NEW FUNDAMENTALS:
THE BOB JONES STRATEGY FOR CONVERTING
NEW YORK CITY

Bob Jones. Just the words are enough to make people cringe. They have come to represent everything that was (and is) wrong with the rural South, everything that is racist, backward, and intolerant. Bob Jones is a fundamentalist Christian college located in Greenville, South Carolina, that originally came to prominence in the 1970s during a thirteen-year legal battle with the federal government. The IRS threatened to take away the school's nonprofit status because of its ban on interracial dating—a ban it lifted only a couple of years ago. At the same time, Bob Jones has gained a reputation for anti-Catholicism—the result of statements made by its administration suggesting, for instance, that the Pope is the "anti-Christ." Despite the outlandishness of such attitudes in the twenty-first century, the school probably would have been relegated to America's dustbin of little-known fringe institutions—the subject of an occasional human interest story in the *Atlanta Journal-Constitution* or a religion brief in *The New York Times*—were it not for the fact that every Republican presidential nominee starting with Ronald Reagan has made a campaign stop at Bob Jones. The concern that the school comprises a real political constituency, one taken seriously by mainstream politicians, continually pushes Bob Jones into the headlines.

And so most people have heard about Bob Jones. Indeed, whenever I mentioned my upcoming visit to the school, I received reactions like these: "Have they ever met a Jew before?", "Maybe you shouldn't mention your boyfriend is black," or a simple roll of the eyes. One elderly relative actually feared for my safety, muttering the word "lynching" under her breath. After two months of these conversations, only one response surprised me. At a wedding I attended in Atlanta the weekend before my trip, a young woman suggested I make the most of the visit to Bob Jones by spending some time in the school's world-renowned art museum. The what? Ignoring my skepticism, she explained that as an art history major at the University of Georgia, she visited the impressive collection of religious paintings at Bob Jones and found it thoroughly worthwhile.

My tour of the museum a few days later lasted an hour and a half and I barely had time to study more than one painting in any of the over twenty chronologically arranged rooms. The works, which include a Botticelli and Tintoretto, are mostly scenes from the New Testament, though there are a number of Old Testament works as well, including three different depictions of Queen Esther. The paintings are complemented by period furniture, and many of the rooms were specially designed to accommodate portions of gates and walls and ceilings rescued from old European religious sites. The Bob Jones University Museum and Gallery, which celebrated its fiftieth anniversary recently, has been praised in publications from *The New York Times* to *Better Homes and Gardens*.

At eleven A.M. conversation in the school's pristine seven-thousand-seat auditorium comes to an abrupt halt. A man rises from one of the twenty-five imposing armchairs on the stage and steps forward to the podium. After he leads the school in an austere rendition of "Jesus Saves," every one of the 5500 assembled faculty, students, and administrators recites the Bob Jones University creed:

> *I believe in the inspiration of the Bible (both the Old and the New Testaments); the creation of man by the direct act of God; the incarnation and virgin birth of our Lord and Savior, Jesus Christ; His identification as the Son of God; His vicarious atonement for the sins of mankind by the shedding of His blood on the cross; the resurrection of His body from the tomb; His power to save men from sin; the new birth through the regeneration of the Holy Spirit; and the gift of eternal life by the grace of God.*

Students must sign the creed when they apply to Bob Jones. And, not surprisingly, since they recite it at chapel four days a week, the students and faculty all know it by heart.

After some brief practical announcements, in which students are threatened with disciplinary action if they do not check their e-mail regularly, the chapel leaders move on to the main theme of the service: missionary work. To introduce this topic, a racially diverse group of teenagers files onto the stage. Described by the man at the podium as "a choir of international students who have been converted as the direct or indirect result of missionary work in their homelands," the message is underscored for students: You could change the lives of people like this if you choose to go on a mission.

During each chapel meeting this week, the students are told, a missionary who has served in a different part of the world will lecture about his experience, and then spend the day on campus, available to answer questions. The idea is to let these religious groups recruit in the same way that businesses or graduate schools do. The missionary speaking today has worked mostly in Asia. He is forthcoming about the difficulties of being out of one's element. "After four years in Muslim countries, I came back here and wanted to kiss the ground." In fact, he confesses, "I never liked anything about New York City before but I was happy to see it then. I was glad to be an American and glad to be a Christian American."

Many of the students I interview are interested in missionary work abroad, and among those who are not, a significant number plan to participate in ministries domestically. Proselytizing is a vital element of fundamentalist religious practices, and the students are taught to engage in it fully and constantly. Bob Jones offers students as many opportunities as possible to practice evangelism during their time at the school. After the terrorist attacks, for example, about twenty students traveled to New York City to minister to the spiritual needs of people there. They passed out a brochure with a picture of the twin towers and the words "Day of Horror 2001. WHY?" underneath. On the inside there are a series of questions such as "Does God love me?" and "Why did God allow this to happen?" Each is answered with a quotation from the Bible.

Of course, Bob Jones students are not oblivious to the fact that such messages can offend people. Michelle Berg, a junior I meet in the student center, believes that the tireless evangelizing of Bob Jones students and graduates is responsible for the university's anti-Catholic reputation. "We love them," Michelle assures me, referring to Catholics. Rifling through her trendy short-handled purse, she explains, "We have a way for them to be saved from hell and go to heaven." But they become offended, says Michelle, because "we have to tell them what they believe is wrong. And people don't like that. No one likes that, but we have to." Unfortunately, she laments, "People don't see that as love."

And, for the record, what is the problem that fundamentalists see with Catholic beliefs? Rick Pidcock, a sophomore with a small face and bushy eyebrows, who participates in a local ministry, gives the theological position: "We want to see Catholics come to the point where they understand that their efforts to *work* to try to get to God are not going to get them to God.

The only way they can get to God is accepting Christ alone. It has nothing to do with what we *do*," and, he insists, with a certain frustration, "That's so much easier. You just accept Christ by *faith* and he will save you and be your savior forever."

Fundamentalists might find common ground with conservative Catholics on any number of issues from school prayer to premarital sex. But they are entirely different religions, with entirely different sets of beliefs. Jim Berg, Michelle's father and the school's dean of students, said he might join in an anti-abortion protest with Catholics or Jews, but he tells me categorically that he would never pray with them. His daughter explains that her religion and others are mutually exclusive. "Jesus says 'I am the way and the truth and the life.' We can't then turn around and say 'God is a mountain and you can climb whatever side you want.' That's not what we believe." Michelle concludes, "We can't be hateful about it or unkind, but we also don't adopt parts of other people's religion so they think we're nice."

Both Rick and Michelle have grown up in seriously fundamentalist homes and have had the strong support of their families behind their religious beliefs. Right now, though, they are in a crucial phase of their intellectual and spiritual development, and, as Phil Smith, the school's provost, explains, it is the mission of Bob Jones to help them fortify their religious foundations as they move into adulthood.

"Bob Jones is a hothouse environment, where students are being cared for during their formative years," according to Smith, whose career at Bob Jones has spanned fifty years. He recalls the original mission of the school's founder, Bob Jones, Sr., or Dr. Bob as he is affectionately called. During Dr. Bob's travels from evangelical camp to camp in the early part of the century, Smith notes, "he kept running into young people whose faith had been shattered by going to state schools or so-called Christian schools and he felt there ought to be a place where young Christians could come and be nurtured."

And it seems to be working. The students tell me that the environment at Bob Jones has made them so confident about their faith that evangelizing becomes second nature. Sophomore Chris McAviney tells me he is only home a few weeks a year now because he spends all of his summers and vacations doing evangelistic activities. He is currently a Bible major and wants to go to seminary when he graduates and then become a youth pastor. Michelle Berg tells me her boyfriend wants to be a pastor in Europe and she would like to do mission work there as well. Josh Jalinski wants to be a pastor, among his other professional goals. Rick Pidcock wants to start his own music ministry. And a young woman I meet in the cafeteria line tells me her fiancé already has one.

The students who haven't considered either the ministry or missionary work as at least a part-time vocation are in the minority at Bob Jones. Sophomore Janice Martin reveals almost ashamedly, "Not all the students always think about evangelizing here. I don't think about it all the time." She reflects it's "probably something we should think about more." Janice just changed her major from biblical counseling to political science. Worried that the former "would have gotten me nowhere," she explains that her dream is to go to Duke Law School and then go into politics eventually. She admits, though, "I can't picture myself in the state senate and saying 'Well, God says . . .' Maybe that's my pride because I don't want people to think of me that way."

But maybe Janice shouldn't feel so bad. Given the strong focus on converting nonbelievers, I received surprisingly few nudges in this direction. A couple of the students ask me about my own faith but none try to talk me out of it. Only Jim Berg gives me what one former fundamentalist calls the "hard sell." Looking at my résumé, he asks, "I saw your Hebrew credentials. Are you by any chance from Judaism?" When I reveal that I am Jewish, he prods further. "You're coming into a lot of colleges that talk a great deal about Jesus Christ. Is that troubling to you?" When I tell him it's not, he continues, now with a couple of tears falling on his cheeks, "We love the Jewish people and we are very grateful to the Jewish nation. I hope our country never changes its position about Israel. Your people provided our messiah and I hope one day that you accept him as yours." Though it was an uncomfortable few moments, there was no mention of hellfire or damnation.

Like many of the students at Bob Jones, Angela Miller grew up in Greenville. Her mother went to Bob Jones and homeschooled her two daughters with the intention of sending them there as well. Angela says she went through a brief phase during her high school years when she was "rebellious" and didn't want to come, but she grew out of it. When I offer to have dinner with her on Main Street in Greenville, a nicely redone strip of shops and cafés, she tells me she'll have to get a recommendation for a restaurant from a friend. Acknowledging that she has led a pretty sheltered life, Angela confesses that she has never eaten down there. At the pizza joint we eventually choose, Angela seems distracted by the sexual nature of the lyrics she hears on the easy-listening radio station, but when I ask her if she would like to leave, she tells me she can ignore it.

Besides these environmental factors, there are financial reasons, as well, that Angela does not frequent restaurants downtown. Though Bob Jones only charges $5,400 per semester for tuition, room, and board—a fraction of most other private schools and still significantly less than most public universities—Angela pays for most of it herself. Her father, who is a guard at a maximum-security prison nearby, is only able to contribute a hundred dollars a month to his daughter's tuition. Angela comes up with the rest of the money working with her mother and younger sister (who will be starting at Bob Jones this fall) at the local Baskin-Robbins. Over the summer, she puts in seventy hours a week, and during the school year somewhat less.

Having lived on campus for a semester, Angela now stays at home to save money, but she doesn't seem to mind. She tells me she may actually have more freedom living at home. She doesn't think, for instance, that her parents would require her dates to be chaperoned (as Bob Jones does), and they might not enforce the Bob Jones strict ban of any physical contact between the sexes. But Angela's father has warned her, "If you ever got pregnant, I don't know what we would do." Mr. Miller doesn't have much to worry about. Angela's own standards are pretty high: "It's fine to hold hands with someone you're dating," she tells me. But as for kissing, that will wait until she is engaged. "Kissing leads to other things. And then you could end up pregnant." Of course, this is all immaterial for now. Angela did not date in high school and has not been on a date in college, either. Though she is hardly unattractive, at six feet tall, she laments, "The boys are always too short."

But Angela insists she is not at Bob Jones to find a husband anyway. She is majoring in political science and wants to go into state politics some day—working behind the scenes. Already she can break down for me the various constituencies at Bob Jones. "There are three kinds of students at BJ." First, she explains, are "the faculty and staff brats who are always flouting the rules." They don't usually escape without punishment for long, but Angela does think they get away with a little more than the other students. Then, there are the "bo-jos." Having made their way through elementary, junior high, and high school at the adjacent Bob Jones Academy, these students "walk around all the time with their rule books in hand correcting people." Finally, there are the people in between, among whom Angela counts herself, who try to follow the rules but "sometimes mess up by mistake."

For instance, during the first semester of school, Angela received ten demerits for missing her mandatory freshman tour of the art museum. It would have been twenty-five—the amount for a missed class—she explains, but the discipline committee cut her some slack since she was in the library studying when it slipped her mind. Accumulating 150 demerits will get you "shipped out" of Bob Jones (a phrase used by a number of the administrators I talk to). But there are some offenses for which the administration has "zero tolerance." Drinking, stealing, and premarital sex are among the ones mentioned. To put it mildly, the school's administration has a strong in-loco-parentis bent, evidenced by the ban on televisions in the dormitories, the regulations governing which routes students may use to walk to class, and a light bell at eleven P.M. and 6:55 A.M. signaling the times when students should go to bed and when they must get up (feet should be on the floor).

Chris McAviney tells me he is unfazed by the rules. "Light bell is fine with me because I'm so exhausted anyway. After a year of it you don't notice." But other students are not so submissive. When I spot Kyle Caldwell, he is slumped on a couch in the lounge with his arms crossed, his teeth clenched, and his eyes angry. His parents, who live in Columbia, South Carolina, always wanted him to come to Bob Jones after high school but he did not; so he started at the University of South Carolina. After a semester, though, Kyle gave in and enrolled at Bob Jones because his mother was so upset with him being at a non-Christian school. Kyle is annoyed with a lot of the rules at Bob Jones, beginning, he tells me, with the dress code that forces him to put on a tie every morning.

Though Jonathan Pait, the school's director of media relations, makes a point of trying to get outsiders to focus less on the Bob Jones rules and more on the other aspects of the school, it is a losing battle, particularly since the other administrators continue to emphasize that the rules are an integral part of the school's identity. According to Jim Berg, the focus at Bob Jones on "attention to detail, including arriving on time, and doing your assignments on time" is vital in helping the school "to develop the best in human character." He is very up front about the school's atmosphere. "You'll see a lot of difference between this and a military establishment, but you will also see a lot of similarities." And just like at a boot camp, Berg tells me, "some students come already conditioned. They've been thinking about this school all their lives." Others, he tells me, "come pretty flabby."

Among the "flabby" there are those, like Kyle, whose parents force them to attend Bob Jones. Berg believes this population is "decreasing," but three different students mention to me their impression that the number of unmotivated students has gone up this year, the result, they believe, of large scholarships offered in honor of the school's seventy-fifth anniversary, which have made parents who might not otherwise have considered Bob Jones eager for their kids to attend.

Berg, for his part, is more interested in the other group of "flabby" students—those who "come to us and say, 'I need this. I'm not sure I'm ready for it but I need it.'" He gives an example of a girl in his office the previous day because of a disciplinary matter. Berg tells me, "After she got done talking to her mother and the dean of women, she said, 'You know what my problem is? I'm a spoiled brat. I've always gotten my way.'"

But Jonathan Pait is right that the project of character formation at Bob Jones involves much more than just the rules. It's about the total environment. For instance, students are assigned a new roommate each year to ensure that they interact with different groups during their time at Bob Jones. Instead of the dormitory, then, the basic building block of campus social life is the "society." There are about fifty such groups on campus—half male, half female, and ranging in size from fifty to two hundred—whose activities are funded mostly by student fees. They would seem a little like sororities or fraternities, except that students are required by the administration to join one and the societies have no say about whom to accept. Each society is given an equal sized square of space on one of two neatly kept bulletin boards, where it may post announcements about weekend events, most commonly intramural games.

Since Bob Jones does not participate in intercollegiate sports (so it's not bound by the rules of any outside organizations like the NCAA), intramural teams organized by the societies are enormously popular and competitive. And most students seem satisfied, if not proud, of the school's sports program, more than one citing to me a statement by the head coach of the University of South Carolina's football team to the effect that Bob Jones has the best intramural program in the country. Not surprisingly, then, watching intramural games is the big weekend social activity at Bob Jones. Vanessa Ball and her boyfriend, for instance, have been attending soccer games together ever since they met at a post-match bonfire around Thanksgiving last year.

Since couples must remain in public locations at all times, the options for spending time with one's significant other are limited. Encouraging wholesome courtship rituals is another means by which the Bob Jones administration can engage in a particular sort of character development. Aside from attending society events, students may also spend time in the dating parlor—which many refer to as the "furniture store" for the obvious reason that it's just a vast lounge with dozens of couches—where a chaperone is always on duty wandering among the couples. But most of the girls I talk to imply you have to be in a very serious relationship before you would even think of going there. Michelle Berg tells me that she and her boyfriend of one year, Matt, sometimes "pray together there. It's a good place to go for quiet."

The administration mandates that couples have a chaperone in order to leave campus. But, as I learned during the few days I spent at Bob Jones, there are a few reasons why this rule is not as restrictive as it sounds. First, students who do not live on campus are not required to comply. Second, students who have completed their undergraduate degree and have decided to stay for a master's degree (a fairly common choice), and the undergrads dating them, are not bound by it. Third, the chaperone can be a friend who is in the MA program. The result is that romantic outings at Bob Jones more often resemble double dates with friends who graduated the year before than couples being observed from across the table by their fifty-year-old English professor. This is not to say, of course, that the dates are anything but G-rated.

After graduation, Jill, an outgoing junior with dark long curly hair, plans to attend medical school. She hopes one day to combine her missionary drive with her love of medicine by going to practice in a developing country. I have lunch in the school's vast dining hall (it seats about three thousand people) with Jill and her friend Sarah. We leave our bags and jackets out in the hall. (It would be a fire hazard to bring them in, I'm told by the attendant outside, and no one at the school ever worries about theft.) Over baked potatoes and chili, Jill, who is originally from Pennsylvania and whose mother attended Bob Jones, tells me about her plans.

First, she wants me to know that she has never worried that the reputation of Bob Jones would hurt her chances of getting into medical school. Even though Bob Jones is not accredited (like the NCAA and ROTC, an accreditation agency, the administration worries, might try to impose its rules on the university), it has a long established reputation, and medical schools, particularly the University of South Carolina, where Jill would like to go, take a number of BJ graduates each year. It helps, also, that the Bob Jones registrar is very accommodating, providing graduate schools with extensive information on the university's curriculum, so that they may better evaluate students' transcripts.

All this is not to say that a significant percentage of Bob Jones graduates are headed to top graduate degree programs—Jill is among an elite few. But that is due in part to the school's very open admissions policy. Gary Weier, professor of political science, tells me, "If you have a high school degree and you take the ACT you will be accepted at Bob Jones." The key, though, he explains, is that "you might not be able to get into certain majors." The school can offer, for instance, rigorous science classes because there are a number of areas of study that require students to pass a test before they declare. Others cull their ranks by asking students to maintain a minimum GPA. Many of the less qualified students are siphoned off into the School of Applied Studies, whose mission, according to the school's literature, is "to train students to effectively serve the Lord and to equip them for careers in ministry or trade professions."

But for the students like Jill who qualify as premeds, the Bob Jones curriculum is a demanding one. Her science classes are no different from those at other schools. "We learn everything in the textbook," Jill explains, "but we learn that some of it is wrong." When I express my surprise to Jim Berg that the students at a fundamentalist school are being taught evolution, he tells me that he does not see a contradiction. "I can study Nazism and the Third Reich without agreeing with them." Students, Berg argues, should understand how other people think because they'll be interacting with them after graduation. Moreover, he believes that this wider "liberal arts education" is what separates Bob Jones from the small Bible colleges that dot the southern and midwestern United States. "We're not just teaching them the Bible. We're also teaching them the rest of the world." When I question whether differences of belief between Bob Jones graduates and their peers, particularly in the area of science, won't affect the chances of students' professional success, Berg suggests that opinions on evolution are immaterial: "A doctor doesn't have to know where the cell came from, they just have to know how they deal with it."

But Jill's friend, Sarah, cannot seem to write off the contradictions so easily. She is studying counseling, which means, she explains, that half her classes are in experimental psychology and the other half are in Bible "to make up for it." Berg, who also directs counseling services at the school, acknowledges, "Psychology classes here are not taught in a manner favorable to the world's view of these things." Though he does not dispute the categorizations of behavior that modern psychology has arrived at, he does question its solutions. His take could be summed up as less Prozac, more faith. Again, though Berg believes that the religious and secular views of psychology are in many ways directly conflicting, he emphasizes that students need to understand both in order to be professionally competent.

But professors face another obstacle in preparing their students: Most of the young women and men matriculating to Bob Jones come from intellectually sheltered environments. Thirty years ago, almost all of the school's students came from public schools, but as the public school environment changed—public prayer and strict dress codes were dropped—Christian education began to take off. The rise in the homeschool movement has occurred a little more recently but it has also had a disproportionate effect on the conservative Christian community. Now, 75 percent of BJ students have gone to Christian elementary and high schools and another 10 percent or so are homeschooled.

Camille Lewis observes that though her homeschooled students are "very disciplined, and have good study skills," they have experienced a kind of intellectual isolation that can prove problematic. Lewis tells me about one young woman who was looking for a topic for a speech to give in class. Instructed to go to the library and flip through some news magazines, she came back to Lewis and said, "There's a whole world out there I never knew existed." On the other hand, when Lewis insists, "They adjust quickly," it is not hard to believe—the students I meet are enormously hardworking. Compared to those she taught as a graduate student at Indiana University, Lewis tells me, her students at Bob Jones are probably on the same level in terms of their intellectual ability, but the latter group seems to care more about what they are learning. In terms of her own discipline, Lewis observes, "Hands down, the students here are better public speakers here than at IU." She attributes this to the fact that they see a need for the skill in a religious context, that is, for preaching and proselytizing. "At IU," Lewis notes, "they are more detached."

Lewis believes her students' connection to the work is particularly evident when she teaches the writings of religious authors like George Whitfield or St. Augustine, but many of the professors try to show their students a religious dimension to works that are considered secular. Dean Berg gives the example of an English professor teaching Jack London's *Call of the Wild*. "Here," Berg suggests, "is a very vivid portrayal of life in the wilderness, of mankind surviving and ending in despair." Berg explains how a class might discuss this in religious terms: "We would say [London] had it right. Life without God does end in despair. He had it right but he didn't have the answer. It was just an unfortunate conclusion." Lewis takes very seriously this charge of helping students to see the religious elements in their secular studies. "I have a responsibility to students to help them carry out their missions, which means when I teach ancient and contemporary rhetoric and we're reading Socrates and Plato, I'm compelled to get my students to think of . . . how [these texts] will affect our daily lives. I see study in rhetoric as affecting the way I live."

For Bob Jones students, religion defines politics. Among his students, political science professor Gary Weier tells me he observes a "seriousness of purpose." Most students, he thinks, read the newspaper regularly, even if they are not in classes that require it. "Without TVs on campus, Bob Jones students may be more informed" than their counterparts at other schools, according to Weier, "because it forces them to turn to more sources that provide them with more balance and in-depth coverage. They have to invest the extra effort. We can't sit around and watch C-SPAN all day."

But the interest in political science is more than intellectual. When I ask Weier why students at Bob Jones are zealous in their political participation, he answers with the following: "We hope that our students here take life seriously, that they render unto Caesar the things that are Caesar's. You should do what you can in the world around you, including with government." For decades students at Bob Jones have voted at a much higher rate than other college students. Though the numbers have fluctuated somewhat, Weier estimates a 60 to 70 percent voting rate at Bob Jones compared with a 30 percent voting rate at other colleges (according to a recent Harvard study). Of course, students generally vote Republican and there is a lot more contention on campus during the primaries than during the general election. For example, Weier offers, during campaign 2000, "you would assume that the campus overwhelmingly supported Bush but there were a lot of McCain supporters and Keyes supporters, too."

Notably, this involvement with politics does not extend to some usual college student practices like staging protests. Weier contrasts his students with the young people he saw demonstrating at Bush's inauguration. The latter, he explains, "are young people looking for a cause. It wasn't so much that they were against George Bush, but rather they were looking for something to sell themselves to. It happens a lot on college campuses—young people are just trying to find their way in life and that's the way they set themselves apart." But, for the students at Bob Jones, it seems, that way is already decided—it's their faith.

When I ask David Haskins and Josh Jalinski out to lunch, their first instinct is to introduce me to the wonders of Southern cuisine, but when they learn of my aversion to pork, they settle instead on a Mexican dive called Corona. The beer is flowing generously at the tables all around us, and the atmosphere seems pretty far from the clean environment of the school just a few blocks away. David orders for himself and for Josh in Spanish, explaining to me that he learned the language from his mother, who is Cuban. (Josh chimes in that even though the interracial dating policy also applied to Hispanics and

Asians, David's parents were living proof that no one really thought about the rule anyway.)

David first started coming to Corona when he was attending the public high school just across the street from Bob Jones. His friends from that high school—especially the Catholic ones—find his choice of college a little odd. But it seems understandable when you find out about his family. His father, who passed away in 2001, was one of the better known graduates of the school. Speaker pro tempore of the South Carolina state house, the elder Haskins's renown came most recently from his role as the cochair of John McCain's presidential campaign in South Carolina. When the campaign decided to attack Bush for speaking at Bob Jones, Haskins resigned his position. According to Gary Weier, Haskins remained friendly with McCain until his sudden death a few months later, and McCain attended Haskins's funeral, which was held in the Bob Jones auditorium.

Having lived on campus his freshman year, David is now at home helping out his mother (who took over his father's House seat after a special election) with his younger siblings. David tells me that he too has political aspirations. His friendly smile and easygoing demeanor certainly make a political career seem plausible, but generally David seems content to act as wingman to the more outgoing Josh. Though they hang out a lot together—they are members of the same society and share a political science major—David jokes that Josh gets all the girls. It's easy to see why. On a campus where there seems to be a higher than usual proportion of awkward young men with acne and little fashion sense, Josh's Gap ad good looks make him stand out. He casually flirts with the girls in his classes—Angela tells me she gets a big kick out of both Josh and David. When Josh is late getting to his class with Camille Lewis, he apologizes, flashing her a smile, and she laughs off the infraction. Later in the afternoon, Josh tries to introduce me to a friend of his who transferred from a secular college. He knows where and when her classes are, but they're not dating, he assures me. He already has a girlfriend who is a graduate assistant.

Josh applied to three schools his senior year: Harvard, Cedarville (a Christian college in Ohio), and Bob Jones. He was accepted at all three, but he decided he wanted a serious religious education. So the choice, he tells me, was simple: Harvard wasn't religious and Cedarville wasn't academically serious enough. He doesn't seem to have any regrets. Though he admits his fellow students may not be of Harvard caliber, he thinks he is getting the right education for what he wants to do. And what is that? Well, first, he wants to get a master's degree from Westminster Theological Seminary, and then use that as a transition to get into a PhD program in history at either Columbia or Yale. His eventual goals are to become mayor of Asbury Park, New Jersey, serve as a pastor for the community, and start a Christian school there.

The confidence with which Josh and David discuss their futures in the secular world is uncommon among Bob Jones students. Having attended a public school before coming to Bob Jones, Josh and David have an edge over their home- and Christian-schooled classmates, who seem unsure and even worried about the kind of day-to-day social contact they will be expected to have with nonbelievers. Tara Rodman, who graduated from BJ two years ago and has been pursuing a master's in rhetoric while working part-time as a counselor in the admissions office, acknowledges that even though "in the Christian faith you love other people, it makes it harder to have really close friendships with people of other faiths." She worries, "If you got into a discussion [with a nonbeliever] it would be hard because you'd be arguing and the way you're looking at things is so different." For Tara this problem hits very close to home because her own extended family is not fundamentalist and her fiancé's family is Catholic.

Janice Martin tells me, "I do have some unsaved friends. I don't think they're my closest friends." Though Janice doesn't think "isolating them does any good at all," she certainly does "not hang out with them all the time." Other students tell me they have no interest in leaving the large fundamentalist community of Greenville, if they can help it, because they enjoy the comfort of being around their coreligionists. And that's just a sample of the students who are willing to talk to me. Though I prominently display the press badge that Jonathan Pait gave me when I arrived on campus, many of the students—who were warned during the presidential campaign not to speak with reporters—look at me with suspicion when I approach them and turn down my requests for interviews. Others ask that I don't tape their interviews.

Lewis tries to explain the mentality in the fundamentalist community regarding outsiders: "We're taught that we're separate. We're in the world but not of the world. And sometimes that leads to thinking that is passive aggressive. We think everyone is out to get us. And that's not good." "Passive aggressive" accurately defines the attitude I receive from Jonathan Pait, who goes from friendly and even solicitous one minute to standoffish and defensive the next. From behind his impeccably neat desk, with only a few papers and a plastic jar of individually wrapped beef jerky sticks on it, Pait, the director of media relations, flatly refuses to provide me with a copy of the student handbook, offering that they have had bad experiences with people using it "to make fun of us on the Internet." I am told that not even students can receive a handbook before arriving on campus to enroll in classes, for fear it might fall into the wrong hands. Pait does offer to let me speak with one of the admissions counselors, who will not give me a list of the rules but who will be able to explain the ones that I already know about.

The close monitoring of how the school is presented to the outside world is evident also in the student newspaper, which is sent out to alumni every week. As Melissa Johnson explains, "We don't want to put the university in a bad light. Before it goes to press, the paper is read by a faculty member and the provost." The paper is completely dull, with headlines like "Dorm Décor Differs on Two Sides of Campus" and "Love of Soccer Opens Door of Ministry." When I ask Melissa whether the lack of controversy in the paper bothers her, she tells me, "I haven't thought about it." But it wouldn't matter. The administration would never allow anything spicier. Pait's explanation for the administration's concern is simple: The school has been wounded repeatedly by the media. Not just during the 2000 presidential campaign either. A few years ago, he tells me, he was interviewed about the school for a segment on ABC's *Nightline*. He believes the producers took his quotes out of context and cut off his conclusion, completely distorting the meaning of his comments.

Pait also thinks that in their zeal to accuse the school of anti-Catholic bias, the media "sifted through thousands of documents" put out by the school over the years to find the quotes they wanted, and then those too were taken out of context. As far as the comment referring to the Pope as the anti-Christ, Pait explains, "It's a statement we mean in a technical doctrinal way." Pait insists that orthodox Catholics understand what fundamentalists have in mind by it, and are often less offended than nonbelievers. On the other hand, he acknowledges that the Bob Jones community has to work on a way to say things less offensively. For instance, when I bring up the subject of Brigham Young University, he tells me he believes that "Mormons are not Christians," but emphasizes that there is a way to get across the doctrinal differences and still show respect for the people you disagree with.

Ruth Crumley is originally from Africa. The adopted daughter of two now retired missionaries, Ruth, who is now a senior, has never been able to afford Bob Jones. "The whole reason I've been able to stay here is people have given us money." As recently as two years ago, she thought she would have to drop out, but she recounts, "One lady who had died in our church gave me money for my junior year. She told my mother she knew I wanted to finish at Bob Jones. All the money has been totally of the Lord."

Last summer, Ruth tells me, the Lord stepped in again—this time, in the form of the Bob Jones administration, which announced it would be offering need-based scholarships to minority students. After filling out the applications and meeting with two of the people on the scholarship board, Ruth was informed that she would receive five thousand dollars for the semester. In addition to being excited about the scholarships because they will allow her to continue her education at Bob Jones, she is also optimistic about their larger effect. "I am hoping that if kids really want to get a godly education and an education in liberal arts they will come here. For those minority students who are hard up and think there is no way they can get the money, this will help."

Though Ruth's friends from Detroit cannot understand how she can go to Bob Jones given its racial attitudes, Ruth doesn't see the problem. When I ask her about the interactions among the different races at Bob Jones, she responds, "We all get along so well that no one notices a color difference," a condition she happily attributes to the school's religious identity. In her own case, she tells me: "I guess I look at people for who they are, and I think that's the way Christ looks at us. We are all sinners. But yet He is willing to look past that if we are willing to believe in Him." Although she doesn't see a problem with racial attitudes at Bob Jones, she does hope that the scholarships will have a positive effect on the school's image. Ruth reluctantly acknowledges, "We are at a college where it will be hard for us to get out of that, for people to not look at BJ as being racist." Ruth is right. The *Tonight Show*'s Jay Leno probably summed up the general population's attitude toward the announcement of the scholarships by joking: "They are actually offering nonwhite students financial aid, scholarships, even their own private water fountains."

Jonathan Pait confirms that changing the image of the school was one of the administration's motives behind the new policy. "We're so often pointed out as being so racist. We want to take a stab, at least, to overcome that stereotype," he told *The New York Times*. But if Bob Jones cares about its reputation, why did it take so long to get rid of the ban on interracial dating? Lewis, who wrote her dissertation on the way that separatist groups represent themselves to the outside world, explains how she believes the situation reached this point. To begin with, of course, until the 1970s, Bob Jones did not admit blacks at all. Once it did, Bob Jones was hardly alone in instituting an interracial dating ban. (Whether or not such rules appeared on the books, they were enforced by the environment inside and outside of the school. Miscegenation laws remained on the books in Alabama until 2000 and one high school in Georgia just had its first mixed-race prom in 2002, only to offer the option of a segregated prom the following year.)

As fundamentalists, professor Camille Lewis tells me, "We want[ed] to be separate from the world, but we also want[ed] to look admirable in the eyes of the world." And there were still segments of the population that found the ban admirable, long after the IRS decided it was reprehensible.

But as for why the ban remained at Bob Jones years after no respectable group would support it—Lewis claims even her "peers on the faculty have wanted to get rid of it for a while"—she believes the school's religious foundations are to blame. She means this not in the sense that members of the Bob Jones community believe in a biblical justification for the ban: no one I ask cites one. Rather, Lewis tells me, "[It's] so imperative to our identity [as fundamentalists] that nothing has changed." Theologically, fundamentalists define themselves by the fact that the same things that guided them seventy-five years ago when the school was founded guide them today. Before the 2000 election debacle, Lewis tells me, "Dr. Bob wanted to let it go quietly," so as not to draw attention to the school changing. In the end, though, according to Lewis, this aversion to change had to be put aside in favor of a more pressing matter—the school's public image.

Jamin Jantz, the sports editor of the school's newspaper, explains, "Dr. Bob saw how [the ban] was affecting the school's [reputation]. . . . If people are going to blow up over this and completely write off Bob Jones because of this, then it's not worth it." But it doesn't seem as though the ban affected applications to the school (which continued to rise steadily before and after it was dropped). And the current students, even Josh and David, don't seem to be particularly bothered by it. Most of the ones I speak with have little idea of why the policy was instituted in the first place, let alone why it was the cause for so much vitriol from forces outside the school.

Michelle Berg, who was a freshman when the policy was changed, shrugs. "Who knows why it was started? I don't know. I don't know if it was more for socially proper reasons. You'd never see anyone complaining about it. You didn't think about it." And she concludes: "When it was changed, nothing looked different the next day." Melissa Johnson, the editor of *The Collegian,* sums up the attitude of most of her classmates. "They say Bob Jones is imposing these rules on the students, but most of the students come here knowing the rules. What does it matter to the outside world if our school has that rule?" Even the minority students like Ruth Crumley said they didn't really see it as much of an issue: "It wasn't a big deal that I wasn't allowed to date white guys. I knew the rules coming in. Big deal. Life goes on."

And if the students interested in Bob Jones will apply regardless, why does the administration care about the school's portrayal in the media? "On a fundamental level," Lewis answers, "we're just trying to get students," but there is another dimension here, says Lewis. "We are also worried that our graduates won't get jobs because of what's said on the nightly news or that our students won't get into graduate schools." Similarly, when it came to a *GQ* magazine picture spread satirizing the school's interracial dating ban published in 2000, Lewis suggests, "We were not so worried about the *GQ* spread because of enrollment but because of the effect on our graduates and the effect on our overarching testimony." Ultimately, in other words, the school has a vested interest in being taken seriously by readers of *GQ* and watchers of the network news. Though that may not be the audience interested in enrolling at Bob Jones, they are the intended recipients for the evangelizing efforts of the school's graduates.

A concern with public relations has only just begun to shape the university's decisions with regard to race, but it has long been true that many of the school's curricular and extracurricular decisions are determined by figuring out how to most effectively bring the school's religious message to the outside world. Education at Bob Jones is essentially "a means to an end," according to history professor Carl Abrams. "If you're going to reach Western culture with the gospel, then in a sense you have to play that game." Abrams is not simply referring to the necessity of teaching subjects—like the theory of evolution or the ideas behind Nazi totalitarianism—that will help students get into better graduate schools. He is also talking about the less tangible ways in which the school tries to help students connect with their secular counterparts.

For instance, the school has a strict policy against allowing students to listen to any kind of modern music, including Christian contemporary music (CCM). But students are allowed to listen to any kind of classical music or opera, even secular opera, and even the secular operas with somewhat risqué themes. "Why classical music?" Camille Lewis reflects. "There is a sense in a way that we try to identify with an upper-middle-class aesthetic, that if we appeal to this higher level we will give ourselves more credibility." "Fundamentalism has historically been associated with lower classes, and if we can push that off so we don't look like country bumpkins, we can not only improve ourselves, we can improve our message and make it more effective and get a different clientele." She warns, though, "You won't hear that from the administration."

You won't hear it from students, either. Most, like Rick Pidcock, whose devotion to his music major extends to his choice of a black necktie with blue musical notes on it, think the policy is the result of the administration's belief "that a rock beat is inherently evil."

And that may certainly be part of it. But Carl Abrams, who has written extensively on the social history of fundamentalists, believes Lewis's assessment is not far off. Though he doesn't think it was "the explicit intention" of the people who made up the music policy and thus not given as an explanation to the students, he does believe "it was in their minds." In fact, he finds Bob Jones's cultural environment, including mandatory attendance at classical music concerts and opera performances, to be "not just middle class, [but] high class." When combined with the school's extravagant Shakespeare productions and extensive art collection, Abrams believes the school is fulfilling the original vision of Bob Jones, Sr., training professionals "who will move within the culture." Abrams thinks that the kind of cultural knowledge that students gain at Bob Jones will help them better relate to nonbelievers on an individual level. And by giving the Bob Jones students the basis to make those relationships more likely, Abrams claims, "the college becomes a means of evangelism."

As much as Abrams agrees with this idea of teaching students to appreciate art and music and literature in order to reach upper- and middle-class America more effectively, he believes there is a tension embedded in it. "There is a contradiction because we think the world is going downhill, but here we have an attachment to the culture." And it's hard, Abrams acknowledges, for some students to reconcile the urgency of their missionary obligations with the demands that they spend their time learning about literature and opera. Though the school is divided on exactly how the world will end— the premillennialists believe that the world is going to get worse and worse until the rapture and the postmillennialists believe that it will get better before the end—there is no question that it could be any day now. (A number of students believe that the attacks on the World Trade Center may be a sign that the apocalypse is imminent.)

So how should students see their role in secular America given the possible brevity of their time here? "I don't really know which way the world is going to end," Lewis confesses, "but I do know I have a social responsibility to change my world." Berg concurs: "We live for other people." Surrounded by lower class neighborhoods, Bob Jones encourages students to serve the community. They provide an alternative Halloween celebration for children (a party without the pagan symbols), organize fund-raising events for the March of Dimes, and arrange neighborhood cleanups. Berg adds, "Those aren't evangelistic opportunities. Those are statements we want to make to the community." But it's a little difficult to figure out where the religious element ends and where the service element begins for Bob Jones students when Berg—alluding to Jesus' admonition to the Apostles in Matthew 5:13-16 to be the "salt of the earth" and the "light of the world"—tells me, "We become very salty and get out there and permeate the society."

The relationship the university has with its immediate neighbors is a kind of microcosm of its interactions with the outside world generally. "There was a time," Phil Smith remembers, "they felt we were cloistered. We once had a row of trees in front of campus." But Smith tells me that the school has in recent years tried to be more open, for instance by inviting the community to visit more regularly. "We have an open house for Thanksgiving, and we have a tree-lighting ceremony at Christmas. There is also the artist series which is open to the public." And what became of the row of trees? Well, Smith says, "We replaced it with a low fence."

CHAPTER THREE

BEYOND THE FIGHTING IRISH:
NOTRE DAME'S RACE QUESTION

It's obvious that Notre Dame's appearance can't explain the mythical status it has achieved in the American Catholic mind. Indeed, more than a few drivers must nod off during the hour-and-a-half trip from Chicago to South Bend, Indiana. The road doesn't offer so much as a bump to keep one interested. What's more, there is no particular moment of recognition as you approach Notre Dame—nothing like looking across the Charles River at the sun shining on Harvard's golden domes, or suddenly coming upon Yale's grand Gothic presence after driving through the slums of New Haven. Surrounded by largely empty parking lots that fill up only when the Fighting Irish play a home football game, the campus is spread out, and the buildings along the perimeter are mostly relics of dull sixties architecture. Visitors can take their bearings from the unremarkable library building, one of whose walls sports a mural of what students call "Touchdown Jesus"—Christ with his hands reaching out at an angle resembling a goal post. (Directions always begin, "If you're facing Touchdown Jesus . . .") Notre Dame's older buildings are scattered around the center of campus, and the school's munificent endowment has kept them beautifully preserved inside and out. The landscaping is meticulous, too.

Students and faculty refer to the Notre Dame "mystique," an aura, partly cultural and partly religious, that draws generation after generation of students to the school. Mike Connolly, the editor of the school's newspaper, tells me that even though no one immediately related to him attended the school, he grew up in a "Notre Dame family." A chubby guy wearing jeans, sneakers, and an old green fleece pullover, Mike tells me they were such fans of the football team, and by extension, the school, that he applied only to Notre Dame. He knew he wanted to be a sportswriter and couldn't wait to cover games at Notre Dame. Though Mike did not come specifically for the religious education, he thinks that the different elements of Notre Dame's identity—the football team, the immigrant Catholic culture, and the religious foundations—are all tied together. In fact, more than fifteen thousand people attend mass after each game.

In the last few decades, though, as other prominent Catholic schools have shed many visible signs of their Catholic identity, Notre Dame has grappled with how its specifically religious elements can survive through the twenty-first century. "The students are not as rah-rah Catholicism as they used to be," Mike acknowledges. But he doesn't think the school is losing its distinctiveness. "Notre Dame's religious nature will never die or become a sidelight. It won't ever become a regular university with a few priests."

Still, Notre Dame is at a crossroads. Will it become more secular or more Catholic? Will the school's so-called mystique be enough to sustain it? David Solomon, a philosophy professor and the director of Notre Dame's Center for Ethics and Culture, has his doubts. "The road is already there. Who remembers that the University of Chicago was ever a Christian university?" The difficulty, according to Solomon, is that "the academy is a very antireligious place" and "Notre Dame wants to compete at a high level academically."

Certainly Notre Dame need not look as far as the originally Baptist University of Chicago for an example of the path to secularization; plenty of its Catholic brethren have also lost much of their religious identities in recent years. Georgetown just hired its first lay president; Holy Cross students, along with their counterparts at ten other American Jesuit universities, perform *The Vagina Monologues* each year (some on Ash Wednesday); and Villanova University offers internships at Planned Parenthood.

In some ways, though, Notre Dame remains noticeably different from its rivals—it maintains a student body that is 85 percent Catholic, in contrast to Fordham and Georgetown, for example, whose Catholic populations make up less than half of the total, and its dormitories are still single-sex, as opposed to those of Holy Cross and Boston College. Most of the 15 percent of the student body at Notre Dame who are not Catholic are Protestant; only a very small number are non-Christian. Though the school is hardly unwelcoming to members of other faiths, and indeed holds some interdenominational services, every administrator and faculty member I speak with is very clear on the admissions percentages. And the students in the minority can't help but notice it.

Andrew Hertoff, a Jewish graduate student in political science whose pale complexion reflects long hours in the library finishing his dissertation, acknowledges, "I hadn't really thought much about the religious character of the school when I came here. I was very East Coast, where you have a religious identity but it's more just trimming than anything else." Though Andrew suspected that he might have to read more Catholic authors, he didn't expect anything about Notre Dame's atmosphere to be different from secular East Coast universities. But, he concludes, "the more time I spent here, the more I understood how much it makes a difference."

More than anything else about Notre Dame, Andrew thinks it is the students who give the institution a religious feel. Even the Catholic students are struck by it. Brooke Norton, the student body president, who grew up in a Catholic family and attended an all-girls Catholic school her whole life, still tells me, "It surprised me the pervading sense of Catholicism and faith here."

David Solomon, a large man with bushy eyebrows, looks out his window on the top floor of one of the school's newest and tallest buildings. His office is cluttered with piles of paper and all sorts of state-of-the-art technology—a computer with a sleek black flat-screen monitor as well as a television and VCR—originally meant to make paper obsolete. He asks me to excuse the mess and his hurriedness. He is leaving for a conference in Italy later this afternoon.

Somewhat hopefully, Solomon sums up the school's task. "I think we're the only school left with a chance to be a first-rate research university and retain a Christian identity." Two factors, he believes, have so far prevented Notre Dame from going the way of other Catholic universities. First, its location prevents some of the more liberal East Coast influence. Second, its leadership comes from the CSC (the Order of the Holy Cross), not the Jesuits, who have historically been more open to secularizing trends. Solomon is confident that at least for the foreseeable future, the school has strong leadership. Alluding to Georgetown's recent presidential choice, Solomon insists, "The Notre Dame president has to be a CSC priest. When you read in *The New York Times* that that rule has been changed, Notre Dame will no longer be a Catholic university. That's what holds it together."

Leaning back in his chair and fiddling with his pencil, Solomon tries to tally the university's faculty. Citing as an exception his own department of philosophy, which plays host to prominent religious scholars as Alasdair MacIntyre and Ralph McInerny, he worries that serious Catholics no longer dominate the faculty. And even in philosophy, there are only two Catholics under the age of forty-five. Solomon, who is himself a Baptist, is one of the strongest proponents of the university holding on to its religious identity in the classroom. Indeed, the most important division within the faculty is not between Catholics and non-Catholics, but rather between those who take the school's religious identity seriously and those who don't. The Orthodox Jew in the theology department is said by some to have more in common with his serious Catholic colleagues than other nominal Catholics on the faculty do.

Notre Dame's program of liberal studies, a Great Books curriculum, has long had a group of professors who take this religious mission seriously, but as Rev. Michael Baxter notes, the faculty includes "five people who were formed intellectually in the fifties and early sixties who are now on verge of retirement. They're all very strong Catholics. They don't wear it on their sleeves. They're so Catholic they don't have to. They study Aquinas, Augustine, Newman, the Encyclicals. Who is going to replace them? Are we producing anyone who can reproduce what they've done?"

In response to the concerns of Fr. Baxter and Solomon, Lou Nanni, the vice president for public relations, insists that the school is doing all it can to keep Notre Dame's faculty Catholic. But there are hurdles. First, the school is drawing on a small pool of Catholic PhDs to begin with, a problem that starts early, according to many professors. Even at Notre Dame, it's hard to get many undergraduates interested in academic careers. As Solomon observes, "A lot of kids here are much more interested in professional schools." Looking at the overwhelming percentages of prelaw and prebusiness school students in his classes, he wonders, "Will there be an elite Catholic faculty twenty-five years from now that will be sufficient for us to draw upon?" Nanni believes it's Notre Dame's responsibility to cultivate such students.

Nanni continues his defense of the school's hiring practices: "We're one of few major Catholic universities that asks in the interview process, in the application process, for people's denomination." Currently, the faculty is over 50 percent Catholic, and Nanni wants to make sure that it stays at that level or increases. Financial resources have been made available for hiring top Catholic scholars. As he puts it, the administration tells department heads, "If you have an opportunity to get them, get them here, but we don't want to hire mediocre Catholic academics."

But some professors believe this policy will prove ineffective. David O'Connor, a professor of philosophy, likens this policy to treating Catholicism "as an affirmative action category." Using this method, he argues, it's hardly surprising that the school gets a lot of nominal Catholics. In order to do better, O'Connor believes, "we would have to take seriously someone's ability to integrate their Catholic faith and their intellectual life as a professional qualification. I don't see that happening." He seems to have a point. Unlike evangelical schools, where a premium is now placed on the integration of faith and learning in the classroom, Notre Dame does not ask candidates for faculty appointments how their religious worldview affects the way they approach their discipline. Rather, they just check off a box that identifies them as Catholic.

Once faculty are hired, however, Notre Dame's administration has been making an effort to get them to think more about the Catholic nature of the school through mandatory professional development programs. These include retreats for new faculty, meetings with campus priests, and lectures by top religious scholars. "Some people have kicked and resisted," Nanni acknowledges, "but there is a commitment and a level of buy-in that one would not have expected."

But there is not enough of a commitment for Solomon, who thinks that the administration is sending mixed messages on the subject. "It's no secret," he remarks, "that the provost wants the philosophy department to be in the top ten [in the *U.S. News* rankings] and you don't get into top ten by hiring only Catholics."

Rev. Patrick Gaffney, a Holy Cross priest with a doctorate in anthropology from the University of Chicago, has been teaching at Notre Dame since 1980, and in that time has given a lot of thought to the intersection of his faith and his discipline. I sit in on his Wednesday morning class—a social history of Catholics in America. Fr. Gaffney's long legs move him quickly from one side of the room to the other, as he jokes with each of the students and tosses them their graded midterms. Later, he shows a clip from the movie *Roman Holiday,* in which Gregory Peck and Audrey Hepburn are visiting a shrine, as a jumping-off point for a discussion about the shrine of St. Jude. Fr. Gaffney is an enthusiastic lecturer, but the students on either side of me are busy reading for another class.

Over coffee after class, Fr. Gaffney talks about the history of his discipline. For much of the twentieth century, anthropology of religion studies were "instrumental and materialist" and had little to do with God. And it's easy to see why. Anthropology treats human beings and their cultures as objects for study in a scientific progression of the human race and their belief systems as the result of their environments and histories. It is difficult to square this with a religious educational environment in which a certain set of beliefs are viewed as true and unchanging. Even when Notre Dame finally established an anthropology department in the 1980s, Fr. Gaffney acknowledges it was not much different from the rest of the discipline. Though things have certainly changed, he notes, "People who don't have recent professional familiarity with anthropology see it as a contradiction: Students ask me how you can be a priest and an anthropologist. I'm sure they're thinking of the Darwinian model, where anthropology is seen as a stalking horse for evolution."

But the reason Fr. Gaffney came to anthropology in the first place was that he "wanted to understand how conviction and social structure meshed." Fr. Gaffney originally began writing about Christian cultures, but quickly decided he was too close to the subject. Instead he decided to study the Muslim world, learning Arabic and spending time in the Middle East. (One colleague recalls hearing how Fr. Gaffney's tall stature and ruddy Irish looks made him stick out in the Arab countries he visited, but added that what really shocked locals was his perfect command of Arab "street" dialect.)

All of this study of other faiths has put Fr. Gaffney in an interesting position. He teaches at a Catholic university and is a member of the Catholic clergy, but he doesn't want to tell his students that one religion is truer than another. "God," he believes, "speaks in many expressions and I'm very hesitant to say God is here and he's not there." Though Fr. Gaffney says he is willing to share his Christian convictions and the lessons of the Catholic intellectual tradition if asked, he doesn't want to "take an optic of doctrinal arbitration—who's right and who's wrong." He sees a more important role for himself in teaching students to be open to religious traditions other than their own. "My deep conviction, though I hate to be up front about this in class, is that by studying others they'll appreciate their own tradition. By learning more about Islam and tribal religions, they'll come to see God's creations as ever more rich."

But in trying to broaden his students' outlook beyond the Catholic perspective, Fr. Gaffney acknowledges, he may be largely addressing the needs of yesterday's students. He recalls, "When I was a student here, most students, 90 percent, had been through Catholic parochial schools from first grade. So you came here with a ghetto Catholic inculturation that was really enormous."

"The trick in those days," he explains, "was to break out of it. By contrast, now kids are coming with a longing for a faith tradition." Only 40 percent of today's Notre Dame students come from Catholic high schools. And while many students have grown up in culturally Catholic homes, the professors I spoke with agree that the Catholic intellectual formation is lacking.

Bob Groegler, a relaxed-looking guy wearing jeans and a sweatshirt, came to Notre Dame to explore his Catholicism more deeply, not learn about other faiths. In the lounge of the student center, slouching into one of the large cushioned chairs, Bob tells me (with Regis Philbin, a Notre Dame alum, laughing on the big-screen TV in the background) that although he grew up in a religious family, he hadn't really thought of studying religion in college. But then, during his freshman year at George Washington University, he quickly lost interest in his original field of political science, and decided to take an introductory course on the New Testament. "There were good professors at GW in the religion department and I took a couple more courses on Genesis and Revelation." But he soon realized, "because GW is a secular university, I had to go outside the class to explore how what I learned fits into my faith." That's when he transferred to Notre Dame.

"A moral disaster." That's what professor David O'Connor calls the Notre Dame students. After a small seminar called "Justice" that he coteaches with a woman in the political science department, O'Connor and I have a quick meeting in his office. In contrast to the frequency of random hook-ups between the sexes at other schools, O'Connor observes, "There is a lot of monogamous sexual activity" at Notre Dame. He even acknowledges that most of the students involved are probably in love. The problem, O'Connor tells me, lies with the adults who won't let them get married in college. "Most parents are much more worried about their kids getting married than having sex. There is a notion that educated people don't get married young." The results of the adults' failure to inculcate Catholic ideals about marriage and intimacy, according to O'Connor, are obvious among Notre Dame graduates: "There are so many annulments. I used to think it was terrible, but now I realize they're true annulments—most people never mean the vows." It is difficult to reconcile O'Connor's complaints. On the one hand, he wants students to get married younger—like they do at Brigham Young, for instance— but the students who rush into marriage in order to satisfy their sexual urges might be less likely to "mean their vows."

David Solomon is also concerned about the students' sexual behavior, but he seems less of a scold than O'Connor. Students have been raised with a "liberal individualistic approach" to morality, says Solomon. "They're just as promiscuous [as their peers at other schools], but they feel a little bad about it." Laughing a little, Solomon notes that then their liberal attitudes kick in and "they feel guilty about [feeling] guilty."

A number of students confirm this idea that there is little grasp of Catholic doctrine in the Notre Dame population when it comes to marriage or anything else. Colleen Moore, a petite woman with a silver Tiffany bean necklace, who graduated in 1997 and now works as an assistant rector in one of the girls' dorms, entered Notre Dame with only a passing familiarity with Catholic doctrine and ritual. For the first couple of years at the university, Colleen tells me, she and her classmates "didn't know what we believed." During those initial years, there would be moments where she would finally comprehend the prayers she had been reciting in church for so many years. David Solomon tells me that students in his medical ethics courses often hold Catholic positions but don't understand them. "People tell me they like taking my course because I show them why their arguments are right."

Aside from giving them in-class instruction on what the Catholic faith says about various moral issues, Notre Dame tries to maintain an "in loco parentis model" of governing students' behavior. Vice President Nanni argues this is "much more appropriate than "saying, 'Hey, you're eighteen. Go out there. If you fall down, pick yourself up.'" In addition to keeping the dorms single-sex, the administration has tried to crack down on alcohol use on campus. And many faculty think that effort has been a success.

But there is reason to doubt this assessment. Mike Connolly tells me that the priests are not very strict about the rules: The administration "tells parents there are no drugs, drinking, or sex at Notre Dame, but then you get back to your dorm and they tell you that alcohol stays in your room, and you should register your party, and tell us how much alcohol you're having at your party." Mike, who admits to spending most weekends drinking, offers one scenario: "So you know you're eighteen years old and you walk down the hall to your RA's room and say, 'We're having a party, we're expecting seventy-five kids, we have twelve cases of beer,' and they say 'Okay' and write it down."

"He's a disciple of Christ. When he walks into the room, when I hear him talk, there is a strong presence—a presence of God," junior Erica Hayman says of Rev. Michael Baxter. Indeed, Fr. Baxter has got a bit of a cult following among students. Wearing black jeans and a red shirt with sleeves rolled up and a black wool vest, he looks to be about forty, but he has a very casual air about him. Curling up in his small desk chair, arms wrapped around his legs, he seems a little too cool for a priest, perhaps, but his concerns are nothing if not serious. Fr. Baxter wants Notre Dame graduates to be "the kind of people who will go out and change society through service to others and do that in a very unapologetically religious way, whether they be counselors or work at Catholic Worker houses for the poor." Smilingly, he concludes, "I'm into that. I like that some of my students are doing that."

But he's into other things, too. Erica says that "sometimes [Fr. Baxter] is very radical with Pax Christi [the pacifist group on campus] and with his ideas, and some people criticize him." Indeed, on a campus where most students tend to be more conservative, everyone seems to know about Fr. Baxter's activism. Referring to Catholic professors who teach that joining the military is acceptable in the eyes of the Church, he stares at me pointedly as he remarks: "My question to them is, 'Why are you so patriotic when it comes to a country that protects by law the destruction of 1.5 million unborn children every year?" But Fr. Baxter is generally respected by people on both sides of the political spectrum for his involvement at the center of the school's service programs. He regularly encourages the administration to use some of its large endowment to fund both volunteer programs for current students and also loan forgiveness for students who choose do to service after graduation.

More than 11 percent of Notre Dame's graduating class does at least a year of service after graduation, a higher percentage than almost all secular schools and most Catholic ones as well. The Alliance for Catholic Education program, which sends Notre Dame graduates into Catholic high school and elementary schools; the Holy Cross Associates, who sponsor service programs domestically and abroad; and the Peace Corps are three of the most popular choices. Indeed, much of the students' Catholic identity seems to be channeled into these service pursuits.

Colleen volunteered with the Holy Cross Associates when she graduated. Eyeing her South American–style embroidered handbag, she explains, "I went to Chile for two-and-a-half years and worked in schools and parishes." Colleen became interested in this kind of service work during her undergraduate years. The school's Center for Social Concerns, she reports, offers a variety of service opportunities, from tutoring local kids to helping out at homeless shelters. But she was particularly interested in the programs offered during school vacations. She participated in an "urban plunge," which sends students to various cities to perform service work. She describes her experience in Chicago:

> We went to a Catholic parish on the South Side. They had the people who run the parish come in and give us an idea of what kinds of programs they run, what kind of neighborhood it is, what kinds of issues they face. A lot of the parishioners were facing poor housing. The elderly people in the neighborhood needed groceries, so the food pantry has a delivery service. We got to see how they run the pantry. They brought in speakers that help youth in the area with gang prevention. It gave us a sense of what goes on in the community. The church is not just there to offer mass.

But at a school with the cache of Notre Dame (not to mention its high tuition) it is hard to get students to resist the temptation of well-paying jobs after graduation. "The economic boom bred some really awful habits in people," says David Solomon. Students would tell him, "I'll make my fortune by the time I'm thirty-four, get my Mercedes, and join the Sierra club." Perhaps even more than the recent economic downturn, Solomon believes, the terrorist attacks have had an effect on spiritual life at the school: "Since 9/11 you don't hear students saying the ridiculous things they were saying in the last few years."

Still, not everyone is so gung-ho about Notre Dame's focus on volunteer work. Though he admires their ethic, John Cavadini, chairman of the theology department, worries that Notre Dame students who "do volunteer work for a year or two and then launch into their careers [represent] a kind of dichotomized thinking: You can either be good or make money." He calls this attitude symptomatic of a "poverty of imagination." Cavadini thinks it is the responsibility of the Notre Dame faculty to teach graduates, no matter what profession they enter, to bear a witness in the world. He wants them to be able to draw on their Catholic education to guide their actions. Cavadini, a tall, gaunt, gray-haired man who looks like he has been up many a night turning over these questions, thinks that students should be separate from their secular surroundings: "They should not just be swallowed up by whatever cultural norm comes along."

The question of how to meet the demands of religious life while at the same time being able to influence the wider culture is at the heart of Notre Dame's mission, and indeed the mission of every religious college. Nanni explains:

> I look at a world in which one percent of the population has a college degree, and one of the questions we ask ourselves on a regular basis at Notre Dame is "How do we make ourselves relevant to the other ninety-nine percent?" Not only are we trying to develop the God-given talents of our students, we're doing it for one reason—so they can serve others more purely and more abundantly. That might be from research, from professional careers, as husbands and wives, fathers and mothers.

Even after students graduate, they can find resources for answering these questions at their alma mater. The Center for Ethics and Culture, for instance, invites 100 alumni who are doctors back to campus for a conference on medical ethics every year.

"There are calls for prophets and teachers and calls for people to share their many different talents," notes Nanni. "It's clear that we should be in the world, because how can you evangelize otherwise?" The word "evangelize" is not one that comes up often during my visit to Notre Dame. Though the campus ministry does print a list in the school's newspaper of everyone who has become a confirmed Catholic that semester and the people who have sponsored them, it is clear that Notre Dame students and faculty do not usually have anything so explicit in mind when they talk about trying to influence the larger culture. According to Fr. Baxter, the question is "How can we make our faith attractive to others? It's a certain way you live. Maybe you live simply. You don't watch so much TV. You try to reach out to the poor. Or be poorer yourself."

Kelly Pascual, who is sitting alone flipping through the school newspaper, the *Observer,* when I spot her, tells me that although she appreciates the school's spiritual atmosphere (she attends mass every week and acts as a eucharistic minister in her dorm), she is not a fan of the political environment. Looking very cheerful in a long-sleeved yellow shirt with a blue flower, Kelly smiles and tells me quietly that the school is very conservative. "That's one of the more negative aspects of it." During the 2000 presidential election, "you rarely saw a person voting Democratic. I was uncomfortable in a lot of political discussions." Kelly even seems a little uncomfortable telling me about this.

Whereas a few decades ago there was generally a Democratic sweep of the Catholic vote, the combination of the Catholics' successful climb up the country's economic ladder and the Democrats' rejection of many socially conservative positions have made Notre Dame's campus predominantly Republican. Though they may be religious and conservative, Notre Dame graduates do not become what many think of as religious conservatives. They are more likely to end up like graduates of East Coast Ivy League schools, as professionals in the cultural, financial, and political centers of the country. Still, Kelly's pro-choice stance puts her in a distinct minority at Notre Dame.

Though the school does have an officially recognized pro-choice group, there is no abortion counseling on campus. David Solomon, who becomes slightly agitated when I ask him about this, explains the administration's position: Even though many other Catholic schools have capitulated on this issue, "we believe there is a clear line between talking about stuff and doing stuff." He notes, "There is an abortion clinic four blocks off campus and everyone knows about it. We have said within this couple of square miles, damn it, we're not going to give brochures to tell you where to get an abortion."

In recent years, though, the abortion debate has taken a back seat to the issue of homosexuality at Notre Dame. When I ask Brooke Norton about controversies on campus, this is the first one she mentions. Last year the student government helped the gay student group rewrite their constitution so that it would be approved by the administration. She glances down at her large black organizer covered with Post-it notes, and takes a sip of coffee as if to emphasize the extent of her effort in this area. "We tried to give [the leaders of the gay group] feedback about how it would be easier to get recognized. They took advocacy out of their constitution. They became more of a social and programming oriented type group. But it wasn't approved." Clearly disappointed by this, Brooke adds, "It's hard. . . . They want to have their own group. They have the sense that we're leaving them out."

The group has continued to meet, but without being officially recognized, it cannot use university facilities or put up posters on campus. The administration has also tried to prevent the group from advertising in the school's newspaper. But Mike Connolly, the *Observer*'s editor-in-chief, has refused to comply. He says that as long as the ads do make it clear that the group is unaffiliated with the university, the paper will not deny them advertising space. And so far, apparently, the administration has been unwilling to exert any real pressure. Of course, Mike tells me, with overconfidence, that the administration couldn't force the newspaper to do anything even if it wanted to. "The paper is independent," he notes, explaining that 75 percent of its revenue comes from advertising, though the rest does come from an annual six dollar student fee. This issue goes to the very purpose of the paper, according to Mike, which is "to open up debate."

"In addition to covering the attempts of the gay student group to be recognized," he tells me, "we covered Ex Corde [the widely publicized encyclical, *Ex Corde Ecclesiae* (1990), which offers guidelines for restoring the Catholic identity to institutions of higher education], which was an attempt by bishops to take more control of the university." On the editorial page, says Mike, "just about anything goes. There was a column today about how we need more sex at Notre Dame." Trying to hold back a smile, he acknowledges, "Some lines were questionable, but I let it roll because that was [the writer's] thing, his opinion, his column. I don't agree with it but it's not my role to censor things I don't agree with."

* * *

South Bend is a long way from home for Jason Villareal, but the educational experience at Notre Dame has convinced him that leaving his Hispanic community in Texas to come to here was the right decision. "In San Antonio, I am the majority. I'm used to growing up where the street names are Hispanic and everyone speaks Spanish. It's good for me to see the way the rest of the country is." Jason believes most of his fellow students knew they wanted to come to Notre Dame from a very young age, but for Hispanic students from Texas, California, New York City, or Chicago, coming to rural northern Indiana is not high on the list of college priorities. "A lot of people are afraid to make that change," says Jason. "It was good for me, but some minorities don't think that way."

It's a good thing for Notre Dame that Jason came. He embodies in so many ways what the school is aiming for. To begin with, he appreciates Notre Dame's approach to academics. "In [his public] high school," he recounts, "there was no such thing as truth. You searched and you questioned and you felt scholarly and philosophical, but that seemed to be the goal." By comparison, he tells me, in Notre Dame's theology classes, "You'll say this is what the Catholic Church teaches." At a lot of schools, Jason believes, people will not say such things for fear of offending others or out of some sense of political correctness. "But that's not what I wanted. Not to be rude and not to say, 'You're not with me so I don't like you,' but really to know what the Catholic Church teaches. I feel like I'm getting that."

Majoring in theology and Russian, Jason reports being very pleased with the integration of religious topics and secular ones in all of his classes. For his Russian class, Jason did a report on the Russian Orthodox Church and the effects of Communism on it. His theology classes have often discussed the Eastern churches, from both a political and a theological point of view. Outside of class, Jason can find people talking about the topics that interest him. "A priest, who came to speak at the basilica last week," he recalls, "was talking about how Eastern and Western churches are like lungs. You have to have both to breathe and a lot of times the Eastern ones are forgotten."

Jason praises dorm life as well, even, surprisingly, their single-sex status, which he credits with keeping dorm residents close: "I've talked to other people—friends from high school—they say life here is unique. We don't have frats or sororities. I've heard people at other colleges will not know their next-door neighbors in their dorms. It's just like living in an apartment house." By contrast, Jason says, "Here, dorm life is extremely tight." Students at Notre Dame remain in the same dorm for their entire career. (Indeed, some administrators cite the dorm experience as one of the major reasons for Notre Dame's extraordinarily high alumni giving rate.) Even during his senior year, when students are allowed to live elsewhere, Jason tells me, "I intend to stay on campus."

Jason is also one of the more religiously committed students at Notre Dame—attending mass a few times a week, participating in the liturgical choir at the basilica, and playing the violin in his dorm's chapel. Though he appreciates the Notre Dame community, he does register some disapproval of his classmates' behavior. He thinks they are basically conservative when it comes to sex, but he has a number of complaints about the alcohol abuse on campus. One of the biggest problems is tailgating, which, he translates, "is just another word for getting drunk." In October, his father and younger brother came to visit Jason for the first time. "I got my little brother into student section at the football game, and, of all the times, the girl next to us starts throwing up." He was even more ashamed of his fellow students' reactions, which were unsympathetic, at best. Jason observes "a kind of a double standard: Someone will go to the hospital and people will say, 'I don't feel sorry for him. He should have known what he could handle. He went overboard.' But I see people go almost to that point . . . yet that's okay."

It is easy to see how Jason's easygoing nature, which is not the least bit preachy, would have a positive effect on those around him. And he is looking forward to influencing American politics and culture when he graduates. Jason considers himself a Democrat, but he is strongly pro-life—"so much so that for that reason I voted for Bush and a Republican senator and two Republican judges in Texas" during the last election. He explains that he is "furious" with the situation in his home congressional district. Jason's representative, Charlie Gonzalez, is Catholic, but he votes, according to Jason, "in favor of abortion with the Democratic Party very consistently." He has been hard to vote out of office, says Jason, because the district is well over 50 percent Hispanic, and so is Gonzalez. Jason tells me what the strategy should be:

> You start locally and say Democrats and Republicans are trying to kiss the feet of Hispanic voters. Yet the Hispanics are having to come to the Democratic party on [its] terms. We need to get a Hispanic in there who says, "Look, I have the support of my constituents; they're not going to vote me out. I'm going to vote on social justice issues and economic issues the way that the Democrats want, but I'm going to be strongly pro-life like my constituents." You get enough people doing that, and they're going to have to say we have to listen to you.

Jason, who is active in the campus pro-life group, tells me that there are "varying degrees of involvement" with politics on campus. Some people "pray the rosary at the abortion clinic. I've been trying to go twice a week in the morning." Certainly the majority of people on campus are sympathetic to the pro-life position, with as many as seven busloads of students attending the March for Life in Washington every year on the anniversary of *Roe v. Wade*. But even with such widespread support, he admits the group does generate disagreement, especially "when we do a cemetery for the innocent," memorializing the millions of fetuses aborted since the Supreme Court decision was handed down.

Though his views and activities may make Jason the ideal Notre Dame student, his physical appearance sets him apart from the other students eating lunch at the campus center's Burger King. In addition to his dark skin, he has a small, adolescent frame, with long black hair and a beard. His glasses add an element of seriousness, quickly removed by the backward-facing baseball cap with his dormitory name embroidered across it. Many of the students who walk by us greet Jason. Without exception, though, they are taller, more athletic looking, with lighter complexions and more expensive clothes.

Most of Notre Dame's Catholic counterparts have already pursued more racially diverse student bodies with little regard to religious identity and the results are clear: It's difficult to have a Catholic college when less than half of the student body is Catholic. That 85 percent mark seems to be the line that Notre Dame has refused to cross, when other factors like the composition of the faculty have changed. And the fact that many cite the student body as the most religious element of the school means that the administration's steadfastness in this area has served it well. But whether Notre Dame will long be able to resist giving priority to the diversity mantra—so deep-seated in today's institutions of secular higher education—over the school's Catholic identity remains in doubt.

The issue of diversity on campus is obviously at the forefront of the administrative agenda: According to Rev. Mark Poorman, the vice president for student affairs, "About five years ago, the trustees committed an enormous amount of money to financial aid for diversity." Though he claims, this was mostly to boost "socioeconomic and class diversity" rather than racial and ethnic diversity, the two are not unrelated, and, he argues, "You have to start somewhere." Notre Dame increased the amount of its financial aid grants (not including Pell grants) to $36 million in 2001 from $5 million ten years earlier. Fr. Poorman believes that it's "not only the right thing to do, but also we get better students" as a result. Before Notre Dame began this initiative, it often lost minority students to schools like Northwestern and Duke because they offered better aid packages. Fr. Poorman notes, "We wanted to recover those people. We felt like we were behind the eight-ball and we did something."

But it's not just the scholarships that Notre Dame has used to attract more minorities. A couple of months after my visit, the university was thrown into the national spotlight by its decision to hire an African-American head football coach. *The New York Times* observed, "[Tyrone] Willingham's new position has shown that a black coach can succeed at a major college." The author of a study on the racial makeup of coaching staffs at major universities hailed the choice: "Having Notre Dame make this decision might be the first time that we open the doors to the possibility of a much broader opportunity for people of color to be hired in positions of responsibility." This move could have tremendous positive public relations implications for the school, which is, of course, most visible on the football field. Sure enough, minority applications for the class of 2007 increased by 40 percent over the previous year.

The administration's efforts to foster diversity have not been lost on Jason, who remarks, "I think a lot of people who are minority complain that there aren't enough minorities and I think that's true," but he wishes they would cut the university some slack. His fellow students should know, for instance, that every minority student admitted gets to come for an all expenses paid long weekend in March of their senior year in high school.

Fr. Poorman mentions this recruiting weekend as well. He has the "strong impression that most of our efforts to attract Hispanic and Latino students have paid off. They have the Catholic thing in common. They're very communally oriented and they find the environment here very supportive because of its religious character."

On the other hand, Fr. Poorman suggests, it's much harder to recruit black Catholics. "You have to go to a first-class inner-city high school. And if [you] grew up in the city, it's hard to imagine camping out in rural northern Indiana." Moreover, there aren't many black Catholics to begin with. Despite some efforts by the Catholic Church to reach the black community, the numbers of African-American Catholics in the United States have remained at about two million (out of an estimated 65 million Catholics in the U.S.), and many of those are immigrants. So Notre Dame is fighting an uphill battle.

Even once minorities do choose Notre Dame, there is no guaranteeing that they will feel comfortable. Fr. Poorman believes "some of the difficulty is socioeconomic." And some of that is beyond the university's control. Minority students, who don't have discretionary funds, often have to stay on campus for fall and spring break. "Your heart goes out to them," says Fr. Poorman, "when they have to figure out how to get home to Texas and California. That sort of discrepancy bothers me a lot."

But the differences among students go beyond money. According to Colleen, "Students definitely segregate themselves. There is a general respect for one another but not a whole lot of intermingling." When she was a resident assistant during her senior year, she says, the two African-American girls on her floor sometimes felt left out and would seek out black students from other dorms to befriend. The other girls on Colleen's floor saw the black girls' community as exclusive and wondered, according to Colleen, "'Why do you have to be apart?' It was a tension."

Aware of these problems, Jason nonetheless remains confident that the common Catholic tradition at Notre Dame can help overcome racial and ethnic differences. Now considering pursuing a career in the priesthood, Jason reflects with satisfaction on his own decision to come here. The other schools he applied to were in bigger cities with larger minority populations but, he explains, "I had a really good priest friend of mine who told me I couldn't go wrong with Notre Dame." Now he looks back and wonders whether it was meant to be.

CHAPTER FOUR

"THERE ARE NO DOUBTERS HERE": THE ORTHODOXY OF THOMAS AQUINAS COLLEGE

It's a chilly March morning in the mountains of southern California when I wake up in the guest hacienda at Thomas Aquinas College. I switch off the electric blanket—embarrassed to have needed it in what I expected to be a tropical clime. Impatiently, I flip through the radio stations on the digital alarm clock, unable to find a news broadcast. The room has no television either, so CNN is out. I am not waiting to hear about anything in particular— the terrorist attacks of September are beginning to feel distant and I don't have much money in the stock market—just trying to quell this feeling of isolation that has come over me suddenly.

I saw a newspaper yesterday, but that was in New York, before I flew non-stop to Los Angeles, before I drove three hours—the last in pitch darkness— through the Los Padres National Forest to rural Santa Paula. It was before my cell phone lost its signal, before the twelve-lane highways turned to two, before a student wearing a tweed jacket and carrying an old-fashioned lantern (did I dream that part?) came to meet me at the gate of the college. It was before I arrived in this strange room, with the brown shag carpeting and the crucifix over the bed and the cross on the dresser with the candles on either side.

As I think to plug in my computer and reconnect with the outside world, Dave Shaneyfelt, a tall man comfortably dressed in khakis and a short-sleeved polo shirt, comes to the door. The director of college relations for Thomas Aquinas, Shaneyfelt has assigned himself the task of escorting me around campus. "How did you sleep?" he asks, adding immediately, "You know Mother Teresa stayed in that bed."

"Really?" I ask, unsure exactly what one's reaction to that is supposed to be.

"She even signed the guest book," he triumphantly reveals.

For most colleges, getting Mother Teresa to visit would be an achievement, like hosting Kofi Annan or Jimmy Carter, but for Thomas Aquinas College, it's hitting the jackpot. Students here don't just admire this venerable woman, as if she were another interesting public servant. They actually want to become nuns. Well, maybe not all of them. Though Thomas Aquinas is not a convent—it's a Catholic coed liberal arts college of three hundred students, founded in 1971—11 percent of its graduates have tried the religious life, that is, they have entered a seminary, abbey, convent, priory, monastery, hermitage, or religious house of study, and 7 percent of them have stayed. It's no wonder that Sister Joseph Andrew, who is staying in the room next door to me during her annual recruiting visit to TAC for the recently formed order of the Dominican Sisters of Mary, Mother of the Eucharist, remarks happily: "I like to think of TAC as a preseminary or a prenovitiate."

Jenny Tilley is one of the women Sister Joseph Andrew is here to see. Jenny enters the school's chapel shortly after she returns from a run up in the mountains. Her hair, tied back in a girlish ponytail, is still wet from the shower. Her long flowing skirt and fresh cotton T-shirt cling perfectly to her tanned athlete's body as she makes her way silently to an empty pew near the front. Like the other thirty or so girls waiting here for the four o'clock "holy hour" to begin, Jenny carries only her Bible. After a few words from one of the chaplains, Sister Joseph Andrew moves in front of the altar and begins to recite the rosary. The door at the back of the chapel remains open—there is no noise outside that would disturb the service—lending the room a nice breeze. Jenny looks out the high window at the front of the chapel as she moves her small fingers across the string of beads.

There are a couple of men in the back pews silently reading the Bible, but this service is primarily for women, particularly those interested in a religious vocation. Sitting next to me is a young woman named Marie, with sort of messy chin-length hair, her feet moving in and out of her Birkenstock sandals. Marie, who comes from a family of ten children in northern Virginia, describes herself as "thinking about vocation—but less so than other people here." Like Jenny, she offers.

Jenny grew up in a lapsed Protestant home in a wealthy town in New Jersey, where she attended a public high school. One of her teachers, who used to work at Thomas Aquinas but had to leave because he wasn't earning enough money, encouraged Jenny to come here. She chose Princeton instead. But then, in the spring of her freshman year, Jenny converted to Catholicism. Her family, she tells me, was pretty upset, but then her mother, apparently inspired by Jenny's new faith, converted as well. Her parents weren't necessarily high on her decision to transfer to TAC, particularly since she would have to start as a freshman again. But they got over that, too, she thinks. Now a senior, Jenny, having spent some time at a convent in California, has decided she feels called to be a nun. Her parents, she laments to me, are once again beside themselves.

After the rosary service, everyone goes over to dinner at the home of one of the school's two chaplains, Rev. Wilfred Borden. When Jenny and I arrive the girls are gorging themselves on huge fresh-picked strawberries while they wait for dinner to be served. Fr. Borden is still busy barbecuing chicken legs but already on the table are enormous platters of potatoes and salad and pork and beans. Students help themselves to chilled white wine. Like Marie, not all of the students at dinner are sure about pursuing a vocation, but they certainly see it as a viable option.

An hour or so later, flanked by girls eating cake and ice cream on the floor of Fr. Borden's living room, Sister Joseph Andrew talks about her community in Michigan, mentioning the fact that a couple of the girls in the room actually have siblings there in training. Though her order is an apostolic one—where the women are out in the world doing the work prescribed for the Apostles in the New Testament—she mentions the role of contemplative and monastic communities as well. When the time comes for questions, more than one of the girls ask Sister Joseph Andrew (in different ways) how they will know when God is calling them to pursue a religious vocation, an inquiry to which, needless to say, Sister Joseph Andrew cannot offer an answer they find completely adequate. She concludes her talk by telling the assembled women that nuns have a particularly important mission now. "It's up to [us] to save the priesthood. We have to support the men in their religious vocations."

Indeed, it seems like someone must step in soon. A few days before my visit, Los Angeles Cardinal Roger Mahony dismissed as many as a dozen priests over allegations of sexual misconduct spanning more than a decade. A front-page story in *The Los Angeles Times* quotes the county sheriff's office as saying the cardinal has failed to hand over the names of any offenders to the authorities. Oddly, only one of the Thomas Aquinas students I speak with has heard about the publicity around Mahony, and none of the others offers any particular opinions about the scandals that have rocked the church in the preceding months. They look at me, puzzled, as if I am asking about a different religion. Which is not far from the truth.

It's difficult to generalize about a religious group with 65 million adherents in the U.S. alone, but an outsider might reasonably observe that American Catholics today are a confused lot. It is perhaps not surprising that there is significant diversity of opinion in such a large population, particularly in one that exists in a liberal democracy. A crude view of this spectrum would begin with the far right, say, with Mel Gibson's father, who has built his own chapel in southern California and who became somewhat infamous after telling *The New York Times Magazine* in 2003 that the Holocaust has been vastly exaggerated.

Gibson himself, of course, is on this side of the spectrum. Though he doesn't seem to hold his father's conspiracy theory views on the world, his movie *The Passion of the Christ,* released in 2004, has caused cries of anti-Semitism from some corners—not surprisingly, since Jews in the movie are depicted as sadistically enjoying the torture of Jesus at the hands of the Romans, bearing the bulk of the responsibility for Christ's sentence to crucifixion, and since passion plays (particularly in Europe in the Middle Ages) were used to incite anti-Semitic actions. Gibson's defense actually makes him sound remarkably similar to the fundamentalists at Bob Jones University. In a January 2004 interview, Gibson told the Global Catholic Network, "We're all culpable [for Jesus' death]. I don't want to lynch any Jews. . . . I love them. I pray for them."

In a way, it might seem strange that attitudes about Jews should be used to determine where a Catholic lands on this spectrum. But this question of how other religious groups are to be viewed is at the heart of what's called Vatican II and therefore at the center of the debate between liberal and conservative Catholics. Though many adherents and most nonadherents have come to think of the Second Vatican Council (1962–1965) as being defined by a change from the Latin to an English mass, a less formal relationship between the priest and congregants, or even some form of sexual liberation, in fact the issue of ecumenism is at the heart of this council's work. The Council encouraged respect for Judaism in and of itself, not simply as a precursor to Christianity, and rejected not only anti-Semitism (which other councils had done before) but also explicit proselytization toward Jews. The reaction of any strongly religious group to such changes might be, to put it bluntly, "Well, are we right or not? We can't be violent or anti-Semitic, but why shouldn't we try to convert everyone?"

Leaving aside for a moment that even the desire to convert among these traditional Catholics does not usually imply the same forms of explicit proselytization one finds among fundamentalist Protestants, the attitude toward converting others is certainly one way to divide Catholics today into their liberal and conservative factions. The students at Thomas Aquinas fall on one side of this divide, as we will see later in the chapter, and the students at Notre Dame, for the most part, fall on the other.

Further along the liberal side are the Jesuit universities referred to at various points in this book. A certain gleeful subversiveness has overtaken the faculty and students at many of these schools. Several students and faculty at Fordham, for instance, mention to me proudly how close the Jesuit order has come a number of times in its history to being excommunicated from the Catholic Church. The Catholics on this liberal end of the spectrum have come to define themselves by Vatican II, both in terms of its ecumenism and its more liberal and egalitarian attitudes. Many on this end of things see the current pope as far too conservative. They are pushing for the Church to reverse its stance on everything from contraception to women being priests to homosexuality.

In his recent book, *A People Adrift,* Peter Steinfels argues that it is more than just particular disagreements that plague the American Church today; it is a lack of direction. The conservative and liberal factions, explains Steinfels, have little to say to each other anymore, and the vast majority of Catholics in between have nowhere to turn for guidance. It is a strange situation for a church with a centralized world authority.

Mike Burn, the guy in the tweed jacket with the lantern, grew up practicing Catholicism, but of a much different sort, he tells me, than the kind found at TAC. "My parents were very influenced by Vatican II," he offers me by way of explanation. And they didn't want him to come to TAC because, Mike suggests, "they don't understand a deeper Catholicism." Aleyna Marie Farrell, who converted to Catholicism during her freshman year at the University of New Mexico, tells me her parents didn't approve of her decision to attend Thomas Aquinas either. Though they weren't bothered by Aleyna's conversion, she thinks they didn't want her to adopt such a narrow set of religious views. "It definitely bothered my family that the school was so Catholic. They didn't want me to be in a place where everyone was Catholic. . . . They thought it would be very limiting."

At dinner one night, I meet an alumna who works in the TAC administration offices. Her parents also "flipped out" when her older sister decided to come to the college. Noting that her family only said grace before meals when all of the people in the family were present ("as if that's the only time when God deserved to be thanked"), she tells me she did not grow up in a "very serious Catholic home."

This is not to say that most students at Thomas Aquinas are rebelling against their upbringings by adopting a strong Catholic identity. On the contrary, though Thomas Susanka, the school's director of admissions, describes TAC applicants as "radicalized," it's often because they come from radicalized families. Susanka emphasizes that this "doesn't necessarily mean they are conservative"—though he acknowledges that the school's biggest boost in admissions came when they started advertising in the staunchly right-wing magazine *National Review*—"but mostly they are." Susanka suggests that perhaps "orthodox" is a better word. He describes the typical TAC family as one that "has decided that standard education at Catholic universities is not significantly different than education at public or private schools."

Even before they reach college, TAC families are educating their children differently from typical American Catholics. According to Susanka, many of the 60 percent of TAC students who have attended parochial schools have chosen more "Bible-based" Christian schools over their local Catholic institutions. And of the remaining 40 percent of the student body, fully half are homeschooled. In fact, many of the leaders of the Catholic wing of the homeschool movement are TAC grads. "TAC students," Susanka suggests, "come from families that are thoughtful, in my view, beyond what you might expect, about the nature of education and how it fits with Christian faith. They've talked about the relation between faith and reason."

John Kunz, a senior raised in upstate New York, comes from such a family. One of five children, John emphasizes he was not forced to come to Thomas Aquinas; his parents offered to pay for him to attend any one of four other schools—Franciscan University of Steubenville in Ohio, Christendom College in Virginia, the University of Dallas, and Thomas More College in New Hampshire, all of which would probably describe their religious identity in terms similar to those of TAC. His older brother came here and John visited a couple of times before making his decision. According to John, the identity of TAC is all about "reason in light of faith." He explains, "Whether you go into math class or science class you can't get past that. When you hold your highest notion of truth to be God and the teachings of Catholic Church, you want to look at everything else in light of that." He has found it "strengthening to be able to know that you believe it the same way that ninety percent of your friends do, and . . . comforting to be able to go to mass with the whole student body."

Fr. Borden, who joined the faculty at TAC after retiring from Notre Dame, tells me that Catholicism is more fundamental to the identity of Thomas Aquinas College than to his former school. Though he found Notre Dame's curriculum acceptable, he didn't think the school was strongly directed toward the faith. At TAC it's not unusual to find fifty students at mass during the day, whereas at Notre Dame students usually only go to the basilica on Sundays.

Nicole Gingras, who attended public school in Orange County, was initially reluctant to come to TAC, having set her sights on UCLA or New York University. But her parents told her that they would pay only for either Steubenville or Thomas Aquinas. She tells me now that the advantages of TAC—particularly in terms of nurturing her religious identity—are obvious. At her high school, Nicole tells me, she was "annoyed because I had to keep quiet about my religion." Though there were some "Mormons who were very free-speaking about their religion . . . and some hard-core Protestants," Nicole laments, "you [didn't] really hear much about Catholics talking out. Catholics didn't have much of a place in our school." Nicole finds it "easier to go here and talk about [Catholicism] freely." She likes "how it plays such an integral role in the program and how you can talk about it in class."

It's just before eight-thirty Monday morning and the students in freshman math are discussing their reading assignment from the weekend. As a young-looking professor (at TAC, all faculty are actually referred to as tutors, the reason for which we will come to momentarily) walks into the sunlit classroom with only a crucifix on the wall, all fifteen or so students stand immediately. Responsively, they recite the Prayer to the Holy Spirit:

> Come Holy Spirit, fill the hearts of the faithful and enkindle in them the fire of Thy love.
> *Verse:* Send forth Thy Spirit and they shall be created,
> *Response:* And Thou shalt renew the face of the earth.
> Let us pray.
> Oh God, Who didst instruct the hearts of the faithful by the light of the Holy Spirit, grant us in that same Spirit to be truly wise, and ever to rejoice in His consolation.

Then the tutor, who has taken a seat at the head of the table, skipping over any small talk, first looks at a list of students' names, and then, calling him by last name, asks one sitting to his left to demonstrate a geometrical proof on the blackboard. Taking one final glance at a page about halfway through Euclid's *Elements,* the student leaves the book on the table, moves to the front of the room and begins to write. With total silence from his classmates, it is easy to hear his quiet sighs of frustration. After a few minutes, he stands back, and a young woman seated close to the board blurts out, in a tone somewhere short of sympathetic, "How does that follow?" Puzzled, he replaces the chalk and creeps back to his seat. During the course of the next hour, there is some prompting here and there from the tutor, but most of the questions—and answers—come from students who refer to each other by surname as well and who do not bother to raise their hands.

Peter DeLuca, one of the school's founders, who is now the vice president for administration and finance, explains the reasoning behind the way the math class is structured. "Kids are called on at random to demonstrate any one of four or five propositions any given day without their book . . . so that they acquire a habit of holding long arguments in their heads, and giving reasons for what they say." These are things, DeLuca believes, "that carry over into other parts of the program." In fact, all of TAC's classes, none of which contain more than twenty students, are conducted in a similar fashion, using the Socratic method.

According to freshman Rebekah Shapiro, "The teaching method here forces you not only to understand the material but be able to explain it. It allows you to see things for yourself. The tutors try very little to tell you things and just sort of direct you." Indeed, all the students I speak with rave about the classroom discussions; they say they feel more focused than they would be if it were just a lecture, and more able to retain the information they learn.

All this certainly seems to be true in the classes I attend, despite the dearth of writing students are required to do. Freshmen at Thomas Aquinas write five papers; sophomores, four; juniors, two; and seniors, just their thesis. None of the papers are more than about fifteen hundred words.

Jacob Aguirre, who attended another small Christian college before coming to TAC, argues that this is not really a problem. Writing and speaking, he explains, "are two fundamentally different ways of expressing yourself and they're both important, but I think that talking is a little more fundamental in terms of discovery. Writing is more about communication and laying out what you know already. What we do here is more discovery."

But the teaching method is, in a sense, an outgrowth of the curriculum, which includes only the Great Books (T. S. Eliot is probably the most recently living author taught here). There are no majors and there are no electives. Every TAC student must take six subjects—philosophy, math, language, theology, laboratory, and seminar (juniors study music for one semester instead of language). During their first week at TAC, freshmen, for instance, read Euclid, Plato, Homer, Ecclesiastes, and *The Insect World of J. Henri*

Fabre. With works as difficult as these, one would think that students would need more, not less, guidance from the faculty. But the theory at Thomas Aquinas is that since the students have at their disposal the great teachers and thinkers of Western civilization, they should not depend on a professor—or even another writer, say, in a textbook—to interpret for them.

And because this kind of curriculum and teaching method do not hinge, for their effectiveness, on the expertise of the faculty, any of the tutors can (and do) teach every subject. As DeLuca notes, "No one teaches in this program as an expert. We view tutors as slightly more advanced students who can help the students read the books. You don't have to master all those disciplines." He tells me that during the course of his thirty years at TAC, he has taught about half the program, though he confesses, "it was probably the less difficult half." Faculty members are helped, particularly in these tougher areas, like the advanced math and science classes and the music curriculum, by attending seminars over the summer to familiarize themselves with the texts they will be teaching.

Despite the constant pressure to keep a few steps ahead of the students, the opportunity to teach various disciplines is part of the appeal of the school for many faculty. Andrew Seeley, a tall man with spiky blond hair and blue eyes, talks with me in his temporary office, a trailer next to the school's library. Having graduated from TAC and received a degree in medieval theology from the Institute of Medieval Studies in Toronto, Seeley returned to Thomas Aquinas as a tutor ten years ago.

> *I was personally attracted to come back because I would get to go through all the material again, and get to be learning all the time. There is no danger here—or very little—of getting stuck in a course you do for twenty years. I have always had broad intellectual interests. In a traditional university, I would be doing theology. It would be hard to break out of that box. Here I've done math and science and music theory and philosophy and some theology even.*

The fact that all of the students go through the same curriculum and all of the tutors teach all of the subjects makes the academic discussion on campus more focused and more advanced. Underclassmen can ask upperclassmen for help understanding their reading. Students who are in different sections can discuss readings because all sophomores, for example, are studying the same texts at the same time. The fact that they are in all of the same classes together means they can bring up ideas from other subjects and everyone will be familiar with them. Moreover, tutors can assume a certain foundation of knowledge from each student not only in one subject, but all of them. (This is one reason why students who have been at other colleges and want to transfer to TAC must start again from their freshman year. Over 50 percent of the students at TAC have made that sacrifice.)

Seeley explains the concept behind the TAC education: "We're successful at giving them a breadth of disciplines." For instance, he believes, "We can create an excitement about geometry, because they will actually know geometry instead of just believing it. They will know the scriptures, by reading through them carefully. They will get an introduction to the ancient Greeks, an introduction to Plato and Aristotle. They will graduate with some conviction about what's true in regard to the most important intellectual issues." Though some fault the Great Books curriculum for its impracticality, Seeley maintains that "the most important thing is that we're not educating them to be doctors or lawyers. We're educating them to be men. The most important thing is that they come out with a clear sense of what's really important in life and that they have the habits of conducting themselves and leading others to live for what's most important."

There are a small number of other schools in the country that have a Great Books curriculum and use the Socratic method, most notably St. John's College, a secular school, which has branches in Annapolis and Santa Fe. Many of the students who choose Thomas Aquinas have considered St. John's as well.

In general, one is more likely to find Great Books or traditional liberal arts curricula at schools with strong religious identities. In the last few decades, the idea that there is a single, unchanging truth, about which one can be enlightened during college, has slowly eroded. What has taken its place is the idea that truth is something that depends upon one's perspective. The simplest and most obvious sign of this shift has been the addition of various disciplines— women's studies, African-American studies, queer studies, etc.—that provide some of those other perspectives on truth, and the disappearance of core curricula, authors, and books that everyone was required to study in order to gain access to truth. But at religious colleges, the understanding that there is an eternal truth, however difficult it may be to find, has remained a part of their religious and their educational missions.

There are some, though, who cannot succeed in this kind of educational environment. While DeLuca notes that the retention rate, now at 88 percent, has been improving ever since the school started to have a wait list ("The admissions committee knows they have more choices"), there are still some kids who are not cut out for this kind of work. Of the people Jacob knows who have been kicked out or left, he tells me, "A few didn't have the aptitude. Some wondered why they were here. One guy didn't think he was mature enough; he wasn't disciplined in himself."

But mostly these types of kids don't choose TAC in the first place. Susanka explains that the admissions process is generally self-selecting. "Students are not likely to apply if they haven't got a good chance of being accepted. They look at the reading list and the various demands, and then they look at the number of essays they have to write in the application, and they decide yes or no." The school is also very up front about is rules, its atmosphere, and its religious identity. Susanka puts it bluntly, "There's enough in the literature about TAC that no one could mistake what is going on here, unless you're really a blockhead and then you don't belong here anyway."

The selection process at the school's end is fairly unusual, benefiting those students who act early in the school year. For every applicant, the admissions committee asks two questions: 1) Can this person do the work? 2) Does this person want to be here? In order to determine this, the committee examines SAT scores (the average at Thomas Aquinas is 1300), class rank (most TAC students graduate in the top 20 percent), a writing sample, and essays demonstrating that they understand the school's intellectual and religious aims. If the answer to both questions is yes, the student is admitted. The process is a rolling one, which begins in September and goes on until the class is full. In other words, as the school's president, Thomas Dillon, explains, "We have geniuses left on the waiting list."

The chapel at Thomas Aquinas, which looks like a ski chalet with its exposed wooden beams and grand views of the surrounding mountains, is already mostly full when Dave and I arrive a few minutes before nine. There are three different masses on Sunday mornings to accommodate the Thomas Aquinas community, which includes not only the students, but also the faculty and administrators along with their often sizable families. Dave leans over to ask me if I've ever been to a "smells 'n' bells" mass before, that is, one in which the priest will use bells and incense. When I tell him I haven't, he adds, proudly, "The whole thing is in Latin, too."

Every student at Thomas Aquinas is required to learn Latin grammar and study the mass. There are a few readings in English, but there is no separate English mass for students to attend. The reason offered by Rev. Wilfred Borden, an Irish-looking man of about seventy with reddish eyebrows, is not simply to preserve a tradition. "Latin is concise," he asserts. "So many English words have different shades of meaning." It might be a shock to some of the students who don't have any background in Latin when they come here, but Fr. Borden, leaning back in his beat-up recliner, with his priest collar hanging out of his shirt pocket, assures me, "They get used to it."

Even Catholics who have attended Latin mass might find TAC's a bit more formal. For instance, they don't pass the peace to their neighbors, as often happens after the priest says, "The peace of the Lord be with you" and the congregation responds in unison, "And also with you."

The school's other chaplain, Rev. Bartholomew R. de la Torre, a harsher looking man than Fr. Borden who takes long pauses between sentences, leads mass today. He scolds the students (in English) for playing games in the dining commons on Friday nights instead of coming to participate in the Stations of the Cross. But his face softens as he tells the congregants that he has "been amiss" because "I didn't make it clear how important this is." The guilt of the students around me is palpable, as they shift in their seats and stare at the floor.

If that is the most unnerving part of the service for students, perhaps the most joyous comes when three congregants who are in the process of converting to Catholicism are introduced. Ninety percent of students who enter Thomas Aquinas are Catholic, and half of the remaining ones convert during their time there. Fr. de la Torre calls up to the altar each of the potential converts as well as the sponsors who are helping them in this process. A section of the mass is devoted to asking the community to support them in this venture and appealing for God's blessing on them.

Fr. Borden tells me of a non-Catholic student whom he befriended. "He said, 'You're never going to get me, Father.'" Initially, Fr. Borden recounts, the student had "difficulty with the concept of the Trinity. But after reading St. Thomas he said, 'Well, that makes sense.' And he became a Catholic." Fr. Borden believes there is a kind of pattern to the conversions at the college: "About halfway through their time here, [students] become interested in converting. Many will do it after they read Augustine's *City of God*. That's their sophomore year. It's a great inspiration."

The issue of how to treat non-Catholics is certainly a topic of much discussion even in this monastic and homogeneous community. Some TAC students don't see the zeal to convert non-Catholics as an unqualified good. And even the president of the school acknowledges that some students may have a tendency to go overboard, but he does expect that proselytizing should be a part of the lives of TAC students and graduates. He reasons, "If you think the faith is true and if you think that it's appropriate to live your life for Christ, it's also appropriate to want to draw others into it." But what does this mean for the religious minorities on campus?

Rebekah Shapiro, whom Dave Shaneyfelt initially introduces to me as a Jewish student, but who is actually evangelical (having come from a high school where some of the students matriculated to Bob Jones), does not seem unhappy with the way she has been treated by Catholics on campus. She does acknowledge that word of her religious beliefs spread very quickly on campus. But she understood what she was getting into. "One of the things I knew coming in here was that as a non-Catholic here, you are a guest." The school, tutors, and students are not going to bend over backward to accommodate other faiths. Recently, Rebekah learned a group of students, including some of her closest friends, is starting a confraternity, and she tells me a little dejectedly, "They have decided this group will be just for Catholics." While non-Catholics tend to rave about the curriculum and even appreciate the school's commitment to the religious tradition, they can't help but feel left out occasionally.

Mike Hurwitz, the only Jewish person (and one of two non-Christian students) on campus, feels more than just occasionally excluded from campus life. A tall, relaxed looking man with a reddish beard and mustache, Mike wears corduroys, a navy blue hooded sweatshirt, and unmatched socks. He balances his chair precariously on its rear legs and explains, "There are a couple of girls I know on this campus who kind of view me as just having different moral ethics. They wouldn't touch me with a ten-foot pole." Generally, he thinks, there are "other students who are curious. I have friends who are always nagging me to tell them more about my religion." Though Mike believes most people are outwardly very accepting, "Seventy percent expect me to convert. I get that question all the time. 'When are you converting, Mike?' That bothers me."

He acknowledges that when he decided to attend TAC he hadn't thought much about the school's religious identity at all. After leaving the University of Oregon, he spent some time in St. Michael's Abbey in Orange County, where one of the brothers recommended Thomas Aquinas to him. He was attracted initially by the curriculum and still finds it uniquely interesting. Over the years, Mike has had friendly disagreements with the administration over some dress-code issues, but otherwise does not register to me any complaints with the way the college is run. Still, he looks forward to graduation, when he can live closer to a synagogue and have access to kosher food. Until then, he believes, he is "virtually the black sheep of Thomas Aquinas."

Despite the occasional friction that results, President Dillon thinks it is important to have non-Catholics like Mike and Rebekah among the students. "I'll give you an example of why," he tells me. "When [freshmen] read the scriptures in the first year, the tutor will sometimes ask, 'What does this passage mean?' and the Catholic student will just give a stock catechism answer. The non-Catholic," Dillon suggests, "will say, 'Where's that?' And it turns out it's not there [in the text]. Or it's not there in the way the Catholic thought. Or it's only there if they combine it with something else." Dillon concludes, "There is a kind of freshness of perspective that the non-Catholic brings to theology that's worth our having because we want to know what's true and we don't want to rely on stock answers. It helps awaken all our students to inquiry, to asking the right kinds of questions so they can make progress and learn."

On the other hand, Dillon doesn't think it's important to have non-Catholics on the faculty. "Our faculty are models in some way for the students. So if there is a faculty member who is not a Catholic," Dillon worries, "a student will be asking 'Why? Have I made the right decision?'" As far as how the hiring works in practice, Dillon tells me, the school just takes applicants as they come. If the administration thinks someone can make a significant contribution to the school, they will be offered a job. Though he doubts they would hire a non-Christian, they have had a few non-Catholics. "It would depend on the context. We had an Episcopalian priest on the faculty. We borrowed him from St. John's, and we liked him so much we offered to have him stay. He was clearly supportive of what we were doing." But Dillon emphasizes, "He didn't teach theology."

When Richard Ferrier came to teach at TAC, he was a "completely committed" Episcopalian. Though he had heard of students being pressured to convert, he was not. He tells me, in fact, "Everybody was wonderfully gentle." So how did Ferrier and his wife end up Catholic? In part it was the "charity of the students and the general good will of the community," he says. But the decision was also a political one. In 1984, when he was attending an Episcopal church in Annapolis, Ferrier recalls hearing a statement on abortion from the American bishops read from the pulpit. "It was so this-worldly and mealy-mouthed; it didn't sound like Christ at all. It sort of disgusted me." He pauses for a moment, reliving the irritation. "Here I am telling everyone that Rome and Canterbury are so close and that Anglicanism is just Catholic Christianity for English speaking people. Then when it comes time to speak with the voice of Christ, they speak with the voice of *The New York Times*."

Molly Gustin came to TAC as a nonbeliever thirty years ago and hasn't budged since. When I tell her that many of the students think she is Catholic or "at least Protestant," she laughs lightheartedly. A grandmotherly woman with long white hair pulled back in a bun and big round glasses, Gustin describes to me the efforts of students to bring her into the fold. "They used to say novenas for me and everything. They give me scapulars." But she is not offended. "I have an utterly different view of religion than a lot of people here. But it's never been a problem. I come to their conclusions and I think they like that, that I can come to their conclusions from nonreligious foundations."

Gustin, who is greatly beloved by the students and the tutors (many of whom she had as students) and solely responsible for developing the school's music curriculum, says that even though she could never adopt it herself, she has great respect for the faith of those around her. "I think that religion can do what I don't know how to do. It can make people happy, successful, and good. It can produce marvelous art. Religion does all sorts of tremendous things. I don't know how to do that." Having once taught at St. John's, Gustin believes religion is the reason that "people are happier here than there." In fact, she thinks generally, "Catholics are happy people."

She pauses for a moment to explain, "Look what they have ahead of them."

After mass, which lasts about an hour, I eat lunch with Dave and his family in the school's cafeteria. I think he has four children, but they leave the table frequently and sometimes return accompanied by friends, so it's hard to tell. (TAC pays its staff on a scale depending on experience, but adds an additional sum for each child in the family.) His wife—one of those mothers whose calm demeanor in the midst of her children's chaos astounds those around her—has the look of a former hippie, with wild long curly hair and a handmade colorful sweater. She grew up in Oregon and California, she tells me, and went to the University of Oregon. The fraternity atmosphere of the school did not agree with her. "That's one thing I certainly appreciate about Thomas Aquinas."

There is a monastic feel to life here. The dorms are single-sex, of course, and there are no visiting hours whatsoever. Students caught in the wrong dorm are expelled immediately. (To more effectively enforce all of these regulations, curfew is set at eleven P.M. on weekdays and one A.M. on weekends. Quiet hours begin at seven P.M. on weeknights.) There are no public displays of affection allowed on campus, but students may hold hands and, perhaps, kiss by the reflecting pools on the edge of campus. Students are asked not to date during their first two years on campus because it is felt they are not mature enough to handle a serious relationship (the only kind of relationship TAC students have). Homosexual behavior is also obviously forbidden and the school would not look to well on a student announcing he is gay even if he didn't "practice." (There are rumors that two students were expelled early in the school's history for homosexual behavior.)

There is no drinking allowed on campus, except at official college functions. There is a little area right off campus called "the pit," where students go to drink on Friday nights (it changes to Saturdays during Lent). The administration knows about it, but doesn't seem concerned, perhaps because the drinking isn't really excessive and, more often than not, it involves singing Irish folksongs around a campfire.

Students at Thomas Aquinas live pretty simply and it's not just due to the school's being small, isolated, and rule-bound. There are no intercollegiate sports, and few intramurals, though some students play in local adult leagues. Many of the students take advantage of the lovely environment to participate in quieter, more solitary activities, like hiking, biking, and Rollerblading. Students are not allowed to have televisions, VCRs, or DVD players in the dorms. There is one TV on campus, at Fr. Borden's house, that students may watch in their free time. In addition, since Thomas Aquinas grants some amount of scholarship money to most students (TAC accepts no government funds), the administration proscribes those students from owning cars or purchasing personal phone lines. Shaneyfelt tells me this may sound extreme but the school's administration struggles each year to come up with those dollars; so, the logic goes, if students can afford luxury items, they can surely afford to pay more tuition.

Mary Jane O'Brien admits she found it "a little odd when I read about some of the rules. I mean, what's the problem with a TV?" Having already lived on her own for a number of years, she found the adjustment to the TAC rules difficult, but being one of the older students, she thinks, has helped her. "What do I have to do after one A.M. anyway?" she asks. "The idea at TAC," she has come to understand, is "to limit distractions as much as possible. It's really focused on the studies. That's what we do." Indeed, standing in the center of campus on a gorgeous spring Sunday afternoon, I cannot see or hear a soul. There is no music emanating from open dorm windows, no flirtatious laughter, no frisbees whizzing by. As I walk up the new looking sidewalk between the three dormitories—small, white one- and two-story

Southwest-style buildings—I notice a couple of students here and there, sitting on the steps or on benches in the shade. Some are chatting quietly, but most are reading.

Most of students' free time is spent studying or praying. Every couple of weeks, there will be some kind of school-sponsored event—career day, upperclassmen versus underclassmen football, or a dance. When I ask freshman Rebekah Shapiro whether she gets bored, she explains, "You only really need one thing per weekend because you spend so much time studying that you only need it to take up a few hours." If there is nothing going on at school, some students will visit family or go take advantage of southern California's natural beauty. But Rebekah, who has long red hair and a very pale complexion, tells me emphatically, "I don't like the beach."

Nicole Gingras likes to play pool in her dorm's common room, which, aside from the new-looking green felt table, contains a small boom box, a fireplace, a single treadmill, and a life-size cutout of Luke Skywalker wearing a sign that says "Man in dorm." When Nicole agrees to talk to me, she offers her cue to another girl, and proceeds to sit down on the small couch, Indian-style. An Asian-looking sophomore with tanned skin and well-defined arms, she has a long braid down the center of her back. "I did so many extracurriculars in high school," she recalls, "this kind of program where it's almost purely academic takes some getting used to." There are a few clubs on campus but no student newspaper and no student government. These sorts of groups, according to Shaneyfelt, might serve to divide the campus. "Tutors and students," he says, "should be focused on their common task of learning."

The same justification is used to explain the school's lack of a separate faculty lounge. Looking around the cafeteria over the course of a few days, I do not notice a single table where tutors are sitting without students. This integration of faculty and students encourages the seriousness of mealtime conversations, which, more often than not, are about literature and philosophy and mathematics. Aleyna tells me frivolous conversations do occur sometimes. "About half the time, I wake up and don't want to discuss the big questions in life. I find most of the time you have to start a conversation at the lunch table about the important things. Otherwise they will talk about a movie or the weather." But eavesdropping at the round cafeteria tables of eight or ten, where students may linger for as long as they wish after meals, I hear only a few items of gossip and no discussion about the weather, let alone movies.

Students at TAC debate from morning till night. Teachers who don't arrive for class fifteen minutes early may find the students have begun without them. Students often stay after class has ended to continue the arguments, or finish them over lunch. Andrew Seeley tells me that the school has "a rule that students who go here have to live here." It's because, he explains, there is so much "learning from one another outside of the classroom." John Kunz compares his experience at TAC to that of his friends at other colleges. "I have a lot of friends who went to college to get new life experiences, and maybe they'd go to a few classes and here I think the life experience is from the classes." John pauses and glances behind him. "You see those people on the patio? That's class still."

After their evening seminars, students meet in the coffee shop—The Dumb Ox Espresso Bar—where they can buy fifty-cent cappuccinos to accompany their peanut butter sandwiches scavenged from the dining hall kitchen. There are four big tables, with books scattered all over them, and a chessboard in one corner. Some students are reading, while others are chatting on the couch about the day's reading, occasionally glancing over at the Ping-Pong game in the next room. I do overhear one student complaining about a tutor who keeps them in class so long he finds himself late for his next class. Again, though, no discussion of the news, the weather, or campus gossip.

When I ask Rebekah Shapiro what she would consider the biggest source of controversy on campus—the thing that most often provokes heated discussion outside of class—I have in mind an administrative policy that upsets students or a division among the students over some particular social issue. Instead she offers this: "The big controversy here is the Plato versus Aristotle controversy." Rebekah recalls that she was first introduced to this debate—in which, she acknowledges, "the material is somewhat over my head"—during one of the school's Friday night lectures. The lecture itself she regarded as uneventful, but afterward "there is a question-answer session, and then discussion." The tutors, Rebekah heard, "were here until three A.M."

But the discussion is not quite as free-ranging as one might expect from this group of avid debaters. Jacob Aguirre tells me that one of the reasons he wavered between St. John's and Thomas Aquinas was because he had heard that the former was "more contentious and more skeptical." Though he concluded, "I wanted to have a better foundation of belief in Christianity before I tackled the skepticism," there are times, Jacob acknowledges, that "part of me that really does want to go out and wrestle with that [skepticism]," and it's a problem because "you don't get that as much here."

During breakfast on Wednesday morning, I find some evidence for Jacob's complaint. The two students present are asking me about my travels to other schools, particularly the evangelical ones. I describe to them the situation at

Wheaton College, where, I explain, there are many students who come seek-ing intellectual safety—a shelter from the challenges to their faith that secu-lar colleges would present. What they find instead is an atmosphere that forces them to question their beliefs, even if ultimately it is in the service of strengthening them. Inevitably, I tell them that this results, at any one time, in a certain population of "doubters." Puzzled, these TAC upperclassmen can't seem to understand why a religious school would want to engender doubt among its students. I try to explain that that is not Wheaton's final goal, but sometimes, the professors there tell me, it's a necessary step on the way to bringing serious intellectual strength to their students' faith.

"There are no doubters here," one of the students tells me resolutely. And the other quickly concurs. After a moment, the first adds that even if there were, we wouldn't be able to "see into another student's soul." Granting that, I ask if perhaps there are any outward signs. Students who go through doubt at Wheaton, I offer, will often find themselves emotionally affected by the new and difficult questions facing them. Have they ever witnessed someone experiencing, perhaps, a crisis of faith? They give me a unanimous no.

During the course of our conversation, one of the tutors, Karen Zedlick, sits down at the table. A thin woman with severe features and blond hair, she listens for a moment before jumping in heatedly with a German accent. "You know, this is not a game." She explains that the tutors and the administration have no interest in making students into doubters. But when I ask whether the students are supposed to take seriously all of the authors, including, for example Nietzsche, she nods.

"If Nietzsche is taught with the same consideration as, say, Thomas Aquinas, isn't it likely that at least some of the students will come away doubt-ing the existence of God?" I ask.

Zedlick begins to clench her hands around the edge of the table. She of-fers a story in response. A while back, she explains, she had an "atheist boyfriend," with whom she was completely in love. They talked about God all the time, but eventually they had to break up. It was not, she suggests, be-cause she had faith and he did not, but because he thought their conversa-tions "were just about intellectual sparring, and I thought it's about your soul." I went back to the example of Wheaton, explaining, "I don't think they view the religious education as intellectual sparring. They also see it is about the soul. But they see doubt as a necessary evil in the process to saving souls." Zedlick begins to raise her voice. There is no one else in the cafeteria so it's not quite a scene, but Dave Shaneyfelt, who has been sitting with us, mostly quiet throughout the conversation, seems a little uncomfortable.

Zedlick and I go back and forth a few more times, but then she hurries out, ten minutes late for her class.

As President Dillon explains, the students and tutors at Thomas Aquinas begin with the premise that "this scripture is the word of God." The discussion at Thomas Aquinas centers on "what [that] means," an issue he believes is "tough." For example, he observes, "In Genesis, there is more than one account of creation. What sense do I make of that? What are these days He's talking about? How can there be light before there's sun?" Dillon believes that sort of questioning is "fine." But, he explains, "In our classes we are looking at that through the eyes of faith so we have the view that we're going to be able to solve these things or at least find it's not a complete contradiction." In other words, though the tutors and students at Thomas Aquinas are starting with a basic adherence to the Catholic faith and a belief in the authority of scripture and the Church, everything beyond that is fair game. As Aleyna explains, "A lot of people at TAC assume the same sorts of underlying truths," a condition, she maintains, that makes it "easier to get somewhere [in the discussion]" because "you don't have to explain the bare basics of things over and over."

Many of the students get used to talking with people who share their outlook on the world. Nicole Gingras, for instance, tells me that when you come to TAC, "I think your perspective changes. Your level of intellect changes in the way that you just look at things differently." She confesses that, "Going home and seeing my old high school friends, it's kind of hard to talk to them on the same level. It's not that I want to say I'm better than them." But, she explains, "Your thinking is kind of curbed to just think about higher things." Nicole believes that her perspective is common. Almost every TAC grad she knows who has gotten married has married another grad. "I think it's very rare when you find someone outside of the school who you can relate to."

On the other hand, Nicole says she is happy that she has had the experience of going to a public school before coming to Thomas Aquinas, because, she suggests, the kids who have been homeschooled their whole lives have even less of an idea how to relate to outsiders. Jacob sees a similar problem among many of his fellow students. "We're very educated and we know about the things that we know but we don't know as well how to convince other people." Though he thinks his time at TAC has helped him to "understand the Catholic faith much better," he laments, "when I leave and I try to talk to other people about it, there are a lot of things that are assumed [here] and those kind of things you [can't assume] with outside people. It's hard to communicate with outside people because you have to explain everything and you can't do that."

* * *

Many Thomas Aquinas students describe a certain "decompression period" needed after TAC in order to reacclimate themselves to the world. Peter DeLuca marvels at the variety of professions that students have gone into. One of them is a nun in Mother Teresa's order; many are in political jobs. His daughter works at Voice of America. But a high proportion chooses to do graduate study. Out of the 848 people who have matriculated from TAC over the years, the school currently has information for 752 of them. Thirty-three percent have been accepted into graduate schools, and 12 percent have been accepted into professional (law or medical) schools.

Rebekah Shapiro, a very ambitious freshman, who tells me she was disappointed that TAC didn't have a copy of the Bible in Hebrew, may apply to either graduate school in history or to law school. She was initially "worried because TAC is so strange and our grading system is so strange," but as far as law schools, she has been reassured that they are familiar enough with Thomas Aquinas that it won't be a problem. Graduate studies in history, she understands, might be more of an issue. "I'll graduate without having taken any American history classes or a second language," both pretty common requirements to get into such programs.

Mike Hurwitz's plans for his future haven't really changed much since he transferred from the University of Oregon. He has always been interested in going to graduate school in chemistry and eventually he wants to be a professor, doing research and teaching. He thinks that the math and science curricula at Thomas Aquinas, though different from other colleges, have prepared him well for his chosen field. Before coming to TAC, he explains, "I had taken calculus all the way through to multivariable differential calculus, but I really felt I had no familiarity with it. If you put an equation in front of me, I could do it but I had no idea why it was working. . . . I was just going through the motions." Not only does he understand the reasoning behind the mathematical and scientific formulas he has learned, but Hurwitz thinks that thanks to his experience at Thomas Aquinas, "the style in which I teach will be better."

Though TAC is obviously not preparing its students for specific professions, the faculty expect that whatever profession they choose, they will be forced to confront various moral choices and that their TAC education will help them to make the right ones. President Dillon hopes that no matter which occupation students choose, they will be people "who aren't satisfied with superficial answers and . . . who seek wisdom throughout their lives, not only for its practical effect, but for the good of their own soul." According to Dillon, the "ideal graduate of Thomas Aquinas is one who is intellectually and morally virtuous, . . . both in his career and his private life." Dillon notes that this applies not only to TAC alumni, like the two who work as lawyers in the U.S. Department of Justice, "who have tried to exercise the things they learned here in their daily work," but also to the women "who choose to stay home and raise their children. They, too, are in some way bringing their education to bear [on their daily lives]."

For the women at Thomas Aquinas, raising children generally means homeschooling them. In fact, Molly Gustin is confident that "all of the women at TAC plan to homeschool their kids." Smiling widely at the prospect, she tells me, "All of the faculty wives do. Some of the faculty children who were homeschooled are now married and grown up and homeschooling their own kids." Many of the women do work initially, though. According to Susanka, "Almost a quarter of young women teach almost as a halfway house [on the way to marriage]." But they choose professions that provide flexible hours and that can be abandoned for long periods of time without consequence.

Nicole, for example, would like a career as a massage therapist. "That's kind of a big surprise to people." She laughs. In high school, she tells me, she wanted to be a photojournalist. Though she still practices photography as a hobby, even taking pictures for school publications occasionally, she changed her mind because "I wanted to get into something that didn't take up too much time for me to get into if I wanted to start a family." The training for massage therapy, she notes, "is pretty short and you make pretty good money." Aleyna cites similar reasons when she tells me she is thinking about studying homeopathic medicine, or perhaps going into elementary school teaching.

The administration at TAC strongly approves of the decisions their female students make after graduation, not out of some antiquated sense that women should not be out in the world. Rather, President Dillon understands that the efforts of these mothers to educate their children are the means for achieving a sea change in America. When I question him about the role of schools like Thomas Aquinas in the larger culture, he quickly returns to the subject of family. "I don't think you can sustain this country without virtue and it's hard to sustain virtue without religion," both of which, he suggests, "are inculcated in the family. You can't make your children be virtuous but you can give them the right kind of habits and lead them down the line. Without the family," Dillon says, "this country is doomed, and," he adds—citing everything from the culture's "sexual decadence" to its "gross entertainment"—"the family has been under attack the last thirty years."

Molly Gustin cannot say enough about the way TAC alumni raise their families. "They do wonderfully when they graduate. We've had two divorces in the history of the school. . . . The students come back and they have these wonderful kids and they're rosy and happy. It's marvelous." TAC may only have a few hundred graduates so far, but it sees itself as very much a part of a larger movement, and not just a Catholic one.

Indeed, Rebekah Shapiro, despite her evangelical faith, seems to feel she has a lot more in common with the Catholic community at TAC than with the secular world. Being at Thomas Aquinas has changed her view of the country. Rebekah recalls, "There were times in high school when I was feeling like there was an approaching crisis, that America was becoming too secular, that the religious people are being marginalized. Here, I guess because I see the religious part of the country as much larger than I did a year ago, there doesn't seem to be as much of a crisis. Being here increases your optimism."

CHAPTER FIVE

THE HATFIELDS AND THE McCOYS:
A DIVIDED YESHIVA

It's a formidable line. Hundreds of professors in full academic regalia mingle with learned rabbis in dark suits and hats, standing on the Amsterdam Avenue sidewalk waiting for the ceremony. As they process from the warm autumn sun into the packed auditorium in the Beit Midrash (literally, "House of Study") the small ensemble in the front of the room plays "Pomp and Circumstance" as well as the "Ode to Joy."

The investiture of a university president, that is, the ceremony in which the authority and symbols of that office are first conferred, is a celebratory occasion, but it must also be an anxious one. The responsibility for leading a large educational institution has always been tremendous, but in recent years, the duties of fund-raiser and legal expert have been added to those of scholar, teacher, adviser, and public figurehead. Certainly, many of Yeshiva University's students and faculty are wondering what the new president, Richard Joel, will do to continue his predecessor's legacy in making the school more competitive: How will Yeshiva bring in the best professors? How will it attract the Orthodox men and women who can attend Ivy League schools with big Jewish student programs? Where will the money for these improvements come from?

But Joel may have an even more difficult road ahead of him than many of his counterparts. As Stephen Trachtenberg, the president of George Washington University, who offers greetings at the investiture on behalf of "the university community," cannot help but point out, Joel is the first president of Yeshiva who is not also a rabbi. Trachtenberg, whose words for Joel are kind if religiously tone-deaf, finds Yeshiva's choice similar to that of Georgetown's recently installing a lay president. He notes that both institutions were looking for the "best person for the school as it is today." Though Trachtenberg is himself Jewish, his concerns are more with Yeshiva's academic reputation than its religious identity. So he "applaud[s] the departure" of Yeshiva from the tradition of having a president with a rabbinical degree.

Loud whisperers from students in the row behind me hope that Yeshiva will not go the way of its (now almost secular) Catholic counterpart. But for the Yeshiva community, ensuring that its students remain committed to Orthodox Judaism is not a great source of worry. Rather, the question of whether Yeshiva's religious message should inform its secular education at all is an open one, and perhaps the biggest one. If the forces that believe the sacred and the secular must remain separate prevail, it is unclear whether Yeshiva graduates will have an influence on American life that is distinctive at all from graduates of secular colleges on the one hand, or from the significant Orthodox Jewish population who never attend college on the other.

Since Yeshiva's Rabbi Isaac Elchanan Theological Seminary supplies a great percentage of the country's rabbis, and graduates of its Azrieli Graduate School of Jewish Education fill American Hebrew schools and Jewish day schools, the university's influence on Orthodox Jewish life is much greater than that of any one other school profiled here on its own faith. Indeed, given the amount of influence that Yeshiva University has over the future of Jewish life, it is hardly surprising that the selection of Joel, only the fourth president of the university in its 117-year history, was a contentious process, with a final vote of thirty to two.

The search for the new president lasted almost three years and considered candidates like Dov Zakheim, the undersecretary of defense (who withdrew himself from the running when a furor erupted over his alleged lack of qualifications for the position), and Rabbi Jonathan Sacks, the chief Orthodox rabbi of England. Ultimately, the university's trustees decided that Richard Joel's experience as president of Hillel (an international foundation for Jewish campus life), Bronx assistant district attorney, associate dean of Yeshiva's law school, and parent of three Yeshiva grads would make him the right man for the job. But if there was any doubt in Joel's mind about all of the competing factions with which he would have to contend in setting out a new direction for the university, the investiture ceremony on September 21, 2003, should have settled them.

The secular music selections at the investiture are followed by a decidedly religious invocation from Rabbi Zevulun Charlop, dean of the seminary. While acknowledging the various ways in which Yeshiva has changed over the course of its existence, Charlop waxes about how it has stayed the course. He notes that the refusal of the original institution to be subsumed by the American melting pot has created a stronger institution, one that still "resonates as surely as ever with the sounds and excitement of Volozhin [the home of the Lithuanian yeshivas], the model and progenitor of the idea of yeshiva for the last two centuries." Charlop speaks of the need to "bring the divine and unchanging message of our faith . . . to every nook and cranny of Jewish life."

The religious faculty has not been enthusiastic about having a non-rabbi as president—a break from tradition. Some of the more ultra-orthodox rabbis, who see religious studies as the primary reason for attending Yeshiva and the secular studies as a necessary evil in order to gain employment, worry that a lay president might send the wrong signal to students about the relative importance of the two sides of the school. According to the *Jewish Week,* many of these rabbis and their student followers "recited Tehillim (Psalms), a prayerful response to times of crisis and danger," in anticipation of Joel's election, while 15 percent of respondents to a recent survey in the school paper believe "Joel's presidency will be a disaster for Yeshiva." To make matters more complicated, some of the more centrist members of the university and seminary faculty worry that Joel's not having a rabbinic degree will prevent him from garnering enough respect from the religious leaders of the school to keep the rabbis in line.

Meanwhile, the reaction of the secular studies faculty to having a non-rabbi has been similar to Trachtenberg's. Some of them see the ascendance of Joel as a sign that they need not worry about the administration trying to bring religious ideas into secular disciplines, a move, they believe, that would impinge on their academic freedom.

There is much reason to believe that, unlike his counterpart at Georgetown, Joel will not be leading Yeshiva down the path toward secularization, or maintaining the current separation between religious and secular education. Joel is not only strictly Orthodox himself but he spent his fourteen years as president of Hillel trying to bring a greater level of observance and Jewish learning to a generation of Jews at secular colleges and universities. (During Joel's tenure, the annual budget at Hillel increased from $14 million to $52 million and the organization opened 26 new facilities.) Nor is it likely, given the respect he seems to command in the Orthodox community, that the more extreme rabbis will be able to ignore his leadership.

Of course, Joel was not picked because he was the most religiously learned of the candidates. As the presence of New York city mayor Michael Bloomberg at the investiture suggests, some parts of the Yeshiva community are trying to take seriously the role of the school's graduates in public life. And Joel is a man who clearly feels a strong commitment there. His legal expertise was not only put to use for the people of New York during his years as assistant district attorney in the Bronx, but two years ago, Joel presided over a commission investigating the sexual misconduct of Rabbi Baruch Lanner, the director of the National Conference of Synagogue Youth, the Orthodox Union's educational arm. The report not only forced the OU to come clean about the misconduct but also about the three decades' worth of failures by high-ranking staff that surrounded it. Joel's investigation, which rejected the idea that these matters should only be discussed privately within the Jewish community, eventually led to Lanner's prosecution and conviction.

Discerning the Jewish community's relationship to American public life is only one part of the equation, as Israeli Ambassador Daniel Ayalon reminded the investiture audience. He noted that so far, two thousand Yeshiva alumni have "made their lives in Israel." Here, among Yeshiva families, there are young men and women who have no plans to stay in the U.S. a moment after graduation, who are here only to get their degrees, and have little or no commitment to life in America. Joel's own son recently made *aliyah*. But the question of how a Jewish university in America talks to its students about Israel—should they give up their safe lives here and put their families in danger in order to ensure Israel's survival in this time of crisis?—is another one that Joel will have to face.

By the time Richard Joel begins his own address, more than an hour into the ceremony, he seems anxious from all of the duties he has been charged with, and impatient to get started. Taking off his academic cap and adjusting the yarmulke underneath, Joel, a large man with a deep, friendly smile, recalls the journey that has taken him to this point: a father now passed away, who left Lithuania for South Africa and then America, his own bar mitzvah forty years ago to the day, his education under the tutelage of various members of the audience, the rearing of his own six children.

Mostly, though, Joel talks about Yeshiva's future. He announces particular steps toward a better university: a genetic research facility at the medical school, a more active campus life for undergraduates, a more student-friendly administrative attitude, higher standards for secular subjects, an extensive community service program, a stronger professional education component at the seminary, more faculty who are devoted to both religious and secular learning, an expanded student internship program in Israel, and more interdisciplinary contact across the school. What is the vision behind these disparate initiatives? Joel takes stock:

> [We] gather at a time when universities have been in retreat for a generation. While pursuing achievement and proficiency, the university has turned from . . . poetry, and has become too much a place of prose. . . . A new generation comes of age, longing for what William Raspberry calls a

life that makes sense, feeling profound existential loneliness, while living in a shrinking world that, paradoxically, produces feelings of anonymity. Our children long to matter, yearning for an informing vision of values that makes life work. They confront a madness of license on one hand and extremist, hateful fundamentalism on the other that seeks to extinguish the light of ideas and the lyric melody of values. . . .

A great university must rebuild a spirit of free inquiry, while embracing the immutability of life values that are non-negotiable. It must teach the skills of navigating the terrain, while reaching for the cosmos. Its challenge is not to defend Western civilization, but to advance Western civilization.

Looking at the efforts of the men and women who have come before him, "Yeshiva," Joel notes, represents "a yearning for all that is sacred in our humanity and all that is human in our sanctity."

When you come above ground at the 181st Street subway stop, there is little sign of Yeshiva University—or any Jews for that matter. The small bodegas all around sport signs in Spanish with some broken English translations underneath. Unlike most neighborhoods in Manhattan, there are few recognizable franchise stores. Though the last ten years have gentrified many of the city's poorer areas, this part of Washington Heights has not been deemed safe enough for many chains to move in. Two blocks north and east of the subway stands the first security booth marking Yeshiva University's perimeter. Even from this closer vantage point, there is still no campus to speak of. No grass. Just a lane of the street permanently closed off from traffic where a few benches and some concrete flowerpots sit.

Though this school is now fairly well known as the flagship educational institution of Orthodox Jewry in America, its current structure and education are still quite foreign to many Jews and non-Jews alike. Yeshiva today is a university with almost three thousand undergraduate and more than four thousand graduate students in its seven graduate schools all over New York City. The prominent Albert Einstein College of Medicine, the Cardozo School of Law, and the Wurzweiler School of Social Work, along with the highly selective Yeshiva College for Men (the focal point of this chapter) and Stern College for Women, its female counterpart, have combined to give the university a rank of 40 in the *U.S. News & World Report 2003* national survey, the same as Boston College's.

The graduate schools outside the seminary are secular, but the 1,300 men in the undergraduate divisions of Yeshiva (Yeshiva College and the Sy Syms School of Business, which occupy most of the Washington Heights campus) all spend their mornings in the reddish stone Beit Midrash, engaged in the study of the Torah, learning and debating the meanings of thousands of years' worth of rabbinical commentaries. Some finish their religious education at one P.M. while others go all the way till three before they begin their secular classes, mostly in the modern twenty-story black stone and glass Belfer Hall, which towers over the neighborhood.

How did the school arrive at this arrangement? It all began in 1886, when Yeshiva was just a small house of Jewish study on the Lower East Side. From its earliest beginnings, Yeshiva has had a Beit Midrash, however small, but Belfer Hall, with its classrooms and laboratories, was obviously a more recent addition, and the role of the secular education it represents at the school remains tenuous. Yeshiva has long been engaged in a great debate over how—and whether—to translate the Jewish education of Eastern Europe to the new American context.

A hundred years ago, as Jeffrey S. Gurock recounts in *The Men and Women of Yeshiva*, the school's almost entirely first- and second-generation immigrant student body wanted additional courses in English, public speaking, and Jewish culture and history. But the rabbis were reluctant to adapt. In 1908, after students had twice gone on strike to demand secular classes, the administration determined that the school would have to become an institution of both religious study (Torah) and worldly learning (Madda)—hence the school's motto, *Torah Umadda*.

In the late 1920s, a true liberal arts curriculum was added, along with a library, dormitories, and a basketball team. But Torah Umadda would not become a fully comprehensive vision until the arrival of Rabbi Joseph B. Soloveitchik in 1941. An eminent Talmudic scholar who also held a doctorate in philosophy from the University of Berlin, Soloveitchik was hailed by one disciple as having formulated "a creative philosophy, conservative and progressive, keeping intact our Jewish tradition even as he was developing it further." Soloveitchik, whose name remains on the lips of every student at Yeshiva even today, was uncompromising in his practice of Orthodox Judaism, but philosophically, the Rav, as he was endearingly referred to, brought about a major shift in Jewish thought and recreated the university to mirror it. In his most widely read work, *The Lonely Man of Faith*, Soloveitchik defines himself not simply in terms of Jewish thought, but also in the context of modern philosophy. Littered with footnotes to thinkers from Descartes to Kierkegaard, the book draws on Soloveitchik's secular education in physics, mathematics, various modern and ancient languages, and philosophy.

As committed as Soloveitchik was to the idea of a well-rounded person having both a religious and secular education, he did not believe in synthesizing the two. Mark Gottlieb, the principal of the Maimonides School in Brookline, Massachusetts, which was founded by the Rav and his wife, describes Soloveitchik's notion that a student must maintain "the integrity of each discipline, and not to assume that there is a theological solution at the end of the road." Instead, according to Gottlieb, Soloveitchik believed the "knowledge of Torah teaching and the Western legacy of science and philosophy are twin peaks," between which "we must build bridges." (This is distinct from the "integration of faith and learning" found at many of the Christian schools studied in this book.)

The Rav's views on the Jewish role in civic life were also revolutionary. Indeed, he argued that it was possible to lead a fully Jewish life in America, not just in Israel or in a secluded ghetto in Europe. Though he knew some cultural adjustments would have to be made in the Jewish community, like ensuring the formal Jewish education of women, he maintained they would be worth it in order for Jews to participate fully in American life.

Soloveitchik's theories were put to the test when he presided at Yeshiva during the most turbulent times in the century for any university—the 1960s. The civil rights movement and the war in Vietnam brought Yeshiva's students and faculty beyond the question of how to balance secular and religious studies to the more fundamental issue of YU's interaction with the world outside. As Gurock writes,

> Within the range of opinion, there could be found those who believed that the causes of general society had to be Yeshiva's not only because those were what concerned other colleges and their students, but, more essentially, because such concerns were intrinsically a part of the agenda of Orthodox Judaism. Others perceived distinct philosophical and practical limitations for both the Jew, and most importantly, the man of Torah if he became involved in the world's social and political arenas.

Soloveitchik argued that his belief in the dignity of man forced him to count himself among the former group when it came to the growing threat of Communism in the world. During the Vietnam War, Soloveitchik told one of his disciples, "If you don't oppose Communism in Southeast Asia, it will spread." But he also told those students who disagreed with him that they had an obligation to protest the war, albeit with a degree of decorum not found on other college campuses.

Citing Soloveitchik's influence, Steven Bayme, national director for contemporary Jewish life at the American Jewish Committee, describes the "incredible intellectual excitement" that prevailed at Yeshiva when he was a student there in the early sixties. "At what other school in the world could you study Genesis through the eyes of traditional rabbinical commentaries *and* Genesis through the eyes of Thomas Mann?"

"I would imagine that a lot of professors probably think we're wasting our time in the morning. And a lot of the rabbis think we're wasting our time in the afternoon," says Naphtali Weisz, a slight young man with a neatly trimmed beard who chooses his words carefully. A recent graduate from Yeshiva College and now enrolled at the seminary and the law school, Naphtali tells me that if he could change one thing about Yeshiva, he wishes his religious and secular studies teachers "would have more respect for each other."

It's easy to see why he complains. For all his professors and rabbis seem concerned, Naphtali and his classmates might just as well be attending two different institutions. As he mentioned in his speech at the investiture, Rabbi Charlop, dean of the seminary, believes that the school must take its bearings from the great yeshivas of Israel and Europe. He and many of his colleagues only grudgingly understand that in order for students to enter professional fields, they must devote a significant amount of their time to their secular studies. Many of the rabbis actively discourage students from taking classes that might run counter to religious belief, such as an art class that studies nudes or a literature class that reads material with sexual themes.

Another common objection to the secular classes by the ultra-orthodox (or "right-wing," as they are sometimes called) rabbis is that they teach Christian themes. Noyes Bartholomew, a music professor who has previously taught at secular universities, sometimes finds himself caught in a difficult position, not wanting to offend his charges' religious sensibilities, but knowing that music students should at least understand the "technical ramifications of Christianity, from the music of antiquity through the Renaissance Church." Bartholomew used to publicize the New York Philharmonic concerts in local churches, but has stopped. Not only will students refuse to attend because of the location, but, the professor laments, "If I put up posters, they will tear them down or deface them."

Perhaps most importantly, the rabbis encourage "the Yeshiva shuffle." Shai Barnea, the tall, lanky president of the Yeshiva student union, says that at least 40 percent of the students "are here to learn Torah and to get out as quickly as possible. To do that, they will pull as many strings, as many fast ones as possible to get out of classes, get out of various [requirements], get their diploma, and get out." In order to keep their nights free for religious study, Shai notes, "[they will] find the easy way out." And the faculty—in big ways and small—helps out. More than one alumnus describes to me how certain professors use the same exam year after year, so students acquire copies from their siblings or friends who have previously taken the course.

Other students and recent graduates report a significant amount of blatant cheating in secular classes. According to Joshua Stern, chairman of the Student-Faculty-Administration Senate (a group that meets on a biweekly basis to address issues of academic concern at Yeshiva), "There are definitely problems here." Though he doesn't think cheating is a disproportionately large problem at Yeshiva, he does find it mildly surprising that it doesn't happen less than it does.

"I didn't expect this to be a perfectly clean type of school," he says, "but I suppose that I expected there might be a slightly higher level of integrity than in other places." Some students even saw the rabbis as encouraging blatant cheating in secular courses. It became so common that the school's rabbis were recently driven to sign a document saying they do not condone it.

But students say that an equally pernicious message is being sent by some of the school's secular faculty. Yaakov Green, vice president of the student union, tells the story of a speech professor who regularly scolds students for letting their tzit-tzis (fringed prayer shawls) show from under their shirts. In fact, it's not uncommon to find secular faculty members who seem to believe that a strict Jewish belief system is a little passé. At one meeting of his Social Psychology of Evil class last semester, professor Maury Silver explained why he is an atheist. "Polytheistic religions are more advanced than monotheistic ones," he elaborated to me later, because they solve the problem of why there is evil in the world. Even Silver's outfit for class—a bright magenta shirt, gray track pants, and sneakers—makes him seem like an outsider on this campus where khakis and button-down shirts seem like the uniform for class.

And then there is the matter of Israel. Though few students at Yeshiva have much time for extracurricular activities, most of the student body belongs to the Israel Club. But the faculty is hardly part of this consensus. In discussing an article from the *New Yorker* about a group of Israelis who tried to blow up a Palestinian girls' school, Silver's message is one of moral equivalence, suggesting that suicide bombing is a tactic common to both sides of the conflict. Not only does he criticize the actions of Israeli leaders and suggest they are responsible for the current situation, but he refers to the entire land of Israel as "occupied Palestine," leading more than one student to walk out of class. Silver tells them to "understand we're bracketing the question of whether violence is right or wrong for the moment and we'll open the brackets later."

A couple of years ago, history professor Ellen Schrecker signed a petition that appeared in *The New York Times* calling on the United States "to make continued aid [to Israel] conditional on Israeli acceptance of an internationally agreed two-state settlement." When the editor of the school newspaper, the *Commentator,* wrote an article criticizing what he found the ridiculous, if not offensive, idea that a professor at Yeshiva University should take such a position, other faculty members leaped to her defense. Physics professor Gabriel Cwilich wrote a letter responding to the article. "His opinion was a little bit narrow minded," Cwilich tells me. "I tried to tell him: Listen, professors can have different opinions. [Students] have to be respectful of any opinion. Even if ninety-nine percent of the students actually happen to agree with the policies of Sharon that doesn't make any difference to me."

But Steven Bayme, who has taught history at Yeshiva off and on for the last couple of decades, explains that Schrecker, like many of her secular colleagues, "has zero influence on students" because her views are so far from theirs. "What is the value of a history education that has no impact on its students?" he asks.

In the hours after he announced his candidacy for president in the fall of 2002, reporters were invited into Joseph Lieberman's childhood home in Stamford, Connecticut. As the Democratic senator talked about faith and family values, his eighty-eight-year-old mother urged everyone to nosh on a little rugelach. This cozy scene provided an attractively ethnic picture to accompany Lieberman's all-American themes. But it is a scene that looks to Orthodox Judaism's past—not to its future.

Although Lieberman is often hailed as a pioneer—the first Jewish presidential candidate, and one who is not shy of talking about how his Orthodox faith informs his positions—one would be hard-pressed to find a coreligionist in Washington who is following in his footsteps. While Mormon, Protestant, and Catholic members of both parties are increasingly comfortable discussing their religious beliefs in the public square, Jews serving in Congress, like Eric Cantor, the chief deputy whip of the Republican caucus, rarely mention their faith in connection with their public lives. (While Cantor told the *Weekly Standard* that he has become more comfortable talking about his commitment to Judaism, he still says, "To me, religion is a very private thing.")

Lieberman traces his uniqueness to the particular Jewish world he was raised in. (Though he did not attend Yeshiva, his wife, Hadassah, has expressed interest to some community leaders in discussing the future of the institution.) As he told the *New Yorker,* "It was a different time, in a way, for the Orthodox movement in the fifties—much more centrist, if I can put it that way. . . . It was all about making things better—*tikkun olam,* improving the world. We had an obligation to reach out." But over the last twenty-five years, Orthodox Judaism has moved increasingly to the right, religiously and culturally speaking. In addition to becoming more observant of Jewish rituals, a larger portion of the Orthodox have turned away from the secular world. While other religious colleges are producing graduates confident about bringing their faith into the mainstream, Yeshiva has been moving strongly in the opposite direction. Today, the growing separation of the religious from the secular has made Yeshiva an institution at war with itself.

Indeed, the seventies brought Soloveitchik's delicate balance of the secular and the sacred to an end. Undermining both his belief in the importance of secular education and his determination that religious Jews must remain engaged politically and culturally with their gentile neighbors in America were rabbis at some borderline fundamentalist yeshivas in Israel. Over the last 25 years or so, more and more young orthodox students began to spend a year or two at one of these schools before beginning college in America, and Yeshiva has encouraged it, offering credit for classes taken at those institutions.

Over dinner in a booth at the kosher pizza place across the street from the Beit Midrash, upperclassman Josh Goldman explains that "most [of my classmates] do their thinking in Israel and then [they're] done. You shut off your mind and go home." Joshua Stern, one of the editors of the school's newspaper, acknowledges there is some truth to this claim. Many of the schools in Israel, he tells me, "do try to de-emphasize the value of the secular education because they feel that religious education is really their primary goal." Beyond that, though, many of them also instill a sort of disgust with modern American culture in their students. Finally, since a significant number of students determine after their time in Israel to move there permanently, their interest in America is already waning by the time they enroll at Yeshiva.

But Soloveitchik's vision was weakened from within as well as without. Those bridges that he tried to build between the peaks of secular and religious learning began to collapse under the weight, oddly enough, of New York state law. In 1969, concern over the school's financial stability led administrators to apply for state funding. New York's Blaine amendment, which stated that public funds should not be used "to aid schools under the control and direction of any religious denomination or in which any denominational tenet is taught," required that Yeshiva become a nonsectarian institution. As a result, its graduate programs all but erased their religious identities, and the seminary was legally separated from the school's secular divisions. Undergraduates began to enroll for their religious education at the seminary and their secular education at the college.

So what have thirty years of legal separation between the secular and the sacred wrought? When I ask Rabbi Yosef Blau, the *mashgiach ruchani* (spiritual guidance counselor) for the undergraduates, whether all students who attend Yeshiva are required to observe the Sabbath, he tells me that they can only require it of the ones on campus. "The lawyers [say] that it can be done in a dormitory, but it cannot be done in the college." In other words, a student in campus housing can be told to turn off his radio on Shabbat, but kids who live in a private residence can do what they want.

The lawyers have played a prominent role in other decisions about student life, like the administration's determination in 1995 to recognize an organization for homosexual students on campus. Despite the fact that such a group flies in the face of the school leaders' religious beliefs, the president at the time did not feel those could override the school's legal obligation to behave like a secular school.

On another occasion during my visit, Rabbi Blau mentions the case of a new young French professor. Several students, it turns out, have complained about her risqué mode of dress. (When I saw her she was wearing a knee-length skirt and low-cut blouse.) Again citing the lawyers, Blau tells me, "The maximum that I could do would be to speak with her, which may or may not have an impact. It probably won't." There is no official dress code for professors and the school may not institute one lest it seem as if they are trying to force religious strictures on secular faculty.

Indeed, so determined is the administration to make sure that the secular faculty do not feel they are teaching at a religious institution that they never mention during interviews the fact that all of the students are Orthodox Jews. English professor William Lee tells me that at his job interview, religion was irrelevant. When I ask business school dean Charles Snow whether he discusses the school's mission, Torah Umadda, with job candidates, he replies, "Not at all. . . . Some of these people don't even know what Torah is."

Sometimes, the drive to convince visitors that the school is not religious becomes laughable, as when Snow tells me the reason for recent heightened security on campus. Instead of the obvious explanation that Jewish institutions have had special reason to fear since the beginning of the current intifada in Israel and the events of 9/11, he suggests that it is people like the D.C. sniper they worry about.

Norman Adler and Joyce Jesionowski, the dean and assistant dean of Yeshiva College respectively, talk to me in general terms about the idea of religious colleges. Neither Adler, who became an observant Jew late in life, nor Jesionowski, who is Catholic, seems to place much import on the peculiarly Jewish nature of the school. Adler compares Yeshiva to historically black colleges: Both, he thinks, provide a dimension to the liberal education that secular colleges do not. Adler describes to me an address he gave at the University of Pennsylvania several years ago, in which he quoted an old Indian proverb to the effect that "what we give our children is our roots." But neither Adler nor Jesionowski will explain specifically how Judaism shapes the core identity of a Yeshiva student.

Perhaps most strangely, the deans of both undergraduate men's divisions agree that Yeshiva "is not a religious college" at all. And the YU media relations office supports them. When I first contacted the school to ask about a visit, I received this mysteriously worded rejection: "Unfortunately, YU does not 'fit' into the . . . categories of Jewish higher education in America you are exploring. We do not 'inculcate Jewish faith and learning' in our curricula."

Aaron Levine, a short, bald economics professor who is also an Orthodox Jew, seems discombobulated when he comes to meet me. Trying embarrassedly to organize the tower of books and folders he has been carrying, Levine smiles, revealing a large space between his front teeth. Jewish law has something important to say about everything in business, according to Levine, from contract negotiations to performance appraisals to corporate disclosure regulations. "Jewish law is two thousand years old. It's a developing law that developed in different societies, very different from ours. The idea is to extract general principles and apply them to new situations." Levine, who has written extensively on the intersection of Jewish and American business law and economic principles, explains, for instance, that there is a Jewish law against creating false impressions in business dealings, a principle he believes would have applied in the Enron case.

Along with Levine and a rabbi named Shalom Carmy who teaches courses on bioethics, there are a few rabbis and professors who seem open to the idea of the integration of religious and secular studies. William Lee, an imposing figure with blue eyes, a full head of gray hair, and a beard, looks a little too WASPy to know much about Torah, but says he has "made it [his] business" to learn about the religious side of the school since arriving at Yeshiva. Some alumni cite Lee in particular as a professor who was interested in helping students see connections between their religious and secular studies. Though Lee explains, "I think it would be ludicrous for me to try to teach Torah," he does hope to "open the door [in class] for students to try to integrate their Torah learning with their secular learning."

Left to their own devices to figure out whether their religious education has any relevance to their secular one, some of the students at Yeshiva College have made do. Yaakov Green, the vice president of student government, who spends some of his time working with Orthodox children, tells me his vision of Torah Umadda. "I explain to them that it's looking at your entire world through a specific lens and that lens is Torah." For instance, he offers, "I'm looking at biology. Oh my God. Wow, the world is a beautiful place. Look at the unbelievable creation of God. Or look at the unbelievable artistry in this piece of literature, in this piece of art. It's a wonderment that God created this kind of a world." He concludes: "When you live your life, Torah Umadda, you're understanding the importance of Torah, as well as the importance of Madda, because they're not different, they're not separate. To separate them out, I think, is to lose sight of what this university is supposed to represent."

Naphtali Weisz, who wants to be a rabbi and a lawyer, offers his take on what Yeshiva should be doing with regard to religious and secular formation:

> The Jewish education that we're getting here is supposed to teach us how we're going to live our lives in the legal world or whatever. The idea is that there's more to life than your salary and your job. A lot of it is incorporating what you're learning into your field your profession and holding yourself to a higher standard. But [it is] also being able to have a more meaningful life as a lawyer.

Shai Barnea tells me he has already seen the practical applications of this idea, for instance, when he interned for a congressman over the summer and wrote a position paper on stem-cell research that included some Jewish perspectives. Shai, by the way, probably represents the majority of students at Yeshiva in being impressed with the way that Lieberman has combined his religious views with his political ones, though there is a not insignificant minority who are concerned about the senator's level of observance.

In order to encourage the examination of the intersections between religious and secular learning and the question of Orthodox involvement in the outside world, a small cadre of students have begun to form organizations and journals devoted to the task. Chaim Strauchler, a recent graduate of Yeshiva who went on to Oxford, was concerned about the difficulty of the task students had in figuring out Torah Umadda by themselves. So he helped found *Mima'amakim,* a journal that explores religious themes in art, poetry, and music. Another recently founded organization that tries to get at the question of how the traditional Orthodox Jew should relate to his surroundings is Edah, which regularly holds lectures and conferences at Yeshiva. "Fully committed to Torah, *halakhah* [law], and the quest for *kedushah* [holiness], Edah values open intellectual inquiry and expression in both secular and religious arenas; engagement with the social, political and the technological realities of the modern world; the religious significance of the State of Israel; and Klal Yisrael,"—the unity of the Jewish people.

Edah and *Mima'amakim* may get students to think more about the question of the relation between religious and secular learning, but the answers are far from obvious. Joshua Stern tells me he is trying to get as much as he can out of both his secular and religious studies while at YU, but "I find synthesizing very difficult because realistically very often the values that each is espousing often come into outright conflict." More specifically, he explains, "Religious studies are based on a sort of dogmatic type of *halakhah.* It's essentially a set of rules and regulations based on biblical law passed down through rabbinical law and interpreted according to context by different rabbis, etc. The general philosophy of a collegiate environment is probably what you would call, you know, challenge everything. Fight for the right answer; if you don't like the answer, fight on." Put simply, Joshua believes, "the thrust in religious studies is not really the same as in a [secular] academic environment, because not all options are truly open. There is a determined end point on certain major issues." Josh is right. This tension, which is at the heart of religious education, is not easily resolved, but avoiding a discussion of it hardly seems like the right answer.

* * *

"It's like the Hatfields versus the McCoys," says Yaakov Green, student government vice president, about the relationship between the modern Orthodox and ultra-Orthodox students on campus. As a general rule, the ultra-Orthodox, sometimes referred to derogatorily as "oreos" because of their black suits and white shirts, follow a stricter set of social codes, shunning social contact with the opposite sex and any form of popular culture, and spending all their free time in the Beit Midrash. Their modern Orthodox counterparts, who dress like college students anywhere, with the exception of their yarmulkes and tzit-tzis, generally show more interest in American culture and secular education. The paths of these two groups continue to diverge after graduation, often leading them to different synagogues. And while most Yeshiva graduates become professionals, the ultra-Orthodox almost never go into politics or academia, as a fair number of modern Orthodox do.

There are exceptions, like Naphtali, who wears the ultra-Orthodox garb but maintains a sort of modern sensibility, but for the most part, there are so few crossovers that students find the formation of a coherent campus life difficult. Yaakov tells me about a concert that the student government recently sponsored. They had to find a singer who would attract the modern Orthodox students who normally listen to American popular music, but who also had some religious message so that students who don't approve of popular music would come. They set up the room so that the modern Orthodox could talk with women in the back of the room while the ultra-Orthodox could be apart. The event was held at 10:30 P.M. on a weeknight, so that students would be on campus, but study in the Beit Midrash would be over. Though Shai and Yaakov were pleased with the large turnout, each group in its own area of the room, they emphasize the near impossibility of planning this sort of event.

Josh Goldman tells me he wishes the groups had more contact with one another and laments the fact that most people leave Yeshiva just the way they came in. They tend to surround themselves with peers who are at a similar level of observance, according to Chaim Nissel, the school's personal counselor. "People tend to be friends with similar people—that's in their personal lives and in their school lives as well."

Partly as a result of this divide, but also as a result of the students' heavy workloads, campus life at Yeshiva is virtually nonexistent. Though there are occasional Shabbatons (weekend spiritual retreats featuring outside speakers or themed discussions along with religious services), the vast majority of students tend to leave school on the weekends and visit family or friends for Shabbat. And though the school's admissions officer mentions that obser-

vant students who choose Yeshiva over secular schools will be able to participate in more activities because they won't conflict with Jewish holidays,
campus organizations, with the possible exception of the newspaper, do not
seem to garner much of the students' time or enthusiasm.

At the reception following the investiture, the university's gym has the trap-
pings of any academic celebration—the ice sculptures, the balloons, the music, the decadent chocolates. Thousands of students, faculty, administrators,
alumni, and local celebrities crowd the hot food tables with kosher delicacies
that mirror the ethnic diversity of New York: sushi, falafel, stir fry, stuffed
peppers. Richard Joel is surrounded by dozens of people who want to shake
his hand, but some members of the rabbinical faculty stand off to the side,
looking much less comfortable in this gymnasium than they did a few minutes ago in the Beit Midrash.

To put Yeshiva's contradictions in a positive light, many students and professors tell me that the religious and secular worlds should be held in tension
with each other, that there must be a sort of dialectic between the two. Certainly each side of the school is thriving enough to present students with
each side of the dialectic.

Yeshiva's secular program is extremely competitive, with faculty drawn
increasingly from Ivy League graduate school programs or recruited from positions at other top colleges. The average SAT scores of the student body
have steadily risen over the last several years even as the number of applications multiplied. Indeed, despite the implicit battle with the school's rabbis
over the importance of secular study, many professors wouldn't dream of
leaving Yeshiva because of the high quality and dedication of the students.
Students who have compared their workloads with friends at other colleges
are surprised by how much more Yeshiva students have to accomplish. Professor Lee tells me that his best students at Yeshiva are as good or better than
the students he taught at Harvard. And the students who are not in the top per-
centile, "in terms of raw intelligence," Lee finds are still a pleasure to teach
"because they're more motivated."

Many professors are surprised to find that their most motivated students
are often the ones who are enrolled in the most rigorous Jewish studies programs. And the rabbis acknowledge that despite the increased rigor of
Yeshiva's secular education, the religious education is taking place at an extraordinarily high level, with many students devoting more time and energy
to it than they did thirty years ago.

But sitting in the crowded old basement cafeteria, Rabbi Blau describes what he sees as a bleak situation. Through bites of fried fish and kasha varnishkes, and sips of milk, Blau laments that students are less inclined now than any time in recent memory to examine the intersections of their religious and secular educations. "They are satisfied knowing that someone else has thought through these issues and they don't have to." While Blau wants to talk about matters like the growing influence of evolutionary biology on society, he explains, "The students want to discuss the evils of modern culture." The intellectual curiosity on campus, he maintains, is waning.

How is it possible that the students are more serious in their secular and religious studies, but are less intellectually curious? Observers chalk it up to an emphasis in the secular curriculum on preprofessional studies. Much of the growth in the undergraduate population has been in the business program, but even in the liberal arts division, students view science, for example, as a route to medical school and political science as a route to law school rather than subjects with any intrinsic worth. Though the professors I speak with acknowledge that this is true to a large extent at any university, they are disappointed that such motivated students are generally uninterested in pursuing academic or research positions.

Business school dean Charles Snow does not have a problem with this at all. In fact, he thinks it is much easier to reconcile a religious education with vocational studies than with liberal arts and offers religious support for his position:

> The Torah itself recognizes the fact that a person has to go out and earn [his] keep. You take a shovel and start to plant oranges and tomatoes or you can go learn about accounting or about the medical profession. The true Torah Umadda fellow is one that says, "I recognize the primacy and supremacy of the Torah. And, I recognize that were I independently wealthy there would be no need for me to work and I would certainly submerge myself in learning Torah the entire day." However, the Madda part comes in because that's not the case with ninety-nine percent of the people.

Indeed, Snow finds problematic the way in which the school's motto has been presented. "Through the years there's been an attempt to talk about a synthesis of Torah and Madda where they occupy an equal plane, an equal plateau. It can't be. In the Jewish world there's nothing that competes with the primacy of Torah. That is it. That is our oxygen, so to speak."

But his idea of secular learning as the equivalent of planting oranges to make a living—something you wouldn't do if you didn't absolutely have to—is a problem for students and faculty who want to see themselves as part of a liberal arts college or even part of a university that is supposed to value learning for its own sake.

Mark Gottlieb, who graduated from Yeshiva in 1990 and is now the principal of the Maimonides School, tells me that when he was a student, "You could count on one hand the students who were committed to a solid liberal arts education and nonvocational training." In fact, when he applied to graduate school in philosophy, he found it hard to get into a good program because Yeshiva didn't have any standing in the humanities. After one round of unsuccessful applications, Gottlieb was eventually admitted to a doctoral program at the University of Chicago.

Looking back on his life as an undergraduate, Gottlieb acknowledges he managed to find a "small coterie of like-minded individuals," and a few professors and rabbis who were "role models," mostly disciples of Soloveitchik himself. But he is unhappy with "the larger picture of the university." Gottlieb, who dreams of eventually starting a college of his own—a Jewish Great Books school on the model of Thomas Aquinas College—says the situation at Yeshiva is partly the result of the school's financial struggles (which led it to accept state money and the strictures of state law along with it) but also of an administration "trying to keep up with the Joneses of higher learning in America." He describes university leaders concerned that their school not appear too parochial, wanting to prove that Yeshiva can be on a par with schools like NYU and Brandeis and Columbia. Competing with these secular schools has led Yeshiva not only to hire faculty without regard for the school's religious mission, but also, Gottlieb complains, to forgo any kind of distinctive core curriculum.

"As sad as it is for me to admit," Gottlieb, who sends several of his high school's students on to Yeshiva every year, tells me, "Torah Umadda is least articulated and least comprehensively lived at Yeshiva." Oddly, for the largest and most successful Jewish university in history, Gottlieb laments, "They never got into a discussion of what is an educated Jew."

CHAPTER SIX

AN INTEGRATED WHOLE:
BAYLOR'S VISION FOR THE FUTURE

Leaving Franklin's, a Southwestern restaurant in Waco, Texas, on my first evening in town, I hear an indescribably loud squawking. In the suddenly darkening sky, I see thousands of small black birds swarming overhead. A man nearby turns to offer me an explanation, but I can barely hear him. Rather than wait around for the conclusion of the Hitchcockian scene, I make a run for the car.

When I return to the Judge Baylor House, a small bed and breakfast a few blocks from Baylor University's campus, I describe to Dorothy, one of the proprietors, what I have seen. She nods knowingly. "Oh, those are grackles. A lot of Texans want to take out their guns and shoot them, but we're told they're endangered." After agreeing with my assessment that they don't look endangered, Dorothy reflects for a minute and then adds, "Actually we also have another infestation problem. You may have noticed the stench in the living room. We have a squirrel decomposing in the chimney." I haven't noticed the smell but I make it a point to avoid the living room over the next few days.

The Judge Baylor House was, not too long ago, a residential home. Dorothy and her husband, Bruce, have three children, who all attended Baylor, and when they moved out, the couple decided to open their home to guests of the school, naming each of the bedrooms in honor of one of their children. Staying in Allan's room over the course of a few days, I meet a variety of people visiting the university, including a violinist and his wife from the Netherlands, a professor interviewing for a job in the economics department, and two sets of parents stopping in on their children at Baylor.

On Sunday morning over French toast, I find myself sitting with the four parents. Three of them are Baylor graduates themselves. Three are originally from Texas as well, and to them, Baylor represents part of the quintessential Texan experience—a big university with good sports teams, decent academics, and a long tradition of fraternities and sororities. Though the families do all go to church regularly—they play the name game and find that they know some of the same people through their local parishes—they do not consider themselves overly religious, and when I ask whether the school's Baptist identity was a factor in their decisions to come here or send their children here, they say it was not. About 70 percent of Baylor students are from Texas, but, generally speaking, it is those who are not from the area who tend to be most attracted to the school's Christian identity.

As we are finishing breakfast, a red Mustang with a license plate that says CA CHIK pulls up outside. Though the driver, Jenny Ebbeling, is obviously from out of state and she has been specifically enlisted by the administration to take me to church, I would not have pegged her as a committed Christian. She is tall with long, blond hair, blow-dried to perfection, and wears a long black skirt, with black leather boots, an off-white sweater with gold sparkles, and a camel-colored suede coat with faux fur around the collar. As we drive, she periodically glances down at her substantial engagement ring and checks her French manicured nails. The inside of Jenny's car is impeccably clean and she complains to me that whenever she washes the outside, it immediately rains. That doesn't happen in San Diego, where Jenny spent about half her childhood.

When Jenny's mother decided to come to Baylor a few decades ago, the school's Christian identity was not a factor, but Jenny is an entirely different story. As a National Merit Scholar, she considered attending Harvard, UCLA, UCSD, Pepperdine, and Wheaton. She was admitted to all but Harvard. Jenny became fairly sure during her senior year that she wanted a Christian atmosphere at college. "My parents are academics. They know what goes on in a classroom." Jenny tells me she thought that at a secular school she would be "getting attacked daily in the classroom." She was not fearful of it, but rather, she decided, it would get old.

"I didn't want to be around people all the time who were constantly against everything I believe," she says.

During a visit to Pepperdine (which is affiliated with the Churches of Christ), she says, she was put off by the fact that most of the students were into partying and there was just a small group who actually cared about faith. As for her decision not to attend Wheaton, her father's alma mater, Jenny tells me she was a little skeptical of because of the school's rules (which, at the time, included a prohibition on drinking, dancing, and smoking). She says she needs "to have reasons behind the rules people give her."

She "sort of understands" the no-dancing policy at Wheaton. "Because of the disgusting kind of dancing some people engage in," she offers, "it might be a slippery slope."

At Baylor, where Jenny believes she has found a sort of happy medium, she explains, "Maybe not everyone agrees with me, and not everyone really lives [the Christian] way but they understand where you're coming from. It's not a constant backlash." Preemptively, she adds, "It can be dangerous to be in an environment where everyone is kind of complacent and accepts Christianity, but at other times, it's very relaxing."

Jenny may feel as though her school has achieved the right balance, but Baylor's religious identity has come under fire in recent years from outside forces. A battle is in the offing between elements in the Southern Baptist Church. On the one side, there are the more fundamentalist elements in the Southern Baptist Convention (SBC) and the individual state conventions who demand that any institution associated with them declare a principle of biblical inerrancy, including, of course, a strict creationist ideology, while the more liberal members take a range of positions on issues like homosexuality, female pastors, and evolution. On the other, there are more liberal elements who favor the ordination of women, the acceptance of homosexual marriage, and a more ecumenical attitude, including the possibility of salvation for other Christian groups.

Though various ministries associated with the SBC and the state conventions (e.g., the Foreign Mission Board, the Christian Life Commission, the Sunday School Board, the Baptist Press) have been caught in this tug of war, Baptist universities have really been the most prominent battlefields for these debates. There are also the financial consequences, particularly for smaller colleges, where the conventions can be contributing as much as 10 percent of the schools' operating budgets.

These schools face demands not only from their religious sponsors, but also from national accreditation organizations that want some kind of reassurance the schools are not controlled by outside organizations, and that there is some semblance of academic freedom. Wake Forest College and Furman University both shed their Baptist affiliations rather than be subject to the demands of the fundamentalists. Most recently, the faculty of Mars Hill College in North Carolina has tried to stave off attempts by this group to install a fundamentalist-leaning president. Indeed, more than a dozen Southern Baptist colleges have loosened their ties with state conventions in the last fifteen years or so.

In September 1990, the Baylor's administration decided to amend its charter to give the Baptist General Convention of Texas significantly less direct control over who was appointed to the school's board of regents. Though it was done secretively, the alumni, students, and faculty generally expressed approval. "This sends the signal," the alumni association's president announced, "that, as far as this institution goes, we want no part of factionalism. We are removing ourselves from the argument. We can now devote 100 percent of our efforts to making Baylor again the greatest Christian institution on the face of the earth."

Michael Beaty, the director of Baylor's Institute for Faith and Learning, calls the 1990 charter change "the crucial moment in Baylor's history." Aside from minimizing chances of a fundamentalist takeover of the school, he says this decision also forced many to consider for the first time what Baylor is all about. He explains, "If you do a study, you know that many institutions of higher education who have done this to protect themselves lost their religious identity. The president at that time was aware of it and he was very committed that that not happen at Baylor." In order to prevent such a loss, Baylor's faculty and administration, according to Beaty, began to ask questions.

"What does it mean to be a Christian university?" he asks. "What does it mean to be a Baptist university? There are different answers to those questions. There are disagreements among the various groups at Baylor within the faculty, but there has been a common commitment to that religious identity being serious."

When the current president, Robert Sloan, took over in 1995, many in the Baylor community were concerned that he was something of a fundamentalist himself. The proprietors of the Judge Baylor House recall many conversations among their guests and in the local churches about religious identity. But Beaty was never worried. "[Sloan's] selection by the board of regents made a statement because he is a minister with a deep connection to Baptist life, and at the same time he is an academic, a very powerful thinker. His aspiration is for us to be a first-tier academic institution while having a serious religious identity."

In order to more specifically define Baylor's mission academically and religiously, the school recently adopted a vision statement called Baylor 2012. Over ten years, Baylor plans to hire 220 new full-time faculty members. It's an enormous number and the school will have to raise a lot of money in order to do so. (To begin with, it's borrowing millions of dollars, diverting money from its endowment, and raising tuition significantly.) The additional faculty will allow class sizes to shrink and give faculty lighter courseloads so that they can devote more time to their scholarship. Focusing on both teaching and research, Sloan notes, is rare in a university. "We want to emphasize 'community research' so that faculty and students, including undergrads, share together in the life of discovery."

Sloan believes that Baylor can fulfill a unique niche. He explains, "Some Christian institutions wanted to leave the work of discovery to the secularists. [They say], 'We'll just sort of summarize it and synthesize it and pass it on to our students.' I think that's a mistake for people of any faith. I think we should not sit back and let other people become the discoverers. I think that's a failure of nerve."

In both their research and teaching, Baylor faculty will have to share a commitment to the integration of faith and learning. As Beaty notes: When the school is interviewing candidates, "we don't make faith independent of professional requirements. What we're trying to do is say, 'Look, if you're a faculty member teaching philosophy at a Christian university, your faith is not an extra sphere independent of your professional responsibilities. Part of what you're doing is thinking Christianly, which has philosophical dimensions. And so your ability to bring the faith in an intellectually responsible way in the classroom and do so in a way that real learning takes place is a professional qualification.'"

Baylor tries to get this message across to job candidates from very early in the hiring process, according to Beaty. Not only do they advertise the position that way, but candidates are sent a copy of the school's mission statement and they, in turn, are asked to write about how they would help the school realize it. Beaty notes, "The extent to which the person takes up the issue of Baylor being Baptist and how their teaching or scholarship or both would contribute becomes a factor in whether they'll be invited for an interview."

But no one can tell what Baylor will actually look like in ten years. Indeed, the attempt to remake the university is being resisted strenuously in some corners. In September 2003, the faculty senate passed a vote of no confidence in the president, twenty-six to six. The majority's concerns were twofold. First, they argued that Sloan's attempts to strengthen the school's Christian identity would result in less academic freedom. Second, they worried that making Baylor a top-tier university would take away from its focus on teaching and price many students out of the education. But it is hard to worry about these things simultaneously, that is, an oppressive fundamentalist university, like the one that some faculty claim Sloan is pushing, would be unlikely to find itself in the top tier with respectable secular colleges. More importantly, the Board of Regents met shortly after the faculty to reaffirm their commitment to Sloan's administration.

There are many faculty members who agree with Sloan's vision of a Christian research university, but who have more practical concerns, like whether 220 new faculty members can really be screened, interviewed, and hired in such a relatively short period of time. Philosophy professor Scott Moore acknowledges, "If we're going to fill those positions with the kind of people we want, it will take a concerted effort."

But even with such an influx of faculty members, Moore believes that Baylor will have to be "selective" in what it undertakes. "We are not going to be able to pursue the wide range PhD programs that our friends at the University of Texas or Texas A&M do." Moore believes that will be a benefit to the humanities because it's easier to get top humanities professors than scientists. "With the former you don't have to buy a quarter-of-a-million-dollar lab."

But are there enough qualified people out there to fill these positions in the humanities or the sciences? Moore acknowledges that he doesn't know whether there are a significant number of Christian mathematicians out there who would be ready to describe to the administration how their faith influences their discipline. But in the humanities, Moore says, there's hope. "Without a doubt," he says, "there are a wealth of really good people and they want to be in places that have a confessional identity." Moore offers me the example of his own philosophy department, which had one position open and 175 applicants. Ultimately, he and his colleagues interviewed almost twenty candidates at the American Philosophical Association meeting, "and all indications were that all of these people were confessional Christians and all of them had achieved some stature as aspiring young philosophers." His department is bringing three of them to campus for more interviews, but Moore thinks, "We could draw the name out of a hat and we would get a good philosopher committed to the university's mission."

So far, the school has managed to draw bright young scholars away from more prominent religious colleges with two kinds of incentives: financial and religious. As Moore explains of Thomas Hibbs, who gave up his position as chair of Boston College's philosophy department to come run Baylor's new Honors College: "He's a confessionally serious person and was involved in lots of conversations about the Jesuit character of his former institution, but he also felt that he had no real guarantee about the future of BC. They're interested in pursuing the Jesuit character of the institution, but the Catholic character can come or go."[5]

And though Waco can hardly offer what Boston does from a cultural perspective, the cost of living is so much lower that many faculty families are willing to consider the move. Hibbs, for instance, used to reside in a small cape home an hour away from work with his family, but can now afford what one administrator described as a "Southern mansion on a golf course" very close to his office.

That Moore uses the example of a professor lured from a Catholic school is particularly revealing. For an evangelical institution, Baylor is incredibly welcoming to Catholics. Indeed, they make up the second largest group of students, and the number of Catholics on the faculty will probably rise significantly as the Baylor 2012 vision is fulfilled. The majority of other evangelical schools, which do not hire Catholics, are picking from a much smaller pool.

On a cold, rainy morning in January, students trickle into Scott Moore's Philosophy of Religion class. The twenty or so men and women are almost without exception completely alert during the professor's talk on Thomas Aquinas. After distributing and collecting the quiz, which Moore tells his students is "shamefully easy," they begin a discussion about the existence of God. Moore, who is sporting a tie with little bottles of Tabasco sauce on it, asks, "What does it mean for something to be self-evident?" As the students think of some serious answers and some less serious ones, Moore cracks some jokes but manages to keep the class on track.

Later, over the all-you-can-eat buffet at the faculty club, Moore explains to me what he sees as the class dynamic.

Every year, there are some kids who take a course like this because they don't believe God exists and they want to fight that fight and engage these issues, and it's good to have them in the class. Every year there are people who take the course for apologetic purposes, and they just want to get into some arguments to fight the atheists. I try to disabuse both crowds of their certainties so that they understand that this business of arguments for and against existence of God or of the rationality or irrationality of religious belief is a much more complex business than simply picking teams. Typically

---

[5] See Chapter 4 for comments regarding how Jesuits view their Catholic identity.

my approach in the class is finding out who is losing and helping them
out. I'll pitch in with the underdogs.

Beaty is quick to point out that Baylor's religious identity should be expressed in classes other than theology and philosophy. What does that mean for Ben Pierce, associate dean of sciences and a professor of biology at Baylor? A small man with a beard and glasses, Pierce decorates his office with gorgeous blown-up photos of mountains. "Faith influences the questions I choose to look at in science," Pierce tells me. He notes, "I certainly think that as Christians we are called to be good stewards of the environment."

More generally, Pierce expresses his hopes for Baylor grads: "That they would do more than practice science for science's sake," he says. "And that they would use their science to help the world and help other people and would take a leadership role in those activities."

One program that the school has constructed to help students do that is the medical humanities minor. The courses in this program, which include topics from theology to literature and use Christian texts as well as secular ones, were created with a view to helping students examine moral questions surrounding medicine.

Juls Trinh, a Texan who was born in Saigon but moved here when she was quite young, is taking medical humanities courses along with her premed ones. "I think I will be more prepared than most students going into medical school," she tells me, citing classes on death and dying, the sociology of medicine, anthropology, and the history of medicine.

Juls says her "faith definitely enters into those classes." It helps her to see the medical profession as "human beings treating human beings instead of a doctor treating a diseased organ. It's a different perspective that you may not get at a state school." Juls credits the head of the medical humanities department with stressing the integration of faith and vocation. Ultimately, she believes that her perspective on medicine has really changed since she arrived at Baylor. "I knew when I came here that I wanted to be a doctor, but a different kind of doctor than I want to be now."

Juls has also been provided with the opportunity to put her skills to good use on a medical mission trip to Nicaragua, sponsored in part by the Institute for Faith and Learning. Setting up clinics in each village, Juls took vital signs, gave vaccinations, and shadowed a doctor. She also worked in the pharmacy and helped administer medicine. When the group wasn't performing specifically medical functions they did mission work, going to churches and conducting Bible studies in Spanish. Juls, who was considering going into the Peace Corps when she finished medical school, is now thinking about entering a more religiously oriented medical mission program. She tells me, "My trip amazed me, how little medical care these people get. They didn't have diseases like cancer. They didn't need heart surgery. They just needed an antibiotic. But no one even had Benadryl."

The integration of faith and learning is not always as uncomplicated as participating in a medical mission trip, as the book on Pierce's desk, *Can a Darwinian Be a Christian?*, suggests. In the last couple of years, Baylor has become a flashpoint in the religion-science wars. Its establishment of the Center for Complexity, Information and Design—where researchers attempt to calculate through scientific means just how infinitesimal the chances are that the world came to be the way it is through random genetic mutation, and then speculate that some sort of intelligent being must have instead played a role—led to Baylor's lambasting in the national media by both leading religious and scientific figures.

Dharmpal Vansadia, another premed student, tells me over dinner: "I haven't bought into intelligent design. I think it's okay for the school to have the center but what I hate is their calling it science. One of the basic things about science is that it's repeatable, and what they're trying to do is explain the existence of God by science, which I don't think is right."

But most of the faculty and students seem largely agnostic about the center. Indeed, the controversy over it has proved the exception rather than the rule at Baylor, where most professors and students see their religious beliefs and scientific pursuits as tightly integrated. Truell Hyde, the vice provost for research at Baylor, who has worked on projects for NASA and tried to make it on to the Columbia flight that went down in January 2003, explains, "The chance to see more of God's creation is an awfully big draw for me," he says—both as a Christian and a scientist. "The Lord basically gives you intelligence because he wants you to do everything you can with it to understand the world around you."

Showing students the compatibility, or at least the points of contact and tension, between their secular studies and their Christian faith, is a large part of academic life at Baylor. Jenny Ebbeling is part of the Crane Scholars program, which means that for the duration of her time at Baylor she participates in weekly seminars on faith and learning with university professors as well as prominent guest lecturers. The program has never simply focused on Christian authors or Christian themed works. As Beaty notes, "Christians have to be able to say yes to the culture and no to the culture." So they watch movies and read books by authors in many subjects and then try to examine what a Christian might discern about them.

The program began as an informal gathering hosted every Friday night by biology professor Christopher Kearney and his wife. A few students would come over to discuss books or movies and their relationship to Christian ideas. A few years ago, the Institute for Faith and Learning offered Kearney a stipend for the dinners he provided and put together a more official set of requirements for the group.

Lesley-Ann Dyer, a self-described "military brat" who grew up all over the world and was homeschooled, is also a Crane Scholar. She wants to go on to graduate school and eventually become a professor herself, and tells me she has benefited enormously from being able to speak with the academics about their own experience, particularly from a couple of professors who came to talk about their experiences at northeastern schools that were hostile toward religion.

But Baylor's focus on the integration of faith and learning is not restricted to its more talented students like Lesley-Ann and Jenny. Any student who wishes may participate in the Baylor Interdisciplinary Core (BIC) program. As an alternative to the usual distribution requirements, BIC offers an "interdisciplinary curriculum of course sequences that replaces traditional courses in the humanities, fine arts, social sciences, and physical sciences." In addition to teaching students the connections among various subjects, BIC is supposed to help students see a purpose in their studies and their relevance to life after Baylor.

During the senior BIC seminar that I attend, one student offers a presentation comparing *Gift from the Sea* by Anne Morrow Lindbergh to Augustine's *Confessions* (which the class is reading). They have also just finished discussing the movie *Wit*. About halfway through the seminar, literature professor Tom Hanks asks the students, "Does your personal belief system involve a god figure?"

One student brings up *The Screwtape Letters,* while another offers some thoughts on her experience as chaplain of her sorority. Students seem to feel comfortable going back and forth between their personal beliefs and their studies, in many cases using the words of great authors and theologians to describe their own feelings.

Later that afternoon, sitting in Hanks's cluttered but cozy office, we discuss BIC. In addition to the hours spent in class, the seminar also has "required get-togethers for active physical activity." Hanks acknowledges, "It does sound a little wacko but I am a nut about physical activity." The discussions, of course, continue during the physical activity. "There were five of us on the track this morning talking about difference between lust and desire. . . . I like being able to talk about these things from a Christian perspective."

After a desolate twenty-five-minute drive through vast expanses of brown grass with no trees, where most of the buildings are large and flat and it's hard to tell the difference between the barns and the churches, Jenny and I arrive in the parking lot of the First Baptist Church of Woodway. Inside the main chapel, which seats about a thousand people, has a kind of watermelon theme with light green chairs, pink walls, and a pink and green carpet. Everyone greets each other while music plays in the background. A choir of about forty or fifty people assembles on the dais along with a large band.

Jenny tells me there are enough churches in Waco to go to a different one every week during one's time at Baylor, but there are about ten churches that most students are concentrated in. Some students do not attend church at all, though. According school surveys, about a third of Baylor students attend church three to four times per month. Another 31 percent attend five or more times per month, 19 percent go twice a month and 17 percent attend either only on special holidays or never. Eileen Hulme, the vice president for student life, acknowledges that some students may overstate their religious commitment on these surveys but, having been a Baylor student herself, she doesn't think the numbers are very far off.

Jenny used to go to another church in Waco. "They had great music. The band there is even making a CD," she gushes, "and they turn out the lights during some of the prayers." The appeal of the music in evangelical churches can be irresistible for young people like Jenny. The tunes are catchy and the words are generally projected in large type at the front of the room, allowing even newcomers to participate fully in the service. But many evangelical observers wonder whether the folk rock sounds of evangelical hymns today—a kind of religious version of the Indigo Girls—make college and high school students too dependent on the emotionalism of Christianity, while leaving behind its intellectual aspects. Of her former church, Jenny notes, "I found a great sense of spirituality there but I didn't feel it was helping me to grow as a Christian."

Though the Baylor administration expresses no preference to its students about the kind of church they attend, it's clear that they are trying to move the evangelical youth into a less emotional and more intellectual form of worship.

125

"We want to give them a broadened understanding," Beaty says, meaning a broadened understanding of what it is to be a faithful Christian.

Over coffee at Common Grounds, a run-down shack with tattered furniture that charges New York prices for coffee drinks, Todd Lake, the dean of university ministries, explains to me the way he has changed the chapel program at Baylor to address these issues in the evangelical world. Lake, who bears a striking resemblance to Geraldo Rivera, offers the history: "It used to be called 'chapel forum.' They had great speakers but no religious message. Ralph Nader doesn't help a student form a Christian worldview. Now it's unapologetically Christian. We just had our fourth Nobel Prize winner there. We've had actors, lawyers, social workers, social activists, all of whom are outstanding at what they do as an expression of the Christian faith."

But how will Baylor graduates respond to this message when they graduate? What does it mean to be a Christian citizen or a Christian professor or a Christian friend? Will Baylor grads, for instance, proselytize to their colleagues at work?

Sloan notes that the university's environment does not encourage aggressive evangelization efforts. "We have students here of all faiths. I think Christianity must simply make its place in the market of ideas. I really think students ought to have benefit of vigorous exchange."

Though most faculty at Baylor believe that Christians must be witnesses in this world, they also acknowledge that there are different ways of accomplishing that. Living a life of integrity and not being ashamed to talk about your faith are two ways of being a witness. Sloan emphasizes that faith is something people come to voluntarily and that you cannot coerce someone into it. "You don't want to be obnoxious. There is a balance. Being harsh and polemical is not our calling. Being weak is not our calling." Sloan settles on the notion of "strength with graciousness."

Indeed, he tells me he would be surprised if a Baylor grad proselytized at work. But Todd Lake observes that the excesses of youth can lead sometimes to insensitive evangelizing. "Young excited Christians," he notes, "are not necessarily moderated by wisdom." Lake jokes that some of the students he meets have "reduced evangelism to a Ponzi scheme. 'I tell two people about Jesus and they tell two people.'"

On July 28, 2003, Waco police identified the decaying body they had found in a granite pit just outside of town as that of Baylor sophomore Patrick Dennehy. One of Dennehy's teammates on the basketball team, Carlton Dotson, confessed to shooting Dennehy in self-defense during an argument. Dotson was arrested in Maryland and extradited to Texas to face murder charges. Meanwhile, Dave Bliss, the school's head coach, resigned after it emerged that Dennehy was receiving improper tuition payments in return for his playing on the team. Then, apparently, in order to cover up the source of the money, authorities allege that Bliss plotted to accuse Dennehy of selling drugs in order to make the money. The investigation into the killing also revealed that various members of the basketball team were using drugs. And the Dennehy family is suing Bliss as well as Baylor.

Baylor has always had a reputable sports program but in recent years the pressure to be more competitive increased. In 1994, Texas governor Ann Richards learned that the University of Texas and Texas A&M were about to leave their conference to join the Big Eight; she intervened to make sure that Baylor, her alma mater, would not be left behind. The Big Twelve, as the conference is now called, does not seem to be the place for Baylor. As a *Fort Worth Star-Telegram* reporter noted, "The Baylor Bears have struggled in the new Big 12 to preserve any kind of identity. The football team has won only three conference games in seven seasons, and has yet to defeat a fellow Big 12 team on the road. . . . Baylor doesn't belong in the Big Twelve." As the only private university, and one of the smaller ones in the conference, Baylor does not have the money to improve its programs significantly.

But whether at a religious school or a secular school, big university sports are always about more than sports. They're about alumni fund-raising and national publicity. They're about living within the rules of the conferences while at the same time giving your school the greatest possible advantage. They're about competing in the marketplace—to get better players, more attention, and more money.

Everything that has happened at Baylor in the last six months could have happened at any Division I school. Observers have been quick to point out that Baylor's religious affiliation does not mean that all of its students or staff will be saints. This is certainly true, but the question of whether a sports program at a strongly religious school should be conducted any differently than at a secular school is not unreasonable.

Most students report that athletes on campus are treated differently—special tutoring, special meals, special living arrangements, etc. When I ask English professor Ralph Wood whether he thinks the huge number of hours these students spend on sports might detract from their academic careers, or Baylor's academic excellence, he answers, "The first time Duke won national basketball championships, its number of qualified applicants doubled.

It's counterintuitive but that's what happened." Wood and others among the faculty and administration believe that Baylor's sports programs will push it onto the national radar screen. And it's from this national audience that they will get applicants who are stronger academically as well as religiously.

Beyond using sports to recruit religious students, are there other ways in which Baylor's religious identity and athletic program should be considered together? In an article published shortly after the scandal broke, religion scholar Alan Wolfe argued that the administration was not very humble or contrite in its reaction to these events. He even compared the president's re-action to that of various higher-ups in the Catholic Church after news of the recent sex scandals broke.

More important than the administration's reaction after the fact, is the question of whether Baylor's religious identity influences the way the athletic program is run in general. Division I schools have notoriously low graduation rates for athletes. According to the *Chronicle of Higher Education,* Baylor's overall graduation rate from the classes entering in the 1992–93 school year to those entering in the 1995–96 school was 69 percent. Their graduation rate for the men's basketball team was 64 percent for those years and for the black players on the team, it was 57 percent. These are better than some of the dismal statistics at other Division I schools but maybe Baylor's religious mission requires a higher standard in this respect. (To be fair, the gap be-tween Notre Dame's men's basketball graduation rate and general graduation rate is 30 points and BYU's is 20.) If religious beliefs are not supposed to be-long to a "separate sphere" at Baylor, then presumably its mission must in-clude a religious responsibility to make sure all of its students are getting a good education.

So just how much does the school's religious message pervade life outside the classroom? Lesley-Ann Dyer, one of the more conservative students I meet at Baylor, tells me, "At first I was shocked that a lot of people here, and even members of Christian organizations, drink."

Shrugging her shoulders, Lesley says, "People are inherently contradictory."

But Lesley-Ann's surprise is not uncommon. According to university sta-tistics, 36 percent of students arrive on campus never having tasted alcohol, and only about 50 percent engage in alcohol use on a regular basis. That is about 25 percent less than the national average.

Still, it is more than many students would like. Ben Pierce, the associate dean of sciences, has noticed, "Baylor is a little bit of a shock for people coming from a conservative religious background. We're a big university and we have students of all kinds. And we have students who drink and use drugs and engage in sex."

After church, at McAllister's Deli, I return to the subject of alcohol with Jenny. She tells me that Baylor's students are diverse in their social and religious habits.

"I would say well under half the people drink on weekends. That's what I like about Baylor. People do other stuff on weekends. They go to concerts. There are game nights and sporting events." The social atmosphere, Jenny says, is different from a lot of other schools. "It's not like you walk into class and everyone is talking about how smashed they were over the weekend."

"If you're not partying, you're okay," she says.

But Jenny's own sorority is throwing a Superbowl party tonight at which she expects there will be plenty of alcohol.

Indeed, fraternities and sororities play a dominant role in Baylor's social scene. Though many students seem to believe it's more, Hulme assures me that only 26 percent of students participate in Greek life. "It's a good thing that it's only a quarter of the population. Any more than that and they might have too much influence." Citing their organization of intramural sports and homecoming events, Hulme argues that the benefits of Greek life outweigh its problems.

Fraternities and sororities do not have their own houses, something Hulme says limits their influence. But since just about all upperclassmen at Baylor live off campus and the administration cannot really prevent the members of a particular group from living together, the sororities and fraternities have unofficial residences.

To have most students living off campus at a strongly religious college is very rare. It was a policy that started in the 1960s. As Baylor was expanding and needed more housing, the administration determined it would be easier and cheaper to just let local developers build apartments for students. Only freshmen were left living on campus, and, as Scott Moore notes, the dynamics of a college experience went missing. "You lost the kind of informal hierarchical structure with juniors and seniors living in dorms," says Scott Moore. "The campus lost a lot of its life."

At a religious college, where a certain standard of behavior is demanded, the problem becomes even more stark, since, as Beaty explains, "By not having students on campus, we're saying we're not going to have influence." To fix this situation, Baylor plans over the next several years to bring more of its students back to campus. After forty years, the school is trying to get back into the business of "formation," developing the whole character of the student by keeping him or her close to campus life and its influences.

Some of the students I speak with worry that "formation" is code for the university planning to interfere more in their personal lives, and few students want to live in the dorms after freshman year. Since dorms are single-sex and members of the opposite sex may only be in a student's room until six P.M. on weeknights and ten P.M. on weekends, many students don't miss them. Matthew Flanigan, the student body president, tells me: "I loved the dorm but I would never do it again."

So what kind of in loco parentis role does the university plan to enforce? When President Sloan was first installed in office, a number of faculty members and students recall, he tried to set the tone early by officially lifting Baylor's ban on dancing. (The dances held in secret over the previous years, I am told, were called "foot functions.") Indeed, by taking the first official dance himself, Sloan signaled to the campus community that he is not a fundamentalist on these issues. But that doesn't mean that he is a liberal, either. And with so many of the students under twenty-one, it doesn't seem likely that Baylor will stop being a dry campus anytime soon.

Enforcing the rules on drinking, though, might be the easier part of the in loco parentis formula that the university is moving toward. Trying to ensure that eight thousand undergrads don't engage in premarital sex is a task that almost no college administrator in the country would attempt. Currently, according to recent surveys of the student population, 33 percent of the Baylor population is having sex.

Jenny tells me that she used to be "naïve about sex at Baylor. I thought nobody does that." But even if they don't gossip about it, the way other college students do, she believes there is a lot of sexual activity in the fraternities and sororities. She says, "Sex isn't openly talked about here. It's more clandestine." Jenny has "heard stories from friends at other schools, where that's all there is. The only question everyone discusses is 'Who did you hook up with?'" The situation at Baylor is "much different," she explains.

But if students return to campus over the next decade or so, many wonder how the rules about sex would be enforced. Hulme thinks it would remain what it is today. "Do we do bed checks?" Hulme asks, and answers emphatically, "No." She warns me about the "cultural lore that's out there." Some students believe that if a Baylor student became pregnant, she would get kicked out. Even barring such incontrovertible evidence as a pregnancy, students do not get kicked out for having sex. If it turns out to be a sustained problem—and one wonders how many students repeatedly get caught having sex by school administrators—some kind of action could be taken against them.

It is true that it would certainly be easier for the administration to enforce its rules against sex if students were on campus, but few believe that is the purpose. "Kids are pretty inventive," says Moore. But there is a sense among faculty and administrators at Baylor that students should be asked to hold themselves to a high standard. The consequences if they do not seem secondary. In part, that seems to be the result of a fuller understanding of Baylor's role in molding students who will soon have to face the larger culture. Sloan notes the pervasive "mentality of sexuality in America. There are no constraints, no norms." But the idea, Sloan emphasizes, that sex is just a casual encounter is enormously destructive to the human psyche. "Intimacy is so good and so profound, that when it is misused it becomes a vehicle for enormous pain and ultimately stunts the ability of men and women to develop long lasting relationships."

Among the students, there is a contingent of very conservative Christians, following strict rules about courtship, says Jenny, who seems baffled by their behavior. "You have the girls who date the guy for months and eventually kiss. How do you do that?" Then, there is the "hookup" scene at fraternities and sororities. As Jenny explains, "Guys never ask girls out. You just see people at parties and it goes from there." Jenny is not a big fan of this form of dating either, though she is a sorority member. Between the fraternity scene and the courtship without kissing scene, there seems to be little middle ground.

To add to this strange clash between the old-fashioned courtship of southern Christian ladies and gentlemen and more modern college sexual relationships, a group of gay and lesbian students recently demanded official recognition from Baylor. Most faculty doubt this will occur anytime in the foreseeable future.

When I ask student body president Matthew Flanigan about this issue, he leans back in the beaten-up leather chair in his office, and takes a deep breath. He explains calmly that he agrees with the position the administration has taken. "I sure don't think there should be a homosexual group. That would mean Baylor is promoting it. That's not in line with what the Bible says."

But he acknowledges that the issue of how to deal with homosexual behavior is a difficult one. He doesn't want the school to turn into Bob Jones, where he knows, "they kick you out if you're gay." "We have to love them—and we do—but we can't say their behavior is all right." Flanigan argues that ultimately it's a question of Baylor's being clear about its expectations. (With a freshman retention rate of 84 percent, it seems that most students do come in understanding what Baylor is about.) Just as he "came to Baylor knowing that homosexuality is a sin and something that's not promoted here," he expects that his fellow students understood that as well.

Most administrators would claim that Baylor is being consistent when it comes to the way it treats heterosexual premarital sex and homosexual sex. "While we are welcoming to everybody because we're all sinners," Beaty says, "the administration is not going to affirm homosexuality as an acceptable lifestyle. Neither is it going to affirm heterosexual relationships outside of marriage."

This kind of evenhandedness when it comes to various forbidden acts is not particularly common among Christian universities, notes biology professor Christopher Kearney, who tells me, "Every culture and time period has their own cherished sins."

Though the Baylor faculty and administration seems pretty clear and confident of its position on homosexual behavior—it's a sin, but there are other sins too, and sinners must be loved rather than simply punished—the students are a little more confused. In part, this is a generational issue. (Homosexuality has simply become much more socially accepted over the last couple of decades.) But this is also a matter of students not having worked out the way that their faith influences their cultural attitudes.

Juls Trinh takes a sip of her coffee and looks around to see who has just walked into Common Grounds. Then she turns her attention slowly to a topic she has thought about plenty. "It's really difficult for me," she says, "because I haven't decided if homosexuality is something that you're born with or whether you decide to lead your life that way. I know it sounds cheesy, but I believe everyone is a person and it's not my judgment. God is going to decide these things. If it helps them to have an organization, I would support it."

But there is certainly a contingent of students at Baylor whose views on homosexuality are indistinguishable from those of their counterparts at secular schools. "There is nothing wrong with homosexuality," says Eric Cooper. "There is an exclusion of homosexuals at Baylor. I think they should certainly be allowed a club. Equal access should certainly include homosexuals."

To what does Eric attribute the administration's refusal to recognize a club? "The homophobia is unbelievable. People fear the domino effect, like during the height of Communism. If they allow ten or twenty homosexual students to gather, then thirty percent of the population will become homosexual and then ninety percent of the population will turn out to be gay and lesbian, like it's contagious."

Dean of university ministries Todd Lake says that views like Eric's must be acknowledged on Baylor's campus, and that the administration cannot turn a blind eye to that large swath of the student body who don't know what they think of homosexuality. He tells me, "I would like to see an opportunity for lesbian and gay students to get together and talk." Though he agrees with the administration's position in not advocating homosexual behavior, he explains, "I would like to increase the discussion in the whole realm of sexuality. Where does marriage play in? What about celibacy? We live in a culture that says if we're not sexually active, we're not whole people. If we don't have those discussions, then students who wrestle with those issues will seek out biased sources."

Right now, Lake says, "The only people those students can talk with are those who advocate homosexuality."

Lake hopes to create more opportunities for talk sponsored by the administration so that students can understand the Christian position more fully and have the opportunity to discuss their concerns. Indeed, in helping students to understand the social, cultural, and intellectual issues presented by modernity, Baylor seems to be following Lake's lead.

CHAPTER SEVEN

WHAT REVOLUTION?
HOW FEMINISM CHANGED RELIGIOUS COLLEGES
WHILE THEY WEREN'T LOOKING

In her recent book *Why There Are No Good Men Left,* sociologist Barbara Dafoe Whitehead chronicles what she calls the "female takeover of higher education."

"In a strikingly short period of time," Whitehead writes:

> *young women have become the majority on undergraduate college campuses. A series of milestone years mark their advance. In 1976, for the first time, the female percentage of June high school graduates who went straight on to college exceeded the percentage of male graduates to do so. In 1981, for the first time, the number of women who received bachelor's degrees exceeded the number of men who earned that degree. In 1984, for the first time, the number of women enrolled in graduate school exceeded the number of men. In 1987, for the first time, the number of women earning master's degrees exceeded the number of men who earned that degree.*

Given this educational revolution, then, it should hardly come as a surprise that women are disproportionately responsible for the recent dramatic increase in enrollment at religious colleges. Indeed, the scales at religious schools are tipped more than secular ones. Last year, women constituted a record 58 percent of college graduates generally, outnumbering men in schools of almost every size, in every region of the country, at every level of selectivity, but they made up more than 62 percent of enrollment at the Catholic schools surveyed and 59 percent at other religious schools. At some religious colleges, the disparities are more extreme. Westmont College, an evangelical school in Santa Barbara, California, enrolls twice as many women as men, while at its sister school, Gordon College in Massachusetts, there are three times as many women as men.

While the baby boom generation may understand this flood tide of females into higher education, religious and otherwise, as an unqualified good and the rightful end to centuries of inequality, the success of the movement, critics argue, has also created a lot of unhappy young women. When women ask to be treated just like men, so the argument goes, they may find plenty of professional success, but not personal happiness. Reprogramming women to view sex, relationships, and marriage in the same way that men do may not be possible.

And the evidence of this problem is everywhere, but perhaps nowhere more obviously than in "chick lit." Typified by say, *Bridget Jones's Diary*, this genre centers on what Whitehead calls "a new kind of serio-comic character, [a] romantically disconsolate, endlessly self-monitoring, single woman who has embarked on a desperate, sometimes obsessive search for a good man." But the protagonists of these novels and their real-life counterparts are commonly disappointed.

These well-educated, successful women are marrying later in life than their mothers and grandmothers (an average age of twenty-eight for college-educated women rather than the twenty-five it once was), in part because they have plenty of other options to keep them busy between the ages of twenty and thirty. It is not simply that they can work outside the home, as, of course, women of previous generations have done, but that they can continue their educations for years after college and then have careers that are both intellectually demanding and financially fulfilling.

The fact that many of these young women cannot find suitable marriage partners, some might argue, is the result of men who are intimidated by their success. And while that may be true in some cases, there is another more obvious reason for the problem. A woman in her mid twenties today has had a completely different kind of interaction with the opposite sex than a woman fifty or sixty years older. Ninety percent of women born between 1933 and 1942 were either virgins when they first married or had first intercourse with the man they wed. Today's young woman, by contrast, probably had sex for the first time in her late teens, continued on to least a couple of sexual relationships in college, and now has become used to sex as part of a dating relationship, of which she will have several by the time she is 30.[6]

Which means, in part, as Whitehead and other sociologists have noted, that young women today have really been through the wringer, particularly since they are more likely than men to invest emotionally in their sexual relationships. Combine this with the common practice of living together before

---

[6] See Whitehead for more statistical analysis in this vein.

marriage, in which women—who often think a relationship is moving toward marriage when it's not—will perform all of the duties necessary to run a home, and it's easy to see why Bridget Jones is always bursting into tears. And it's also easy to understand why traditionally religious communities might not be altogether thrilled to find themselves undergoing a similar revolution.

So is the tipping of the gender scales at religious colleges a sign that these institutions have become centers of female empowerment? Or do they prove that religious people will do anything they can to protect their daughters from what they see as the harmful influence of secular universities?

The character of the education at religious schools and the effects on these women have been hotly disputed. There are two dominant theories of what is happening on sectarian college campuses today. On the one hand, it is argued that religious schools ghettoize their populations, cutting them off from the ideas of the secular world, and, by extension, making them unable or unwilling to enter it. Feminists, in particular, fear that such colleges (and traditional religions generally) deprive women of the wide array of opportunities available to them. By sheltering these women from the outside world during their impressionable college years, they argue, religious communities reinforce traditional roles of subordination. On the other hand, a number of sociologists have presented a very different scenario. Sociologist James Davison Hunter has suggested that religious colleges actually contribute to the secularization of their students by exposing them to modern ideas and drawing them further away from the strictures of their families' traditions. The most startling aspect of Hunter's thesis—particularly for professors and administrators at religious colleges—is his claim that these schools, rather than helping students to preserve their faith, are speeding up the process of secularization.

"Contemporary Christian higher education," Hunter writes, "produces individual Christians who are either less certain of their attachments to the traditions of their faith or altogether disaffected from them." Moreover, he finds secularization to be most evident in the area of family and in the students' changing perceptions of traditional gender roles. That is, religious colleges may be furthering, not hindering, a more liberal, feminist agenda.

The experiences of women at religious colleges thus offer fodder for both sides of the debate—to the feminists who protest their religiously conservative curriculum and environment, and to sociologists who believe that such schools may have a subversive effect on their female students' distinctive religious identities. Which is the more accurate picture of women at today's religious colleges? And why are an increasing number of young women choosing religious schools over their secular counterparts?

Professors and administrators at religious colleges suggest a number of reasons why women may prefer to attend religious schools, including evidence that women often tend to be more spiritual and more active in religious life than the men in the same communities. But many believe the disparity can be attributed to the fact that religious parents are less willing to have their daughters attend a secular school than their sons. These parents feel, as one evangelical college administrator put it, "more of a need to protect them."

This protective attitude is, of course, what troubles many feminists. By keeping them from exposure to the broader world, they argue, religious schools weaken the standing of women and reinforce a culture of male domination. *Issues in Women's Studies,* a popular college textbook, sums up the attitude: "As Western Culture is patriarchal, so is its religion, and so is its god." The editors charge that conventional Christian doctrines and practices consign women to "a lesser excellence and status," making "victimization a sacred principle, sacrifice a magic contribution, self-effacement a high." This viewpoint is also captured in an article in *Jane,* a popular feminist magazine, which portrays the April 2002 "Women of Faith" conference in Kansas City (one stop on the twenty-seven-city tour) with a heavy dose of sarcasm: "So women need men to take care of them, and good men take care of their women. In a nutshell, that's the Promise Keepers-on-estrogen message: 'Just sit back, relax and give yourself over to a man, mortal or otherwise.'" But one need not buy into the *Handmaid's Tale* version of events in order to feel concern. In their aim to provide higher education in an environment that conforms to traditional moral standards, religious colleges may not be fully preparing young women for the modern world.

One way of investigating this charge is to compare the future plans of women at religious colleges with those at secular schools. More so than with the other topics in *God on the Quad,* it is both possible and important to examine this data. Possible because the American Council on Education's survey, "The American Freshman," asks numerous questions on the subject to freshmen at religious and nonsectarian schools across the country, and has done so for decades. Important because attitudes about women's roles have become a sort of bellwether for so many other political debates in this country, from abortion to child-rearing to no-fault divorce.

Feminists may find the survey results described here surprising. Data from the fall 2001 survey show that on questions concerning family life, career paths, and graduate education, the responses of women entering religious colleges hardly differ at all from those at secular institutions.

For instance, when asked whether "the activities of married women are best confined to the home and family," 13.1 percent of freshmen women at nonsectarian four-year colleges agreed, compared with 15.2 percent of freshmen women at Catholic colleges and 17.3 percent of the same group at other religious colleges. At highly selective private schools, the percentage increased to 16.8 percent of students who agreed with the statement, whereas at the highly selective Catholic and other religious schools this percentage moved up to 19.2 and 17.7 percent respectively. (Though there are no dramatic differences in the percentages, it is noteworthy that better educated students in religious schools are less likely to dismiss the notion that women belong in the home than their less competitive counterparts.)

When asked which objectives they "considered to be essential or very important," 70.3 percent of freshman women at nonsectarian four-year colleges checked off "raising a family," compared to 76.5 percent at Catholic colleges and 73.8 percent at other religious colleges. Broken down by selectivity, the numbers look similar, with about three quarters of women at highly selective schools choosing this response.[7] The percentage of women who included "being well-off financially" among their important or essential objectives was fairly similar across the board—65.5 percent at nonsectarian schools, 71.9 percent at Catholic schools, and 62 percent at other religious schools. One might attribute this difference to the students' variations in income (non-Catholic religious schools consistently had a higher percentage of freshmen with parents in lower- to middle-income brackets), but on the other hand, poorer students might also be expected to place more weight on financial security.[8]

Contrary to the concern of some feminists, "The American Freshman" survey data show that a significant number of women at religious colleges plan

---

[7] 70.7 percent of women at highly selective nonsectarian schools, 75.6 percent at highly selective Catholic schools, and 73.5 percent at other highly selective religious schools

[8] At highly selective nonsectarian schools, 58.6 percent of women checked "being well-off financially," compared with 67.7 at highly selective Catholic schools and 55.5 percent at other highly selective religious schools.

to pursue advanced academic degrees as well as demanding careers. Nearly 48 percent of women at Catholic schools plan to get an MA or an MS, compared with 44.3 percent at nonsectarian schools and 38.5 percent at other religious schools. The number of women at religious colleges who plan to pursue a PhD or EdD and the size of this group at secular colleges differ only by 1.5 percent. Moreover, the percentage of women at religious colleges who plan to pursue medical degrees is actually 2 percentage points higher than the women at secular colleges.

In fact, though a greater number of women, both secular and religious, listed "raising a family" as a priority than those who chose "being well-off financially" or "becoming an authority in my field,"[9] less than half of one percent of all the women interviewed expressed a desire to become full-time homemakers. This suggests that of all the women who agreed that "the activities of married women are best confined to the home and family," the vast majority were either not including themselves in this category or were considering the question in ideal circumstances.

Not only did the higher percentage of women who thought that women belong in the home not translate into a higher number of full-time homemakers, it didn't even translate into a significantly higher percentage of women pursuing careers that demand fewer hours. One might suppose that religious women would expect to seek jobs that are less time-consuming, but again, the responses did not vary significantly between religious and nonreligious schools. Nearly 7 percent of freshman women at Catholic colleges plan to pursue careers as business executives, the same number as at nonsectarian colleges (but slightly higher than the number at other religious colleges). Likewise, about 5 percent of women at nonsectarian schools plan to become lawyers, compared with 4.4 percent at Catholic and 4.1 percent at other religious schools. A college professorship, which would offer a more flexible schedule, appealed to equal percentages of students at secular and religious schools. The gap for elementary school teachers was a little larger, with 7.9 percent at nonsectarian colleges planning to pursue this career, compared with 12.5 at Catholic schools and 10.5 at other religious schools.

Overall, female students at religious colleges seem more interested in raising a family and less interested in becoming wealthy than those at secular schools, if only by a slim margin. It seems plausible that a few years down the line, these women might reconsider being full- or part-time homemakers when their children are young. This may be especially true of religious

---

[9] 57.3 percent for nonsectarian, 56.5 for Catholic, and 55.3 for other religious schools.

women, who tend to marry earlier than American women on the whole. But it is difficult to say for sure. Because it is based entirely on the responses of college freshmen, "The American Freshman" survey does not account for the effect college life itself will have on the women's attitudes and on the development of their future plans. Moreover, it is difficult to gather reliable statistics on students at religious colleges because, even though it differentiates between nonsectarian, Catholic, and "other religious" schools, the Department of Education (upon whose data the vast majority of the surveys done by independent groups rely) does not distinguish between schools with loose religious affiliations and those with stronger ties to their sponsoring denominations.

But if, as one might conclude from this data, the fears of the feminist camp are not well founded, then what can be said about the commitment of these women to their respective faiths? Are female students rebelling against their religious backgrounds? If the religious colleges are not "protecting" women from the secular world, are they failing in their aim of perpetuating their religious communities?

James Davison Hunter was among the first to conduct research on the process of secularization at American evangelical colleges. In his landmark 1988 study, *Evangelicalism: The Coming Generation,* Hunter chronicled the significant percentage of evangelical Christians who no longer subscribed to biblical inerrancy, whose political views leaned leftward, and who tolerated or engaged in behavior deviant from Christian moral standards. The trend toward secularization, Hunter maintained, was most evident in the area of family. Indeed, Hunter's comparison of the beliefs of younger (eighteen to thirty-five) and older (thirty-six and older) evangelicals concerning gender roles exposed startling differences between the age groups.

While almost three quarters of the older interviewees agreed "that it is more important for a wife to help her husband's career than to have one herself," less than half of the younger set agreed with this statement. Asked whether they "agree that women should take care of running their home and leave the running of the country up to men," 57 percent of the older evangelicals agreed, almost 25 percent more than their younger coreligionists. And while more than three quarters of the older generation agreed "that a preschool child is likely to suffer if his or her mother works," less than half of the younger generation thought so.

Remarkably, Hunter found that the views of the younger evangelicals regarding family issues more closely mirrored secularist views than those views traditionally held within their religious communities. Though acknowledging that "only a minority [of evangelical Christians] has accepted the rigors of feminist ideology," he found a "propensity toward androgynous role definitions" among evangelical students. Hunter concluded that "feminist sensibilities are . . . ingrained within substantial sectors of Evangelicalism and particularly with its coming generation."

A recent report by the Cardinal Newman Society (based on data from the Higher Education Research Institute collected at thirty-eight Catholic colleges) indicates that a similar process of secularization has taken place at Catholic institutions. The study found that the views of Catholic students at these schools liberalize considerably between their freshman and senior years. For instance, in 1997, 55 percent of Catholic freshmen at these colleges believed that abortion should be illegal, while in 2001 only 43 percent of those same students felt the same way. (It is important to note, however, that unlike Hunter's sample, which consisted of strongly religious evangelical institutions, this study did not include the more strictly Catholic schools.)

In their 2002 book *Evangelicalism: The Next Generation,* James Penning and Corwin Smidt, professors at Calvin College, confirm at least in part the secularization thesis. Between 1984 and 1996, the percentage of evangelical college students who agreed that "a woman should put her husband and children ahead of her career" dropped 4 percent, while the percentage who disagreed "that a married woman should not work if she has a husband capable of supporting her" rose 11 percent. As far as the role of men is concerned, 58 percent of the 1984 group believed that "the husband has the 'final say' in family decision making," compared with 41 percent of the 1996 interviewees.

But does this mean that the students are becoming secular feminists? Penning and Smidt's research contradicts Hunter's claims regarding the increasing theological and behavioral laxity of evangelical college students. According to their data, 66 percent of students in 1982 believed that "the only hope for heaven is through personal faith in Jesus Christ," the same number as today. The percentage of students that believed that "there is no life after death" remained the unchanged (at 1 percent) and so did the percentage that believed "the devil is a personal being who directs evil forces and influences people to do wrong" (85 percent).

As for the questions regarding "moral boundaries," as the authors call them, the results are similar. Students in both 1982 and 1997 almost unanimously believed that "extramarital sexual intercourse is always wrong," and while slightly less than half believed in 1982 that "heavy petting" was always wrong, about half believe that today. Indeed, had the Cardinal Newman Society study included some of the more orthodox Catholic schools, one suspects that its results would have been different. In another recent book, *The New Faithful,* journalist Colleen Carroll offers much anecdotal evidence to back up the claims of Penning and Smidt, concluding that there has been a return to Christian orthodoxy within both the evangelical and Catholic worlds. Certainly, the surge in enrollment at strongly religious colleges would seem to support this theory.

What's going on here? Has the feminist camp (unbeknownst to itself) won the battle for the hearts and minds of religious college students? Have women at today's religious schools become increasingly secularized? Or are young people becoming more orthodox in their religious beliefs? What does it mean that attitudes toward gender roles have changed but not views on theology or sexual morality? The picture is indeed complicated, but becomes more readily discernible in interviews with young women at religious colleges.

Rejecting the demands of both radical feminist ideology and the more traditionally conservative views of their religious communities, women at today's religious schools have found a practical balance between the two. The women I spoke with possess a modern sensibility as well as an awareness of the opportunities available to them. Many plan to pursue careers like those of their secular counterparts. At the same time, they have not abandoned their faith or capitulated to the androgynous culture of the secular world. Rather, they pursue education and religious duties with equal vigor, with their respective faiths informing their postgraduation choices. From Brigham Young to Bob Jones University to Touro College, women at religious schools are embracing a third way.

At twenty-seven, Zee Cramer is one of the older undergraduates at Brigham Young University, having switched majors a couple of times and taken two years off to do mission work in Washington state. (Most women at Brigham Young wait until after graduation to do their mission work.) Zee's religious obligations continued when she returned to school. This semester she is in charge of "compassionate service"—ministering to the physical, spiritual, and emotional needs of others in the ward—and part of her duty is to attend all of the ward's social and religious activities to make sure she gets to know everyone, a time-consuming task. But at other times, she has had to devote only one or two hours a week to her calling. Her religious work is clearly central to her experience at Brigham Young. No matter how much time it demands, she explains, "I work the rest of my schedule around my calling."

Beyond the demands of her religious duties, her schoolwork, and her campus job, Zee is also pursuing one of the most important goals for men and women at Brigham Young—finding a spouse. For the large majority of undergraduates like Zee who are not from Utah, and who plan on returning to communities where there is not a large Mormon population, their undergraduate years at Brigham Young present the best opportunity to find a spouse who is a Church of Jesus Christ of Latter-Day Saints member. By the time they graduate, 45 percent of the women and 55 percent of the men have succeeded. Some Brigham Young administrators worry that the early marriage age among Mormons causes some women to come to the school simply for their "MRS" degree, leaving school once they marry. But this has changed significantly in recent years due to the efforts of the administration. Even though the size of the entering class is the same as it was a decade ago, Brigham Young now graduates three thousand more students per year, and women make up two thirds of that increase. "In the past," university president Merrill Bateman explains, women would get married during school and the couple "would value education more for him than for her and so he would finish school. But now they value education for both the husband and wife and they work it out, even with children."

Figuring out a balance between career and family is by no means easy for Mormon women. Jan Scharman, the school's vice president for student life, explains: "I get a lot of young women who come to me and say, 'You have a family and you're a professional. How do you fit them together?'" The Mormon Church, for its part, has tried to emphasize the advantages of higher education for women regardless of whether they plan to pursue careers. Cecelia Fielding, a Brigham Young administrator, seems representative of the school's community when she tells me, "General American culture expects women to be more serious. We expect them to step forward and take a role."

I encountered a similar level of academic seriousness in the female student body at Bob Jones University. One junior I spoke with plans on attending medical school upon graduation, after which she wants to combine her missionary drive with her love for medicine by going to work in a developing country. When asked about having a family, she conceded that she would like to, but felt that God was calling her to pursue this path right now. And she is not alone. Many of the women I interviewed at Bob Jones were charting their future courses independent of marriage or family considerations.

Although most expected to marry someday, their postgraduation plans didn't take any greater stock of that than those of women at nonreligious schools.

With such enterprising attitudes toward their futures, one might expect the women at Bob Jones to have been taught something about feminism. Yet in Camille Lewis's rhetoric class, it's clear that no one is up on her Gloria Steinem or Carol Gilligan. In discussing the political rights of women in the context of two eighteenth-century works on the subject, the students are articulate, but the gaps in their knowledge are revealing. One young woman asks Lewis, "What would a feminist say?" in a tone that intimates she has never met one before. After explaining the basic ideas behind feminism to this student, ideas that most high school students would probably be familiar with, Lewis must offer examples of sex discrimination because her students cannot think of any on their own.

Lewis recalls encountering some prejudices when she wrote her master's thesis at Bob Jones on the history of feminism. "Some of the professors thought I was trying to be a 'libber.'" In general, though, Lewis doesn't really think women are treated any differently from men at Bob Jones. Contrary to the stereotype of religious women being subservient, she explains that women have been in authority positions since 1927, the year of the school's founding. Lewis attributes this to the "pioneering attitude" inherent in Christian fundamentalism. "When the school was founded," she recounts, "they didn't have time to worry about gender roles because there was too much to do. They decided that whoever can do the job should do the job." For Bob Jones University and other fundamentalist colleges, the most urgent task is to proselytize as widely and effectively as possible. In the modern world, this means that women must receive the same opportunities and education as men.

Fundamentalism, as defined by religion scholar George Marsden, is "militantly antimodernist protestant evangelicalism" and can be distinguished from evangelicalism not through any particular theological disagreement so much as through its attitude toward the outside world, "its fierce opposition to modernist attempts to bring Christianity into line with modern thought." While Christian fundamentalists consider secular education primarily as a means of expanding their missionary base, evangelical colleges encourage students to consider their secular studies as intrinsically tied to their spiritual growth. This is a fairly new concept within the evangelical community. Until recently, evangelicals tended to subscribe to what historian Mark Noll calls "a Manichean attitude," which assumed "that we, and only we have the truth, while nonbelievers or Christian believers who are not evangelicals practice only error." This led evangelicals to dismiss most secular ideas and to "[fail] notably in sustaining serious intellectual life."

In contrast, the "integration of faith and learning" at today's evangelical colleges emphasizes secular as well as religious knowledge. Scholarly pursuits are seen as a way of glorifying God, both in studying the greatness of God's world and developing one's God-given faculties. And it is believed that students will bring their faith to bear in their professional lives and other pursuits. This shift in attitude may also be another reason evangelical women have been able to gain equal footing at Christian colleges: The world of serious higher education is relatively new for many evangelical men as well.

After college, Jenny Ebbeling, a sophomore at Baylor, a National Merit Scholar, and a participant in the Crane Scholars program (for students who are interested in academic careers to get together to discuss literature, science, and popular culture in a Christian light) plans to go to graduate school in England to study literature. Though she has given a lot of thought to the question of how to combine her career with having a family, she doesn't seem anxious about it. Jenny believes her Christian faith will make her a better wife and her expectations for marriage and family more realistic. "Coming from a Christian perspective, you get married and you share your life with this person forever," she says. "The thought that you can just move to different people never even occurs to me." Though Jenny feels that she and her fiancé are "perfect for each other," she emphasizes, "there's so much work that goes into the relationship daily. . . . You need a God who will say 'It's going to be okay. You'll get through this.'"

Students at Thomas Aquinas College in Santa Paula, California, can take a marriage preparation class to learn some of these lessons. Not surprisingly, since 28 percent of Thomas Aquinas graduates marry each other, it is a popular class.

Sophomore Nicole Gingras does not have any imminent plans for marriage but she thinks she wants to pursue a career as a massage therapist. Other Thomas Aquinas women opt for teaching or journalism, but almost all of them choose professions that provide flexible hours and that can be set aside for long periods without great consequence. The reason for these career choices is clear, considering that for women at Thomas Aquinas, raising children often means homeschooling them. Unlike other religious women—who might decide to stay home or work part-time when their children are young, and then return to full-time careers when they begin school—some of the women I spoke with at Thomas Aquinas plan to make homeschooling their full-time occupation. Thomas Aquinas president Thomas Dillon emphasizes that those "who choose to stay home and raise their children . . . are in some way bringing their education to bear [on their daily lives]." A future "career" of homeschooling would necessitate that these women receive the strongest possible education.

Women raised in some traditional Orthodox Jewish communities are also encouraged to pursue a broad, secular education—though for different reasons. Smadar Rosensweig, a professor of biblical studies at Touro College in New York, explains how it has become more common for Orthodox women to pursue secular education seriously. "The difference between the men's and women's education is that men have an official [religious] responsibility to study, and therefore, their involvement in secular activities might need more justification. There is not that demand for women, and therefore not as much of a conflict for religious Jewish women to learn secular subjects."

Devorah Ehrlich, dean of Touro's women's division, adds, "Women do have to learn Torah . . . as a means to an end" of making decisions regarding ethical dilemmas they encounter, while men "are commanded to learn Torah" for its own sake. This explanation accounts for the difference between the women's and men's schools at Touro. The men pursue their religious studies for most of the day and then only reluctantly apply themselves to secular subjects. Kenneth Bigel, a business professor, describes the attitude: "You will have a few students that are here just for the diploma, quite literally, and secular education is only important insofar as it provides them with a career—and worse, they may say that everything they need to know they learn in their religious studies." In fact, this did seem to be the attitude of most of the men I interviewed. One student even told me that he felt guilty about enjoying his math class.

The women of Touro, on the other hand, seem enthusiastic about their secular studies (which are integrated with religious classes throughout the day) and ambitious about their careers, even while they look forward to a fulfilling family life. Though many of the female students come from very sheltered families where secular learning is not highly valued, Ehrlich insists that the school wants to provide its students with a serious education.

While women at Touro may take some time off to marry and have children, those who don't immediately finish their graduate or undergraduate degrees often return to school at some point.

* * *

In speaking with students about their parents' occupations, I found a much higher percentage of traditional, stay-at-home mothers in that earlier generation than seems likely in the current generation of religious women. Unfortunately, it is impossible to conduct a rigorous comparison, as there is little reliable data available on strongly religious women from earlier generations. The U.S. census does not ask questions about religion, and most of the surveys (conducted by the Gallup Organization, the National Opinion Research Center, and the Bureau of Labor Statistics) do not begin until the 1970s. Even then, questions on religiosity are spotty at best. (Weekly church attendance, for instance, does not always indicate a traditionally religious woman.) Moreover, categories like "full-time homemaker" did not appear as options on the 1960s "American Freshman" survey, while on the 1970s versions "other choice" and "undecided" were chosen by as many as a third of the participants.

Certainly, though, the anecdotal evidence gathered through my interviews seems to confirm Hunter's thesis about the changing attitudes of traditionally religious groups about gender roles. Even if women at religious colleges are not well versed in the tenets of feminist theory, they clearly understand the options open to women in the twenty-first century and are considering a wide range of them. Statistically, as well as anecdotally, there is no question that women coming out of traditionally religious schools are planning careers like those of their secular counterparts.

But there is another side to the story. What is occurring among young religious women may be less a case of secularization than a sophisticated accommodation to modernity. In some cases, like that of the Mormons, the church's own teachings on women's roles have changed. But there are also religious reasons for women to pursue secular education and professional careers. For an increasing number of evangelicals, secular learning is seen as a path to God. Fundamentalist Christian women, on the other hand, value a strong education and an understanding of the ways of the secular world primarily because it helps them in spreading the message of their faith. Traditionally Orthodox Jewish women study secular subjects and pursue careers in order to allow their husbands to spend more time studying Torah, while for orthodox Catholics, as well as many other religious groups, the practice of homeschooling makes obtaining a broad, liberal arts education indispensable for many women.

Overall, women at religious colleges share a certain attitude about their future—a calm pragmatism. After considering all of their options—all of the permutations and combinations of balancing career and family—they do not seem overwhelmed with concern that they won't be able to do it all. Their religious beliefs allow them to accept the inevitable trade-off between work and family. Another reason they may lack anxiety is that these young women do not see themselves as representatives of a cause. The current generation of religious women is the first within their communities to view working outside the home as a viable, if not obvious, choice. In this way they are similar to the women college graduates of the 1970s. But these latter women's choices with regard to marriage and career were automatically interpreted as political statements—on one side or the other—while today's religious women have no political agenda.

That the personal for these women has not become political can be attributed, at least in part, to their religious views. Many of these female students speak of finding their "calling," in the sense of finding out what God has in mind for each of them personally. This is not to say that their decisions will never be affected by others within their religious communities, but it does mean that they see their personal destiny as directed by God more than by their husbands or fathers.

As the students I interviewed demonstrate, women at religious colleges are reaching back into the foundations of their faiths for guidance in, and justification for, their decisions. They are not a symptom of a trend toward secularization, as they uphold, no less than previous generations, the theological and cultural tenets of their religions. Nor are they throwbacks to a previous era, sheltered from the opportunities that have become open to women in the last half century. Finally, the colleges themselves, rather than speeding along a process of secularization or stopping these women from achieving their full potential, are helping them to consider their futures in a more thoughtful manner, one in keeping with their religious beliefs.

CHAPTER EIGHT

BRIDGING THE RACE GAP:
CAN FAITH SOLVE THE
"LUNCH TABLE PROBLEM"?

In the spring of 2003, the Supreme Court decided that the University of Michigan may continue to admit minority candidates who are less qualified (in terms of their GPAs and standardized test scores) than their Caucasian counterparts to its undergraduate college and its law school. Justice Sandra Day O'Connor, writing for the majority, explained: "The Law School's educational judgment that diversity is essential to its educational mission is one to which we defer." And, as a result, "The Court endorses [the] view that student body diversity is a compelling state interest in the context of university admissions."

Though affirmative action has been wending its way through the courts for a quarter of a century, the Michigan decision was made on novel grounds: the presentation of scientific evidence to show that this population jiggering can produce visible educational benefits, not just social ones. The question then became: If affirmative action can actually improve the learning of the students—something central to the school's mission (and the state's in providing a public university)—are these preferences acceptable? In this case, despite the rather flimsy evidence provided, the court decided the answer was yes. It seems, then, that there are instances in which a college can prove that affirmative action, whatever its harms, should be pursued because it is vital to the mission of the institution. The situation of a public university is, of course, different from that of private religious institutions, but the principle set forth by the Supreme Court has important moral, if not legal, implications for the latter.

In the last decade or so, religious colleges have begun their own push for racial and ethnic diversity. Michael Beaty, the director of the Institute for Faith and Learning at Baylor, tells me, "[The school] didn't admit its first black student until 1965, after the University of Texas had. I'm ashamed of that. It's an indication of institutional sin. That we're open to people of all races now is a good thing." Indeed, some religious colleges pursue diversity as a form of repentance. "Why would having people at Baylor who are not Caucasian be a good thing?" Beaty asks. "It may mean we are doing as much as possible to be open where we have not been . . . in the past."

But what about the many religious schools in the Northeast, which, though they may not have admitted large numbers of minority students in the past, did not have in place explicitly discriminatory policies? Gordon College, for example, was founded in 1889 in Boston, and, according to admissions director Silvio Vazquez, "If you look at some of the photographs going back to the early 1900s, you will see a nice proportion of women and blacks in the class." He maintains that it was only once the school moved to the suburbs that it became almost all white. If pursuing diversity is not about repentance for schools like Gordon, what is it for?

On some level, religious colleges want diversity because secular colleges do. P. J. Hill, an economics professor at Wheaton College (near Chicago), observes, "There is a certain amount of trendiness in the term 'diversity.' Sometimes we haven't thought through fully what we mean by it."

Dharmpal Vansadia, an Indian student from Texas who meets me after his MCAT review class at Baylor, tells me that if his university wants to put itself in the top tier, the administration will need to step up its minority recruitment efforts. Comments like Dharmpal's are not common. Across denominational lines, the reasons for diversity offered by students, faculty, and administrators at religious colleges are, more often than not, religious ones. When it comes to diversity, "Scripture gives us ground on which to stand," according to Baylor chaplain Todd Lake. He cites the letters from Paul "urging Christian unity."

Churches, he rightly notes, are among the most segregated of American institutions, not just racially, but ethnically as well. There still exist predominantly Polish, Irish, and Albanian congregations, for example, thanks to immigrant populations that come here with particular languages and cultural traditions. (Even long after the children and grandchildren of immigrants have assimilated, families will continue to attend these ethnically specific institutions.) And many religious college administrators and faculty feel it should be part of their schools' missions to bring people from these different backgrounds together under one roof. As Corwin Smidt, a political science professor at Westmont College in southern California, notes, "The body of Christ is diverse. If you really believe that Jesus Christ came to save all people, that all cultures, all people are images of God, that no one culture fully embodies the Kingdom of God, we probably would be much richer and more reflective of what the church is, what the body of Christ is, with that diversity."

A conversation with Abby Diepenbrock, a senior at Westmont who attends a Pentecostal church and is one of the codirectors of the school's Center for Christian Concerns, reveals that there is at least as much enthusiasm on the part of students as from professors for the cause of diversity. Abby, whose hair is tied back in a bandana and who looks ready to wield a hammer for Habitat for Humanity at a moment's notice, becomes very excited when I ask her whether the school needs more diversity.

"Yes! Yes! Yes! And you can tell anybody I said that."

She explains the rationale: "People should be taking the best of their Christian cultures and offering it as glory to the lord. It's the Christian message."

Jud Carlberg, the president of Gordon College, notes: "The whole genius of the Christian message is that anyone can embrace belief in Jesus." Others echo this idea of Christianity as an "equal opportunity" faith. As her friend and codirector Jake Reid (who is wearing a T-shirt that says BODY PIERCING SAVED MY LIFE, a reference to the crucifixion) listens intently, Abby cites Paul's speech in the third chapter of Galatians: "In Christ, there is neither Jew nor Greek nor slave nor free nor man nor woman," meaning, she explains, that once people accept Christ as their savior and get into heaven, there are no distinctions among them. And so, Abby concludes, to have a Christian school that is predominantly one ethnicity gives people "the idea that it's the white man's God or the white man's religion. That's completely not true."

Silvio Vazquez, who now sits in a sunlit office in Gordon College's administration building with papers scattered around an expensive-looking computer set-up, cites himself as someone who came away from his own upbringing in a predominantly white, upper-class area of New Jersey with that very impression. Only recently has he rediscovered his own religious beliefs needn't be tied to race. God "is not the God of the white people," he says. He is adamant that "we can't have that type of perspective at Gordon. We need recognize that within the Christian community there is diversity." Vazquez explains that because he is a Latino who wasn't really aware of his own culture until he got married, he is very passionate about the cause of diversity.

Susan Penska, a professor at Westmont who attended Gordon College as an undergraduate, offers another New Testament justification for a policy of diversity. "At a Christian college, we need to take seriously what it means to love your neighbor as yourself and that loving your neighbor requires you to learn about your neighbor." According to Penska, "The only way you can begin to think about your responsibility to others is to learn about them."

But using the Christian mandate to learn about and love your neighbor as a formula for admissions at religious colleges presents some problems. In an essay in *Professing in the Postmodern Academy*, Elizabeth Newman, a theology professor at Saint Mary's, Notre Dame, offers the logical extension of Penska's reasoning. Newman advocates mandating racially, ethnically, and *religiously* "diverse" student bodies:

> *The practice of hospitality, in contrast to [Christian] triumphalism, calls us to welcome the other in all of his or her particularity, even to the point of being willing to suffer [her emphasis] at the hands of another. One of the theological convictions that sustains this risky practice is that the other is a worthy child of God no matter how much we might fail to see this. Even more, however, hospitality relies upon the conviction and promise that God speaks through 'the stranger.'*

But religious colleges must determine how much they are willing to "suffer," and how many "strangers" they plan to admit—that is, how much and what kind of diversity these schools are looking for. (The answer would interest the many strongly religious students who do plenty of "suffering" in secular schools at the hands of "the other," and come to religious colleges for some respite.) Admissions officers at secular colleges and universities, for example, place a premium not only on racial and ethnic diversity. They may also give preference to men or women (depending on the school's gender ratio), gays and lesbians, transgendered students, students with disabilities, older students, single mothers, or, most obviously, students of minority religions. Once a school adopts the idea that diversity is useful for its own sake, it is hard to say where the line should be drawn.

A January 2003 article in the *Chronicle of Higher Education* by Boston University professor of anthropology Peter Wood gets to the heart of this argument, even if the specifics are not quite the same. Wood criticizes women's colleges for their inconsistency in pursuing racial and ethnic diversity while excluding men from their student body. "This large hypocrisy eats away at the foundations of American higher education. Clearly, one answer is to hold colleges to the spirit of *real* diversity [his emphasis]. If diversity is such a good thing, why not, as at least part of the effort to create a diverse institution, eliminate artificial barriers that exclude some categories of intellectually able and otherwise qualified people?" An administrator from such a college might answer that being a women's college is central to the school's identity and educational mission, while having mostly white students is not. And someone from a religious college might similarly respond that a common faith is central to the school's mission, while a common race is not.[10]

Indeed, many students and faculty argue that a racially uniform student body would be downright detrimental to the school's mission. As Abby explains, "It's crucial for Westmont to be open, to be supporting financially and spiritually people of different ethnicities so that we are influencing them." For example, she offers, "I can't reach Korean people as well as a Korean could. I want to partner with Koreans in reaching their people with the gospel." Even Bob Jones University, whose graduates have found some success setting up churches in inner-city areas, is now recruiting minority students who will be able to go back to those communities and lead them from the inside.

However offensive outsiders may find the idea, religious colleges are hoping to use minority students to spread the faith to other ethnic communities. If the mission of the college, ultimately, is to spread the gospel (in its evangelical, Mormon, or Catholic form), then, the thinking goes, it needs representatives in each community who can help to do that. Were religious colleges to present their rationale for recruiting minority students to the Supreme Court, they could add another group to the list of possible affirmative action beneficiaries—the unsaved.

But let us step back for a moment. When exactly, one might easily wonder, did conservative religious communities become so devoted to interracial harmony? To take the most well-known case, blacks were barred from Bob Jones University until 1970, and the first black student did not enroll at the school until four years later. Then the infamous interracial dating ban was adopted by the administration, according to Bob Jones director of media relations Jonathan Pait, "for partly cultural"—in other words, racially prejudiced—"and partially religious reasons." In a 1998 letter explaining the policy, Pait wrote that while racial prejudice is "biblically wrong," there is a religious rationale for banning interracial dating. The destruction of the Tower of Babel in the book of Genesis, he explained, shows that God wanted the races to remain separate. Intermarriage, he wrote, "is promoted by one-worlders, and we oppose it for the same reason that we oppose religious ecu-

---

[10] The issue of the presence of religious minorities at these colleges will be taken up more fully in Chapter 11.

menism, globalism, one-world economy, one-world police force, unisex, etc."
Besides, Pait tells me, it was a classic case of "in loco parentis": The ban simply codified the rules most parents wanted their children to follow.

For much of the school's history, racial discrimination would hardly have
made Bob Jones University stand out in the South. But the ban continued
there long after such practices became taboo. In the 1970s and 1980s, many
fundamentalists stopped believing that the Bible itself forbade racial mixing,
and the administration began defending the ban with appeals to the theological principle of the "weaker brother." Among the early Christians, newer
converts, considered the weaker in faith, would not eat meat, in part because
meat was associated with pagan rituals. The older Christians, stronger in
faith, were comfortable eating meat. But St. Paul said that out of love for the
weaker brother, the stronger brother should follow his customs when eating
together. In other words, even though only a few "weaker" people at Bob
Jones felt strongly that interracial dating was sinful, the stronger were obli-
gated to go along with the ban.

Even as outsiders heaped ridicule on the school, stubbornness helped
keep the ban in place. As Pait recalls, "Once the wagons had been circled,
they didn't want to give up on the issue they had fought so hard about." It was
only a couple of years ago that Bob Jones University finally lifted the ban. And
even if the school's administration came to the realization that they needed to
change its reputation in order to be taken seriously by the educated elite, the
ultimate audience for the Bob Jones message,[11] there has been little in the
way of acknowledgment that there was anything wrong with the old policy.

But other religious schools, whose reputations are not nearly so sullied by
racism, and who have largely come to terms with any past wrongdoing, still
have student bodies that do not resemble the United Nations. Indeed, when
Damon Linker first came to Brigham Young University to teach political science, he says he was struck by "how clean cut and wholesome the students
are . . . how they look like the master race, tall and proud and muscular." At
Calvin College, Latino student Mariano Avila laughs about his "pitch black"
mane amidst a "sea of blond hair." At Westmont College, Kevin Lewis, a senior and a resident advisor, tells me there is "kind of a running joke that anyone on campus who is not Caucasian gets called to appear in the school's
brochures." Leslie Clark, an African-American senior at Wheaton, has over-
heard people talking about how college "was the first [occasion they] had
seen a black person outside of television." Though many religious colleges

---

[11] See Chapter 2 for more detailed explanation of the Bob Jones Strategy for proselytizing.

manage to attract significant international student populations because of the mission work of members of their faith, the schools' records for appealing to American minorities have not been stellar.

The reasons that minority students do not choose religious colleges in numbers as high as the colleges would like are varied and sometimes a little surprising. Leslie, who is originally from Charlotte, North Carolina, tells me that her black and Hispanic friends at home cannot fathom how she could choose to attend Wheaton—a school that (until recently) banned dancing. Though Leslie tolerated the rule, she did register a complaint to the administration when she arrived on campus a few years ago: "I grew up dancing and I love dancing. To say I can't anymore . . ." She pauses. "I see their point. They don't want to cause some students to stumble"—in their faith, not their dance moves. "But I think dancing can be incorporated in the Christian experience and not necessarily take you further away from God."

Leslie suggested to one of the school's deans that eliminating the ban would bring a more racially and ethnically diverse population to Wheaton. "You have people from African-American and Latino cultures where dancing is a part of their culture. It's very celebratory, a way of expression. To make it even seem like it's ungodly, I don't think that's right." Though it's difficult to say whether this was the winning argument, the school did end up lifting the ban in the spring of 2003. (The administration cited as its justification the fact that the Bible does not prohibit dancing.)

Such "cultural" changes notwithstanding, many students believe that their schools are not doing enough to improve the racial diversity on campus. Pointing to a student body that hails in large part from white upper-middle-class Texas suburbs, John Drake, who is African-American and the editor of Baylor's daily, *The Lariat*, tells me, "The students at Baylor aren't really people who have had a lot of diversity growing up for the most part." And when they get to the university, Drake believes, nothing really changes.

Beyond their general reputations, though, religious colleges face other challenges in recruiting "the whole body of Christ." Nisha Kuttothara, an Indian-American student at the Ave Maria School of Law, tells me she knew "from the beginning it was going to be difficult [for Ave Maria] to attract minorities, not just because it's difficult to attract minorities to many graduate programs, but because it's a new school and a religiously affiliated school, which is also different." As Nisha points out, recruiting racial minorities adds another layer to an already pretty specific set of requirements—strong religious belief, good academic qualifications, and the ability to afford a college or law school education.

Moreover, the presence of minorities in some religious groups is particularly rare anyway. Of the approximately 35,000 students at Brigham Young, there are fewer than two hundred blacks.

"That raises concern from people," notes one African-American student at BYU. But that statistic is hardly surprising given the tiny pool of black Mormons in America. Similarly, the number of black Catholics in the United States is relatively small. As a result, it is difficult for schools like Notre Dame and Brigham Young to attract African-Americans while at the same time maintaining the schools' high percentage of people who count themselves members of the school's faith. (Of course, in the case of Mormons, the Church has only itself to blame for the problem since it did not allow blacks to become full members, to "receive the holy priesthood," until 1978, when a new "revelation" made it possible.) Finally, the growing, but still small, population of Hispanic evangelicals makes it difficult for schools like Wheaton, Gordon, and Westmont to attract from this population.

Though Baylor and Fordham do not face this same problem because they admit significant numbers of both Protestants and Catholics, they also have some hurdles to overcome in achieving racial diversity. The minority populations of these strongly religious groups are often concentrated among recent immigrants and working-class families, but children from these families would not normally be on track to attend top-ranked colleges. As senior Kevin Lewis observes of Westmont, "It's such a high-priced school and the majority of people who have that class status are Caucasian." This is an area where religious colleges have been able to make some headway through scholarships. Notre Dame, for instance, has recently increased its financial aid budget sevenfold to $36 million. And the administration at Baylor has just announced a tuition hike of 28 percent, some proceeds of which will be used to dramatically increase scholarship money.

But money is not enough. Religious colleges need to make it onto the radar screens of minority high school students. Notre Dame tries to do this by taking advantage of the network of inner-city Catholic high schools to recruit its freshman class. Evangelical colleges usually take a different route because even though there are a growing number of evangelical elementary and high schools, the epicenter of life for evangelical youth is still in the churches, specifically the youth groups. A few years ago, Gordon College, for instance, started building a relationship with the Emanuel Gospel Center in Boston. According to admissions director Vazquez, the center received funding from the Pew Charitable Trust and Nellie Mae (a federally subsidized provider of college loans) to start higher education resource centers in Lawrence, Dorchester, Lynn, Brockton, and Worcester, Massachusetts, where students may come to research and prepare their college applications. Gordon has also become involved in a program called the College Support Initiative, which, Vazquez tells me, "seeks to identify Christian youth in the city, attract them to the Gordon campus, and then offer them support once they are here."

In many cases, the connections with inner-city churches that are needed to start such programs are already there. The missionary work of students at Westmont in nearby Los Angeles, for example, provides some of these bridges. Students who go on that school's "Spring Break in the City" work with the homeless and tutor in after-school programs. Tim Sisk, the director of the Office of Christian Outreach at Wheaton College near Chicago, understands that the school has to be careful about the attitudes students take with them into these service programs, at least in part because his school wouldn't mind getting some of the minority kids they work with to apply for admission eventually.

"In the ministry office," Sisk says, "we try to do cross-cultural training. We want them to go out there not with a white savior mentality, but as a learner, someone who can learn a lot from other cultures and be a better person." This model can also work in reverse. In other words, if students encounter minorities among their fellow classmates and professors, they will be less likely to adopt a "white savior" mentality when they go out to do their missionary work.

While many religious colleges are sufficiently far from the cities that they must make a concerted effort to build these bridges, others, like Fordham, find themselves in the middle of working-class neighborhoods. Fordham does have some outreach programs (like the Bronx Educational Alliance, which partners students in the graduate school of education with local eighth graders), but the effort to connect with minority populations does not need to be so intentional. As junior Erin Zuccaro puts it, "The campus's location makes for diversity. When you go off campus at Fordham, you are not in the rolling hills of the midwest. You're in a really vibrant urban ethnic neighborhood."

Bernard Stratford, the school's dean of students, explains that aside from its large minority commuter population, Fordham can attract minorities from other areas, too. "If you take an African-American kid from California, I think they like walking down Fordham Road and seeing people of color." Similarly, there is a relatively large minority population in the Virginia Beach area surrounding Regent University. Of the 824 Regent University graduates in 2003, 22 percent were black, 8 percent were Asian/Pacific Islander, and 3 percent were Hispanic. Still, that diversity is concentrated much more in Regent's (much less competitive) education school than in its law school.

Another factor in encouraging minority students to attend a religious college (or a secular one) is the extent to which minorities are represented on the faculty. Whether or not having minority role models improves educational performance, the current wisdom is that their presence makes nonwhite students more comfortable. John Drake points to a front page *Lariat* story about Baylor's seven black professors, complaining that there is a lot of apathy on the issue of faculty diversity. "I don't know that the [small number] really bothers a lot of people." Drake, who was president of the black students' association last year, says it bothered that group. "There has been no movement," he says, "no storming [the president's] door and saying 'Hey, we need to get this campus more diverse.' That just hasn't happened."

Many religious colleges, though, have instituted faculty affirmative action programs. At Calvin, for instance, there is an arrangement in place to pay for the graduate education of minority Calvin students who come back to teach. According to professor Corwin Smidt, "For every two years of funding, they would come teach for one year at Calvin." The program is only a few years old but Smidt laments that it's not as successful as they had hoped. He does volunteer that the school has a "longer standing rule which says that if any department can find a qualified North American minority—qualified in the sense of religiously qualified plus academically qualified—you can hire that person without demonstration of a need in the department. And when the first tenured vacancy in the department that becomes available, that person slips in."

Cheri Larsen Hoeckley, a literature professor at Westmont, describes a similar policy that used to exist there. But Hoeckley adds, "When I checked around, I was disappointed to learn that the policy is not currently being funded."

Many religious college leaders believe that minority faculty serve an important role for the majority students. Rodney Sisco, the director of minority affairs at Wheaton, who is black, explains. "Because many of our students have come from settings where they haven't had a lot of interaction with adult professionals of color, they have not had to challenge some of the assumptions they have. Here they encounter 'Dr. So and So' who is on top of his or her field, and wonder whether 'maybe some of the things I used to think are problematic.'" This idea that adding faculty diversity is not only for the benefit of the minority students but also for the majority is common at secular schools as well, but religious college administrators argue that students' ability to relate to minorities, either professors or fellow students, could influence their ability to proselytize effectively.

"People will see a wider range of human beings," Baylor English professor Tom Hanks tells me regarding the importance of faculty diversity. "They often think they alone are the way things are supposed to be and everyone else is a stranger." Hanks describes how he did not get over that attitude until he started interacting regularly with people of other ethnic backgrounds. "I was raised in a culture where African-Americans were barely human, certainly second rate." And Hanks adds, oddly, that he is still "making his way out of that."

But hiring minority faculty, or directors of minority affairs, or even orchestrating extensive outreach efforts, may not be enough to get these colleges the diverse student bodies they long for. Wheaton professor P. J. Hill sums up the situation. "You can only go so far in trying to recruit and quite frankly, minorities with high SATs are pretty valuable to lots of colleges."

"While I would like for us to have more minorities, if we don't get them I'm going to work with what I have," he says.

Hill tells me he "would prefer not to have affirmative action policies. I think they can be very harmful if they go too far because they mismatch colleges with students in terms of their abilities and then you reinforce particular stereotypes." But others, like Sisco, resent this kind of speculation and wonder why minority recruitment always makes people think there will be a lowering of standards.

Whether or not Sisco is right about the views of white students toward affirmative action, and whether they have any basis for thinking that recruiting students of color means a "lowering of standards," his concern about the students' racial attitudes once they are on campus is an important one, not to be overlooked in all the discussion of student admissions. Indeed, Wheaton senior Noel Jabbour tells me that he thinks it's good that his school is trying to gain a more diverse student body, but thinks it should focus more on "how we can appreciate the diversity we already have."

Though the atmosphere at Baylor, for example, has obviously improved dramatically for minorities over the last forty years, there are those on campus who believe that discrimination still rears its head in campus affairs. John Drake tells me of a recent controversy over the construction of a pan-Hellenic house on campus. As Drake explains it, the eight white sororities will all have space in the building, but because the four black sororities and the two Asian ones do not have the money to contribute, they will be excluded (though they will have access to the public eating area and computer lab). Baylor administrators defend the decision by telling me that the "white" sororities do include minority students, but still, Drake says, "The existence of this building is separatist and Baylor is contributing to all this." Nonetheless, taking account of the larger picture on campus, he acknowledges that there are few complaints from minority students about the way they're treated on campus.

In fact, campus opinion at Baylor is probably typified more by sophomore Jenny Ebbeling, who tells me that she only sees the importance of diversity insofar as students might feel more comfortable around people of the same ethnicity. She explains, "I wouldn't want people who want to get a good Baptist education not to come here because they couldn't find a group."

But Dharmpal Vansadia has observed that very situation: "I have known people who have left because they could not fit in. They couldn't find a group that reflected their values and views." Thinking about the problem for a moment, he adds, "I can see how a black person wouldn't feel comfortable here."

Despite her concerns that all students should feel welcome to get their education at Baylor, Jenny, who is not a part of a minority group, doesn't think that racial diversity should be a high priority for Baylor. "I just think MTV has done such a good job of saying, 'We don't care what race you are.'" Citing as an example of this new political atmosphere the 2003 ballot initiative in California to take the race question off the census, Jenny asks pointedly, "If race is not an issue, why do we care?"

Some students of color share her attitude, adding that they are quite comfortable at religious colleges, even if they are in an extreme minority. Nisha Kuttothara, who is in the first graduating class at the Ave Maria School of Law, is one of just a couple of minority students. "Being here two years now, I'm comfortable with everyone," she tells me. "My fear in the beginning was, 'Am I going to feel like I don't belong or I'm not accepted?' But it didn't happen like that. I think that comes from the whole broad religious basis here. If you're in a Christian school, you're taught to love and accept people for who they are."

There is a considerable amount of disagreement about how faith affects race relations on religious campuses. Ade Brayboy, an African-American student at Regent University's education school, tells me enthusiastically that he does not think race relations on campus are a problem. "The common bond is that we're brought together for a single purpose of the gospel. I'm blessed to be here. I've encountered nothing but a positive experience. I wouldn't trade it for any place else." Some of the students and faculty even offer a utopian-sounding view of the relationship among ethnic groups on campus—like Megan McGrail, the president of the college union at Wheaton, who tells me, "Above and beyond color, we are all brothers and sisters in Christ," and Leslie Clark, who believes that "as a Christian community, we should look forward to how it will be in heaven, where there will be no biases or racism."

In at least one of its goals—creating a microcosm for racial integration that could be taken into American society at large—affirmative action has hardly been a success story. It is difficult to fully explain why, but many critics of the policy have observed that once diversity becomes the overriding concern of a school's administration, then students increasingly see their racial or ethnic identity as their defining characteristic and want to be with other people who share that feature rather than integrating themselves into the community. Michael Beaty accurately warns that, "diversity for its own sake often leaves you with a kind of disunity." He suggests, "You don't have any way of getting these groups together." But what if there were another unifying characteristic to offset the ethnic divisions? Can faith facilitate assimilation at religious colleges?

Even if one does not expect religious schools to be perfect models of racial and ethnic harmony, the idea that a common bond of faith should help bridge differences among ethnic groups seems intuitive. In reality, though, the vast majority of students and faculty I interview express, with a marked sadness, that religious colleges seem no different from secular colleges with respect to race relations on campus. Crystal Twitty, a black law student at Regent University, thinks she was "naïve" when she first arrived on campus, believing "everyone would be nice and friendly because it's a Christian school. But it's not the case." Personally, she has not found it "hard to cross color lines," but looking at the larger picture, she worries, "We are not as integrated as we should be, especially [given the fact that] we are at a Christian university. I haven't seen as many blacks associating with whites as I would have thought given that we have [our faith] in common."

"There is not enough comingling," says John Drake of Baylor. "The races don't relate as much as they need to and student groups aren't doing enough to facilitate that. The office of student life isn't doing enough." But even religious life itself can hinder integration. On Sundays, Wheaton administrator Rodney Sisco acknowledges, you will see students attending the church most closely associated with their ethnicity. "Some churches are intentionally multi-ethnic, but very few."

When I ask Fordham student Erin Zuccaro about race relations, she acknowledges that people "tend to stay within their comfort zones" and her school is no different than anywhere else in this respect. Still, she asserts, "I don't see Fordham as a segregated campus [since] a lot of students overlap. Even if people aren't best friends," she insists, "they're still acquainted with people who come from different backgrounds." Other Fordham students, however, cite the "commuter-resident divide" as a cause for racial self-segregation (since the commuter population includes a much greater percentage of minorities). The school has instituted various programs in place to break down this wall, but most students report they have had little success.

"I think [our school] has a lunch-table problem," Baylor English professor Tom Hanks tells me frankly. "For the most part, black students stay with blacks, Asians stay with Asians, and WASPs stay with WASPs." He adds, "This doesn't surprise me but it troubles me." In this sentiment, Hanks is hardly alone: Self-segregation at religious colleges concerns many students and faculty, but few can explain it. And just as at secular colleges, there is a sense of hopelessness in combating it.

Is it a lost cause? In part, yes. There is certainly an extent to which religious colleges cannot overcome the racialized social environment in which they exist. Secular society's attitudes about race are bound to permeate the walls of these schools. While for the last few decades, that has been undoubtedly positive, causing schools like Bob Jones to change their backward policies, the politically correct attitude that race should be the defining characteristic of a person, influencing every aspect of their character, is one that religious colleges could probably do without. But the schools' own acknowledgment that members of a particular ethnic group are best suited to bring its other members into the fold supports secular society's tacit message that only people of the same race can truly understand each other and can therefore communicate best with each other.

Even if a college is determined to downplay this idea, it is hard to discourage self-segregation. Except within the strictest environments, college administrations do not monitor where students sit at lunch or where they attend church on Sunday. But what about the other facets of college life? Are administrators placing enough emphasis on the unifying religious message of the school or are they advertising the divisive racial one?

Calvin College seems to be leaning toward the latter with its "Mosaic Floor" in one of the dormitories. Senior Mariano Avila tries to explain the theory behind this arrangement to me as we zip around town in his compact car with a press pass from the local paper swinging from the rearview mirror: "It's one floor in a dorm where minorities are kind of invited to live, and you get a tuition cut if you live there. Then, once or twice a week, you have to talk about racism." He estimates that approximately a hundred people live there, a significant population on a campus with only a little more than three hundred minority students.

Avila, who has some interaction with students on this floor through his participation in the Latino student group on campus, was so upset by what he saw as institutional segregation that he complained to the school's president. He relates to me what he said in that meeting: "This is like apartheid." Since the dorm is on the edge of campus, Avila says no one who doesn't live there ever goes over there. "That group becomes so strong as a group that they don't need to interact with nonminorities."

When I ask him how often he goes to the Mosaic Floor, Avila sighs and explains that members of a number of different ethnic groups do their cooking in the same kitchen there.

"Bottom line, that place stinks," he says.

But the biggest problem Avila sees is with the group's meetings. "The people are kind of hostile because they're forced to talk about racism once a week. So of course they're going to think they're being attacked by the racist white man."

At other colleges, programs that try to encourage diversity by separating a minority population from the other students have incurred similar criticism from students and similar defense from faculty and administration. A couple of years ago the assistant provost at Gordon, herself an African American, tried to start a minority-only gospel choir. Sitting in her new-looking on-campus apartment with board games scattered on the floor, Laura Johnson, the editor of the school's newspaper, the *Tartan*, recalls the controversy: "The whole issue of the choir is reverse discrimination. Shouldn't we be integrating rather than separating?" When the *Tartan* exposed the plan for the choir, the uproar on campus was so great that the administration had to open it up to everyone. Mia Chung, an artist in residence at Gordon who teaches piano, seems to have mixed feelings about the incident. She is on the school's diversity committee and attends a church in Boston, in part because there are so many different ethnic groups there, but suggests that perhaps excluding whites from the choir was a little extreme. "We always have to walk a fine line," she concludes. "We have to use our best judgment all the time."

In terms of the students' residential and extracurricular lives, it seems as though religious colleges are encountering the same self-segregation problems as secular schools, at least in part because they are pursuing similar policies. A recent study of college campuses by the New York Civil Rights Commission concludes that, "Segregated housing, courses, and programs disseminate poisonous stereotypes and falsehoods about race and ethnicity." Moreover, its authors claim that such programs "limit interaction between minority and nonminority students, and reward separatist thinking. . . . Although they claim to have minorities' interests at heart, [the administrators responsible for these programs] in fact take the civil-rights movement giant steps backward."

Even if they make the same missteps as secular colleges in attempting to make minority students feel more comfortable, religious colleges may be at something of an advantage in combating racial self-segregation, having at their disposal other means of fostering campus unity that secular colleges do not, like chapel programs. These generally mandatory, but always well attended, meetings of the student body that take place between one and five times a week and offer some combination of spiritual and intellectual stimulation could be an effective means for communicating the priorities of a single unifying religious identity over multiple racial ones. Unfortunately, they are rarely used in this way.

Most of the evangelical colleges have occasional chapel sessions devoted to some multicultural theme or another. At Calvin, where chapel attendance is not mandatory, there is a gospel-style chapel meeting once a week, which minority students regularly attend even if they don't come on any of the other days. Laura tells me she doesn't mind the different musical styles or presentations about other cultures, but she is frustrated that some of Gordon's chapel meetings force the issue of diversity on students. "I leave feeling guilty for being white and middle class." But, she assures me, "I'm thankful I'm here and thankful for the opportunities I have."

Clement Wen, who is the student vice president in charge of diversity at Wheaton, expresses a similar resentment toward his school's chapel program. Clement, a Chinese American, becomes agitated as we talk in an old-fashioned booth inside the school's snack bar. "We get a speaker who comes in and says, 'You guys are type A and you are type B. And type A, you're trash because you treat type B badly. And type B, you're helpless. And then they try to get one side to feel guilty." In other words, he concludes, "The speakers categorize students into the white majority with a history of oppression and all the people of color who can't do anything about it and are depending on the white majority." What bothers Clement most about the situation, though, is that the chapel guest lecturers come in and "lay this big guilt trip and then they go away." The attitude of the speakers, he believes, is, "'I don't care if I get invited back. I'm just here to stir things up.'"

Clement has brought this complaint to the chaplain along with his worry that his fellow students "see someone of color on stage and think, 'Oh man, this is going to be about diversity again.' I'd love to see them bring in people of color to speak about everyday stuff." Chapel programs where minorities speak about the Christian faith, for example, instead of their particular culture might alter the racial situation on campus. In the meantime, Clement believes that Wheaton is behind most other schools in dealing with racial tension, and he tells me, "After five years of being here, I don't want to be in another Christian environment."

Though it seems that religious college administrators have squandered dormitory arrangements, extracurricular life, and chapel as opportunities for creating religious unity among different races and ethnicities on campus, there is one final facet of campus life that still serves this purpose. The strong core curricula found at religious schools, including rigorous theology requirements, may help the students see more of the similarities than differences among them. Such traditional curricula also tend away from the "multicultural" aspects of secular college educations. Students at religious colleges can rarely major in African-American Studies or take most of their classes on Asian-American literature. It is Baylor student John Drake who brings up this distinguishing feature of religious colleges, interestingly, by complaining about it. At Baylor, he tells me, "I think they're trying to create this common experience academically. There are a lot of classes that everyone has to take: the Great Text series, the religion requirement, which includes biblical heritage and Christian scripture. . . . The overall vision is to take away choice [from students], to say this is the experience everyone will have at Baylor." One can't help but wonder, though, whether that common experience is such a bad thing.

CHAPTER NINE

SEX, DRUGS, AND ROCK 'N' ROLL:
HOW STUDENT LIFE IS DIFFERENT
AT RELIGIOUS COLLEGES

In 2003, Yaacov Weinstein and Gil Perl took some time off from their graduate study at Harvard to produce an eleven-page monograph called "A Parent's Guide to Orthodox Assimilation on University Campuses." The two warn that the atmosphere at secular schools—from the classroom, where students are taught that the Torah was not divinely authored and that Israel shouldn't exist, to the dormitory, where the abundance of sex, drugs, and alcohol has now come to include officially sponsored "lingerie study breaks" and "pornography clubs"—encourages young Orthodox Jews to compromise or abandon their faith. Weinstein and Perl observe that even the campus Jewish organizations "often place Orthodox kids in un-*halachic* [contrary to Jewish law] social situations."

Promiscuity, or at least "sexual awareness," has become part of a college education promoted by the administration at secular schools. While she was a student at Williams College, Wendy Shalit wrote an article in *Commentary* describing the meeting in which the residents of her dormitory voted to make the bathrooms coed. When Shalit objected to the idea, "The other girls actually seem[ed], for a moment, to take her part, as the poor benighted miss surrounded by a pack of worldlings patting her on the back, flattering and reassuring her. 'Don't worry, I was just like you once,' one of them [began] condescendingly, smiling with the smug authority of the victorious. 'And then . . . I became COMFORTABLE WITH MY BODY.'" After Shalit is embarrassed into going along with the decision, "The resident advisers," she notes, "take this opportunity to announce that if anyone has problems with the coed bathroom, please do come and talk with them—there are any number of good campus counselors at 'Psych Services.'"

And if you're crazy not to want to share a bathroom with a member of the opposite sex, why not a *bedroom*? Several schools, like Haverford College, have recently added the option of coed dorm rooms as a way of accommodating homosexual students who don't feel comfortable living with someone to whom they might be sexually attracted. Of course, since the schools involved would never question students about their sexual orientation, the policy gives a free pass for heterosexual couples to live together. Few administrators feel as though they have any basis for protesting such an arrangement. Tufts University president John DiBiaggio was able to muster only this half-hearted explanation for his rejection of the idea: "I'm not saying that we are prudish. We are not acting in loco parentis. But we are dealing with life-threatening venereal diseases here."

With administrators backed into a corner like this, unable even to seem like they are taking a moral stance, students at secular universities continue to push the envelope. Life on most college campuses remains defined by the 1960s mantra that college is the time for students to get out from under the thumb of their parents and "experiment."

Rich Powers, the dean of students at Wheaton College, who used to work at a public university in Illinois, recalls how, shortly after arriving in his current job, he telephoned one of his former colleagues. "I asked how are things going, and the person I talked to said, 'Oh man, somebody shot off a gun in his apartment the other day and campus police just had to bust a prostitution ring.'" Powers acknowledges that Wheaton is far from perfect, "but the issues here by and large pale by comparison."

Religious college students generally seem to avoid the kind of trouble that puts secular campuses in the headlines. There are certain exceptions, of course, but on the whole, religious campuses are devoid of the alcohol, drugs, sexual activity, and violence that plague many secular universities. "We have our challenges," says Powers. "We want students to think as critically outside classroom as they do inside of it. We want them to make wise decisions which are honoring to the Lord and good for them and the community."

How do they do it? First, and most importantly, religious college kids *want* to be in this environment. Only a small minority of the students I spoke with claimed their parents told them they had to attend a religious college. Carri Jenkins, who is in charge of public relations at Brigham Young, tells me why over lunch with a few other administrators and faculty:

Many of these students have been in a high school where they are the only one who is a member of the Church of Jesus Christ, and they are tired of having to constantly defend who they are. They want to have fun without getting drunk. This is freedom for them. They come here and they can be who they want to be. They can live their principles.

170

Second, religious college leaders have no problem acting in loco parentis. In fact, the parents themselves often become involved. At Calvin, for instance, there is a parental notification policy for any alcohol use on campus or any other disciplinary infraction. "We've found that to be very effective," says administrator Shirley Hoogstra. "We think that a parent is a partner in the process in terms of discipline."

Administrators at religious colleges, not surprisingly, take a religious approach to discipline. Professor Scott Moore notes that if a Baylor student violates a rule, "any action taken would be redemptive." Most of the adults on these campuses agree that human beings are sinners, prone to make mistakes, and, within limits, it's the job of the college to help set them on the right course, rather than simply kick them out.

Powers explains, "We will hold students accountable for choices, but do it in a gracious fashion, not a punitive fashion." Wheaton's student body president Noel Jabbour finds the administration's attitude useful. "They ask 'How can we help this person to get through what he has done, and explore the reason why he did it?'" Administrators believe the key to successful discipline is creating an environment in which students will come for help before they are caught violating some rule, "when they reach a point where they feel like they are not in control."

Steve Baker, the director of BYU's honor code office, boasts that fewer than 1 percent of students are ever brought to see him. One reason for this is that problems are often handled in a religious context—with a student approaching his bishop or vice versa—before they ever get to the university offices. If a disciplinary infraction does come to the attention of the administration, the student can choose to involve his or her bishop as an advocate. Baker emphasizes that the student is entitled to the "ecclesiastical confidential relationship that no one else is privy to."

Ultimately, religious college administrators are a lot like parents when it comes to the issues of sexuality or the use of alcohol. They offer guidance and help in the process of character formation, which sometimes includes punishment, but more importantly, they are also supposed to prepare their charges for the world outside. Most religious college students do not live in a vacuum. They are aware of how secular culture views dating, sex, marriage, homosexuality, drinking, drugs, and smoking. On some issues their faith may provide clear guidelines regarding what is expected of them in these regards. Mormons, for example, are not allowed to smoke under any circumstances. But in other cases, the gray area is more significant. Are young evangelicals allowed to kiss? To what extent are Catholic students supposed to drink?

How are people with homosexual impulses supposed to be treated? It is the job of religious colleges to help their graduates make these decisions.

Administrators and faculty at religious college tend to agree that the place to start addressing these issues is in the dormitories. Most strongly religious schools have stuck with the relic of single-sex dorms. Many students note they are not comfortable sharing their bedrooms and bathrooms with members of the opposite sex. Moreover, they like the fact that they don't have a "third roommate" (the problem created when a roommate's significant other stays over regularly). Lauren Whitnah, a sophomore at Gordon College, was skeptical of the dorm rules, but says she is now grateful for them. "If my roommate was coming in drunk or with her boyfriend, I had recourse to say, 'That's not okay with me and not okay with the school.' I felt like there would really be someone that would back me up."

Kelly Pascual, a sophomore psychology major at Notre Dame, likes the single-sex dorms because they foster close friendships. Eighty-five percent of the university's student body lives on campus, and there is a general agreement about the positive effects of single-sex dorms. Erica Hayman, a junior, tells me that before she came to Notre Dame, she always wanted to live next door to a guy, and when she arrived freshman year she was irritated to find that on the weekends she could go six or seven hours without seeing one. Since then, though, she has learned to appreciate the value of the living arrangements. She notes, "Notre Dame wouldn't be Notre Dame without single-sex dorms."

The university's visiting hours are, however, some of the most liberal at religious colleges. Members of the opposite sex are allowed in the dorms until midnight on weekdays and two A.M. on weekends.

Few leaders of religious colleges are of the opinion that they can prevent all sexual activity among the students. Instead, most religious college leaders use dorm life as a means of student "formation." What is meant by formation, of course, varies from school to school. At Baylor, it involves a willingness on the part of the administration to adopt behavioral standards, but no one is checking the beds each night.

Some schools have adopted an almost military approach to formation, on the theory that breeding certain habits in students will build character. This has produced mixed results. At Bob Jones, where women and men are not allowed any kind of physical contact, the school's rules may be strict enough to minimize such incidents, but as most administrators will tell you, where there's a will there's a way. Even at Thomas Aquinas College, where students live on a mountaintop, spend almost all their waking hours studying, have a curfew of eleven P.M., and no visitation hours, a young woman was caught having an affair with a married man in a nearby town a few years ago.

At seven thirty on a cold, rainy morning in late April, the chapel at Magdalen, a small Catholic college in rural New Hampshire, is more than half full, most of its students and faculty (all attired, in accordance with the school's dress code, in either coats and ties of muted colors or long skirts and modest blouses) sitting in silence for the fifteen minutes before mass begins. Candles are lit on the altar just as the lights come up in the chapel. Two male students sitting in the third to last row check their voices against a pitch pipe and begin to lead the congregation in song. There is no organ at first, but the congregation's a cappella sounds almost professional. Though the service is slightly more elaborate today because it is the week following Easter, daily mass at Magdalen usually lasts close to an hour.

By the time students leave the chapel to line up for breakfast, where their seats are assigned (differently each day, so as to avoid the formation of cliques), they have made their beds and tidied their rooms. Clothes must be folded neatly, there can be no clutter on desks or dressers, and decorations on the walls are not permitted. Students also carry around an extra pair of shoes with them, and change whenever they walk into a building so that they do not soil the floors. That rule is easily enforced since students themselves do most of the campus cleaning.

"I thought it was crazy, nuts, and bizarre when I came here," says Mark Gillis, who graduated from Magdalen in 1990, and is now a professor there. Gillis, whose parents told him he could either go to Magdalen or be kicked out of the house, remembers his reaction to the school's ten thirty lights-out policy: "I would lie awake for hours. It was like detox." But one day during the spring of his first year, Gillis recalls, "I realized I was happy." Even the students who are forced by their parents to attend, Gillis believes, come to like it eventually. "As you mature, you begin to appreciate things being more or less organized. . . . It's good habits. It's character formation. It's Aristotle."

Magdalen also has the strictest policy with regard to dating—it's not allowed. The rule is actually against "steady company keeping" and most students come to like it after some time. Nancy Carlin, a senior, explains,

The rule makes perfect sense to me. It has allowed me to have deeper friendships with guys than ever before in my life. There was a sense in

*high school that if you sit down with a guy you are attached at the hip.
They will think, "You are mine and I possess you." It's so freeing to be able
to sit at a table with a guy for an hour after lunch and not have people
think you must be dating. [The rule against coupling] fosters a sense of
self-giving.*

"Whereas dating makes your world shrink to about this big," Carlin notes,
holding her thumb and forefinger an inch apart, "it seems love should open
your world."

Many Magdalen students do get married shortly after graduation, and
Carlin thinks they have a better idea of whom they're marrying as a result of
the no-dating rule. "It's pretty easy when you're going out to dinner and a
movie with a guy that you just put on a front."

But at a place like Magdalen?

"It's much easier here to get to know someone. You are part of a group of
friends and you see how they react with other people." Carlin, who grew up
in a family with ten children, thinks that the best reason for putting off dating is that you have a better chance of getting into a solid marriage instead of
a relationship based only on self-gratification.

Both Bob Jones University and Patrick Henry College have strict rules
about dating, as well. PHC requires students to get their parents' permission
before pursuing a romantic relationship, and BJU requires chaperones for all
dates. Though evangelical schools generally allow dating, some of their students have been attracted to the ideas in a recent popular book called *I
Kissed Dating Goodbye*—which advocates that young people put off any kind
of romantic relationship until they are ready for marriage.

Regardless of their rules on dating, all of the schools in this book try to
monitor sexual activity on campus, starting with hugging and kissing. At
Thomas Aquinas, students are prohibited from engaging in any public displays of affection because the administrators believe it is harmful to the formation of community. At Brigham Young University, on the other hand, such
displays are ubiquitous. Even during the "fireside" talks given by leaders of
the church on Sunday evenings in the sports arena, couples are holding hands
and men have their arms around their girlfriends' shoulders. There is a strange
slow movement everywhere you look as students stroke each other's hair, arms,
and faces.

But BYU students do take seriously the rule against premarital sex. Since
most of the students live in off-campus housing, the rule is enforced primarily
through peer pressure. Minji Cho, who only recently converted to Mormonism

and experimented with sex in high school, tells me, "I realized that if I went to a public university there would be a lot of . . . temptation for me. I didn't want to necessarily be around Mormons; anyone with clean morals would have been fine." Knowing how she is struggling, Minji's roommates keep a motherly eye on her.

Like Minji, most religious college students seem thankful they will not have to confront the sorts of sexual pressures they would at secular schools. Rachel Stahl, a sophomore at Gordon, tells me she looks forward to going out with guys there. "I have dated people who aren't Christian and sex is all they want."

But are these students really abstaining from sex? When I asked that question to a gathering of Southern Virginia University faculty about their Mormon students, there was a lot of giggling, and several noted that there would hardly be such an intense obsession with getting married early if students were having sexual contact outside of marriage.

At most of the colleges, though, there is a contingent of students who are not living by the code of sexual conduct. Rev. Mark Poorman, the vice president for student affairs at Notre Dame, is not sure about the percentage of undergrads engaging in sexual activity. He posits that it's rather small, but notes that if the administration finds out about such behavior "from a credible source," they will challenge it.

Indeed, even at schools where students are not watched as closely as they might be at Magdalen or Bob Jones, sexual activity is not flaunted thanks to peer pressure and administrations that are clear about their standards. But an atmosphere where premarital sex is considered shameful and not to be discussed can also encourage what Abby Diepenbrock, a codirector of the Center for Christian Concerns at Westmont, calls "hypocrisy."

"Christian schools and religious schools in general," she says, "have a reputation for saying one thing and then behaving in a different way."

Abby senses that many of her fellow students feel guilty about this disconnect between their words and actions. "You can tell in conversation. People start talking about something that's a little questionable. I hear a lot of people saying, 'Oh, we couldn't do that if Jake were around,'" referring to her codirector. Abby asks, "What does Jake matter? What about the Lord?"

Ben Patterson, Westmont's chaplain, has been surprised by the kinds of things his charges are engaged in.

In areas of [sexual] morality, students are very much affected by their feelings, more than any sense of dogma. . . . It's pretty scary around here how many professing Christian students who are really seriously believers split off there. What they will do . . . in intimate relationships [is] so off the edge. I was at [the evangelical] Hope College for four years and I talked to students periodically who wanted to clean up their sex lives, to get themselves in line with their faith. . . . It took me four years to realize what they meant by that. They weren't having intercourse, but they were doing absolutely anything else. And it just one day dawned on me. Oh heavens. I thought they meant they had very high standards, but they didn't. They went right up to that. That was the only thing left to do. . . . [Westmont students] are in the same place. They'll say, "I feel close. I'm not just doing it with anybody. I care deeply."

The solution to these kinds of moral slip-ups, according to students and faculty, may be early marriage. The median age at which college-educated women marry has increased dramatically in the last few decades. But at most religious schools, getting married young is encouraged, if not expected. (Even at Notre Dame, a number of the seniors remark on their many friends who plan to marry shortly after graduation.) "Ring by spring"—that is, getting engaged by the spring of senior year—is a mantra at almost every school I visit. And there is always a rash of weddings right after graduation.

Because the vast majority of evangelical students do not get married while in college, they use a number of traditions to signify to each other the seriousness of their commitment. Christian Bell and Beth Heinen, the editors of the Calvin newspaper, who are themselves engaged, explain to me the various stages of courtship at Calvin, from the opal, which is the pre-pre-engagement ring, to the pearl, the pre-engagement ring, to the actual engagement ring. (Beth acknowledges that when she heard about the opal, "I was like, 'You've got to be joking.'")

In the Mormon community, courtship does not have so many stages because students often get married while in school, and after a relatively short period of dating. The high rate of marriage among students or recent graduates of religious colleges may be inevitable. Students are, often for the first time, placed in a pool of people their own age who share their beliefs and values.

But with the opportunity comes great anxiety. All of the sexual pressure that students at secular colleges might experience is transformed at religious colleges into the pressure to find a spouse. And it is compounded by the fact that many parents of religious college students found their spouses at such schools. Andrea Ludlow, a senior at BYU, who dates, "but not a ton," explains, some of her classmates "think, 'Oh if I don't get married in college, I'll never get married.'"

Paul Jalsevac, the student body president at the Catholic Christendom College, describes the temptation that arose when he first arrived at school:

You show up, and all of a sudden you discover a whole bunch of people who, well, a whole bunch of girls, who, you know, are pretty beautiful, very nice girls, who share very much the same values and morals as you, the kind of girls you very rarely run into. They are looking for the same things in a relationship and care about the same things. All that ground-work, you know, that you'd have to do back home is not necessary. You have people who actually want a real relationship. They aren't just look-ing for something physical.

The result, according to Paul, is that freshmen get very serious very quickly. "They think, 'Wow this is the perfect match.'" Laura Johnson, the editor of Gordon College's newspaper, sees a similar phenomenon among her classmates. "The guys think, 'Wow, there are Christian girls here. And they're actually cool.' They haven't seen that. The tendency is 'I have to go get that right away.'"

The pressure is also compounded by the lopsided ratio of women to men at many of these schools. Laura tells me that women often complain to her about the ratio (almost three to one at Gordon). "They say, 'I'm never going to find anyone.'"

But, laughing about the "senior scramble," Laura says, "It doesn't bother me. I know that God is going to provide the right person, here or later on in life."

When Robert Sloan, the president of Baylor, finished reading his school pa-per's editorial in favor of gay marriage in the spring of 2004, he was pretty an-gry. In a statement that garnered much more attention than the editorial itself, Sloan explained, "While we respect the right of students to hold and express divergent viewpoints, we do not support the use of publications such as the *Lariat*, which is published by the university, to advocate positions that undermine foundational Christian principles upon which this institution was founded and currently operates."

But the guy who should have really been upset is Karl Rove. Baylor is a Baptist university, serious about its commitment to the faith both inside the classroom and out, and its student body were presumably supposed among those "energized" by Bush's recently announced support of the Federal Marriage Amendment. But if the Bush campaign is searching for the 4 million evangelical voters who stayed home during the 2000 election, they should know that the editorial board of the Baylor *Lariat,* which voted five to two to support gay marriage, is not completely unrepresentative of the views of younger evangelicals.

During my visit to the school, the subject of whether a homosexual student organization should be recognized by the administration was a topic of much discussion. The faculty seems pretty averse to the idea, but among the students it was easy to find a range of opinion.

Though many students strongly oppose it, others seem agnostic.[12] James Penning, a professor at Calvin College and the coauthor with his colleague Corwin Smidt of *Evangelicalism: The Next Generation,* believes, "Students at evangelical colleges today are more likely to believe that homosexuality is something you're born with." (In fact, at no point during my visits to six evangelical colleges did anyone try to promote "conversion therapy," that is, the treatment of homosexuality as a pathology which can be "cured" by any of several controversial techniques.) Such people may be more sympathetic to the homosexual position than someone who believes it is a choice (like, say, abortion).

Smidt and Penning's book, which compares attitudes on "moral boundaries" among evangelical students in 1982 and 1996, offers some interesting statistics in this regard. While the percentage of students who believed extramarital sex was always wrong remained the same over that period of time (97 percent) and the percentage who believed premarital sex was always wrong increased (from 89 to 92 percent), the proportion who thought homosexual relations were wrong actually decreased. Though it was slight (from 94 to 91 percent), Penning believes that the trend has continued in that direction since 1996 and that now there would at least be "greater openness toward civil unions."

Several factors are at work here. First, we are all products of our environment to some extent and the general public has become more accepting of homosexuality in recent years. Second, there is probably a greater awareness of the issues faced by homosexuals today, the result of more gay people being outspoken about their experiences. But the sense that homosexuals are people to be loved, and not necessarily condemned, is at least in part the

---

[12] See Chapter 6 for more on Baylor students' opinions on homosexuality.

product of current evangelical culture, and what Penning calls its "increased emphasis on grace and diminished emphasis on judgment."

Even if the atmosphere seems to be softening, it's hard to imagine how someone with homosexual inclinations would get along in an environment where the vast majority of students live by a strict code of sexual conduct and keep the goals of marriage and family in the front of their minds— let alone why that person would come in the first place.

The question of how to treat gay students was faced as far back as 1995 by Yeshiva College for Men, when a number of students petitioned the school to charter a gay club. Though similar organizations already existed at the Yeshiva University's law and medical schools, those are not generally populated by observant Jewish students. Then-university president Norman Lamm explained his dilemma this way: "As a rabbi, I cannot and do not condone homosexual behavior, which is expressly prohibited by Jewish law. But as president of a nondenominational institution that must accommodate people who reflect a wide range of backgrounds and beliefs, it is my duty to assure that the procedures of Yeshiva University conform to the applicable provisions of secular law." Despite the vocal protests of many Orthodox students, and the fact that the state's nondiscrimination law includes an exemption for religious institutions,[13] Lamm allowed the club's formation.

The issue of homosexuality arose again a few years later when a lesbian student at Yeshiva's Albert Einstein College of Medicine demanded that the administration allow her and her partner to live in the school's married student housing facilities. When the university refused, the student (and the ACLU) sued. Before the end of the trial, though, the university changed its policy to accommodate homosexual couples.

In the spring of 2000, the Yeshiva College community faced the issue of homosexuality once again when a young man running for student body president came out of the closet during a campaign speech. The campus turmoil that followed, among students and between the administration and students, was so great that Yeshiva officials eventually tried to stop all media reports on the subject.

Looking back, the current student body president, Shai Barnea, tells me he thinks the problem that most students had with the campaign was not with the candidate's homosexuality per se, but rather that he "flaunted it."

"It's one thing," Shai explains, "if it's known and you just don't say anything about it. It's another if you sort of do it . . . just to totally piss people

---

[13] See Chapter 5 for more on how this law has affected the governance of Yeshiva.

off. . . . And that's why you had the largest voter turnout ever for an election."
The gay student's opponent received the most votes ever by any candidate to
ever run for office at Yeshiva.

Chaim Nissel is Yeshiva's associate dean of students. He says, "The Orthodox world tends to be homophobic. I tell students that it's very difficult to
be openly gay in the Orthodox world. We've had students that have transferred out because they couldn't continue living a lie. And had they come out
of the closet here, they would have been shunned by their peers, as well as by
the rabbis." So what does he tell students who come to see him about their
inclinations? Nissel, who is not a proponent of "conversion therapy," says,
"Obviously, the [position of] orthodox tradition and the Jewish tradition
would be that being gay is not a sin. But the behavior is explicitly forbidden
by Jewish law. There's no way around that."

Of course, at some strongly religious colleges, students who participate
in homosexual activity are not allowed to remain on campus at all. At
Brigham Young University, for instance, two homosexual students were
expelled when their roommates reported on their behavior. For most
Catholic, Jewish, and evangelical schools, though, expulsion is rarely considered, at least for a discreet and infrequent offender. Most of these colleges encourage students and faculty to adopt a "love the sinner, hate the
sin" approach. When I ask Richard Ferrier, a tutor at Thomas Aquinas College, what he would say to a student with homosexual inclinations, he
replies, "'Then, you have a cross to bear of a more than usually difficult life
of chastity.'"

TAC's president Thomas Dillon thinks there are distinctions to be made
in determining what to do about a homosexual student.

*Here's a case where I hesitate to give blanket answer. A lot depends on the
circumstances. First I would talk to the student. Would I have any problem dismissing someone who announced they were gay? Not at all, because there are a couple of thousand colleges across the country where
they'd be very much at home. They wouldn't be at home here. If someone
said, "I have strong homosexual leanings, but I'm working against it and
don't want to engage in homosexual practices," that's a different question
than someone who said, "I think homosexuality is fine in principle." I
would be inclined to keep the first person here and not the second.*

Dillon notes that ultimately his decision would be based on two factors:
the good of individual and the protection of the community.

* * *

However delicate the administrations might be in dealing with this issue, Cheri Larsen Hoeckley, a literature professor at Westmont, worries that the atmosphere for homosexual students at religious colleges has become a problem. Hoeckley, who has known some gay students—both in and out of the closet—says, "It can be horrible for them here." She even knows some who have come to Westmont hoping to end up straight.

"We don't fix them. We can't." Hoeckley acknowledges that she differs from most of the faculty in believing that being gay and Christian are not incompatible, but she thinks there is some common ground.

"Whatever you think of homosexuality, homophobia is a sin."

In the face of the kind of ostracism and, sometimes, outright hostility that students with homosexual inclinations sometimes receive from their classmates, it is hardly surprising that many gay and lesbian students at religious colleges are taking a cue from their secular counterparts and attempting to start campus organizations. Indeed, the recognition of gay and lesbian student groups by religious college administrations has become the biggest battleground in this war.

Richard Ferrier tells me he does not think the question is likely to come up at TAC since there are no student organizations on campus to speak of. But "if they wanted to start a group, it would constitute public opposition to the Church"—something unacceptable at TAC.

At Calvin College, they are debating whether such a group should exist. According to newspaper editor Christian Bell, the administration has been doing climate studies on campus to find out how open the college environment is to homosexuals and how welcoming the people are to the idea of a group. Christian remarks that the administration is probably more concerned with the opinions of alumni donors than of the students, but "I think also on campus, they just want to ensure that it isn't going to be met with a sort of fundamentalist backlash." He predicts "that they're going to find that the campus is not yet welcoming to such a group, but that people are receptive to the idea of homosexuality itself—[students are] open and willing to talk about it."

Calvin is already different from many other evangelical schools in that its counseling center offers a support group meant for people who are struggling with how their questioning of their sexuality affects their "Christian walk." And counselors on campus do not attempt to provide therapy for the homosexual "condition." Ruth Mueller, a sophomore, who tells me she knows people at Calvin who have questioned their sexual orientation, likes the fact that Calvin has a support group. "I would like to know that if I were struggling with that," there would be someone to go to.

But it is a thin line between a group where students can seek guidance and support and an organization that appears to be condoning, if not facilitating through its social events, homosexual behavior. Heath Lambert, the president of the Gordon College Students Association, explains the problem with Gordon officially recognizing such a group.

"There are people saying we want to discuss homosexuality, its social implications, and that kind of thing, which is a perfectly justifiable thing to do," he says, "but the people starting the club were actually condoning homosexuality in their meetings."

Heath campaigned for president on this issue. "We were clear that there wouldn't be any club like that. We don't need to be hateful and ugly about it, but we do need to have an open, honest statement that this is wrong."

The debate over homosexual groups has reached a fevered pitch at the nation's Catholic universities. Notre Dame Professor David Solomon explains, "We don't allow official groups to be directly in conflict with Church teaching. There is a gay group but it is not an advocacy group. There are no dating parties. The administration doesn't try to change them, but it also doesn't promote that lifestyle." But it's pretty easy to see the slippery slope ahead. At Fordham, one of the more liberal Catholic universities, which has a fully recognized gay student group, the chaplain, Rev. Gerald Blaszczak, S.J., cites this difference between his school and a secular one: "Fordham wouldn't be a place where someone who said homosexuality is a sin would be ipso facto excluded from community. They're repeating a teaching that comes from the Magisterium of the Church. That person wouldn't be branded as a bigot."

It's possible that such a standard is the best some religious colleges can hope for in the future, but there is something odd about an administrator having to offer assurance that someone who supports the doctrine of most Christian churches would not be ostracized for doing so on a Christian campus. On the other hand, maybe it's not surprising. The administrative position on homosexuality at religious colleges is becoming increasingly defensive. For years now, the discussion has been led by students—students starting organizations, students inviting speakers to campus, and students petitioning for greater tolerance of homosexual activity, while administrators just stand on the sidelines.

Some religious college leaders have noted this is a losing strategy, and have started discussing the issue on their own terms. Gordon College, for instance, recently brought in a speaker who, according to Heath, "spent time trying to refute biblical evidence that homosexuality is a sin." But before he did so, one of the school's Bible professors gave a little introduction. He explained the Bible (and the school's) understanding of homosexuality, that it is a sin. And, then, as Heath recalls, the professor said, "'Now, as a community that is both spiritual and academic, we are going to hear the homosexual argument.'"

Administrative involvement in student life at religious colleges goes beyond sex. Like their secular counterparts, if not to the same extent, religious colleges face issue of alcohol use and abuse by students. At Brigham Young, Southern Virginia University, and Bob Jones, the rules with regard to alcohol are abundantly clear and there is little evidence that they are violated with any kind of frequency. The fact that drinking is considered not merely against school policy, but against the will of God, means that students at these schools have culturally absorbed the message and generally would not attend these schools if they did not think they could follow the rules.

Intuitively, though, it might seem that religious colleges would have problems worse than those at secular colleges. After all, if students are coming out of sheltered religious environments, where underage drinking might be even more frowned upon than in secular families, then religious students will have all the more desire to let loose when they come to college. In fact, though, most of them have been resisting such pressure for years and seem pleased to be in an environment where it's common among the students to have fun without drugs or alcohol.

But there are religions in which drinking is not viewed as sinful at all. The evangelical community has experienced a pretty big shift on this issue over the last few decades. Once strictly forbidden, it is now generally accepted. Perhaps the death knell of the alcohol taboo was heard most clearly in 2003 when Wheaton College lifted its ban on faculty drinking and smoking, along with its ban on student dancing (a subject to which we will return).

"Our wisest course," reads the Wheaton administration's statement explaining the change, "precisely because it is so fully biblical, is to draw the college's boundaries where and how the Scriptures draw them, and then stand there come what may."

But it wasn't the sudden realization that these prohibitions were not contained in scripture that resulted in the change. Rather, it was a gradual cultural shift. Mark Noll, a professor of Christian thought at Wheaton, explains the history of these rules: "They came from a time when Protestants of a more rigorous sort defined themselves against urban immigrants who had different cultures and styles. The English-based Protestants defined themselves against European immigrants," the more recent immigrants who engaged in drinking, smoking, and dancing. Some evangelical denominations, like the Assemblies of God, still find these behaviors to be sinful, but, as Chad Nicholson, the student director for orientation at Wheaton, explains to me, "If there is a group [at Wheaton] still offended by [these behaviors], it's a small minority."

In addition to the cultural shifts responsible for the elimination of the ban on faculty drinking, there was also the looming threat of legal action. It turns out that Illinois law prevents discrimination against an employee "because the individual uses lawful products off the premises of the employer during nonworking hours." There is an exception in cases that involve a "sincerely held religious belief" on the part of the institution, but since a prohibition on alcohol does not appear in the Bible (and few on campus would refrain on their own), Wheaton might have had a tough time proving that exception in court.

Perhaps more than the legal issue at stake and the desire to "contemporize" the behavioral code, as one administrator put it, faculty recruitment may have played a role. Mike Leroy, a Wheaton professor of politics and international relations, tells me that the drinking policy has "[kept] us from attracting the best faculty who have vital intellectual projects." Of the faculty who do come to Wheaton, Leroy explains, "Mostly they don't like the alcohol ban." Indeed, faculty members at other top Christian colleges express reservations about teaching at a school with such regulations.

So if drinking isn't considered sinful anymore, why are Wheaton, Gordon, Calvin, and Westmont dry campuses? (Wheaton does not allow students to drink off campus either, while the other three allow students who are twenty-one and over to do so.) For the same reason some secular colleges are: the administration worries that allowing its students to drink will be unhealthy, if not dangerous, for the community.

Heath Lambert of Gordon notes, "I think it's a careful line the school has chosen to tow, . . . [trying] to balance the Bible's commands with the freedom we have in Christ." There are rules that the college sets down because they're biblically mandated and then there are rules that benefit the community, like the campus bans on smoking and drinking. Heath thinks, "It would be easier for the administration to say, 'Here are the rules,' and micromanage the system. But that's not necessarily the best way. The rules now imply a definite responsibility on the part of the students."

Wheaton dean of students Rich Powers takes a similar approach. "Two thirds of our statement of responsibilities for students is about the lordship of Jesus Christ. Students have to realize that the Lord wants them to walk in a personal relationship with Him and respond to Him in a loving and obedient way, as opposed to responding impersonally to a list of dos and don'ts." But if you teach students that drinking alcohol in and of itself is not wrong, the question is how to get them to drink in moderation.

Thus far, binge drinking does not seem to be a significant problem at the evangelical colleges, but some of the Catholic schools, having long allowed alcohol on campus, have more experience with the problem. As Notre Dame anthropology professor Rev. Patrick Gaffney explains, there is plenty of drinking on campus and, more generally, it's very hard to escape in the Catholic world.

The alcohol at Notre Dame certainly has an effect on the educational environment. More than one professor reports students regularly coming into their Friday classes already hung over from Thursday night's parties. But there are more serious effects as well, according to Bob Groegler, a transfer student from George Washington University, who points to "ambulances coming to dorms on a more routine basis than they should be."

Students' alcohol use can obviously harm others as well. Fr. Gaffney notes that there have been a few incidents of violence and sexual abuse at Notre Dame resulting from alcohol. At Yeshiva, meanwhile, several undergraduate men were recently accused of sexually assaulting a female student from nearby Barnard College in their off-campus apartment. The details of the incident still remain unclear and the young woman ultimately decided not to press charges, but alcohol was involved (the students were celebrating the Jewish holiday of Purim). Perhaps the most shocking detail, provided by a Yeshiva administrator, is that a couple of the participants left in the middle of this scene to go recite a prayer in memory of the death of a family member of one of their fellow students.

But there are a number of religious colleges that don't have any real problems when it comes to drinking. At Thomas Aquinas College, students are not allowed to drink on campus except at official college functions (where a little wine might be served), but it does happen at a campfire in the woods nearby on Friday nights, or Saturday nights during Lent. The school's president, Thomas Dillon, makes clear that anyone who returns to campus drunk will be subject to disciplinary action. At the same time, he adds, "I can easily make a distinction between someone who goes down to have a beer and talk to someone and someone who is drunk. The second thing is out of character with our high noble aspirations."

Thomas Aquinas may have an easier situation thanks to the significant number of older students on campus. It means that more of them can drink legally, but it also means that they have fewer students away from home for the first time testing out their freedom.

In order to set the rules, the men and women who run religious colleges must act as filters for the general culture. They want to produce students who know what the tenets of their faith say about their personal behavior, who have been given enough freedom to practice making some decisions on their own, and who are strong enough to go against the grain, if necessary, when they graduate. But making judgments about secular American culture involves much more than simply knowing when and with whom to have sex and whether to drink.

In October 2002, the Indigo Girls played to a sold-out stadium at Calvin College, a school that "pledge[s] fidelity to Jesus Christ," and whose faculty and students almost all belong to an evangelical strain of the Reformed church. For anyone who has ever listened to the folk-rock group in question, the situation will seem ripe for parody. In one of their more popular numbers released a few years ago, "Shame on You," the Indigo Girls sing of a friend who tells them, "Me and Jesus, we're of the same heart. The only thing that keeps us distant is that I keep f—in' up." Though the song's message is in some sense a Christian one, there is something that usually keeps this singing duo distant from conservative Christian venues. Besides supporting leftist causes from the Zapatista rebels to Leonard Peltier, the Indigo Girls are two of the most visible and outspoken lesbians in popular culture today.

In order to deal with the seeming contradiction of its inviting the pair, Calvin organized a campus discussion on the implications of the Indigo Girls' outlook and what Christian students should make of it. Though the panel of three professors didn't exactly play to a sold-out house, the principle behind the combination of the concert and the panel—that Christian college students should be exposed to "the best" that secular culture has to offer, but should be assisted in subjecting it to critical examination through the lens of their faith—merits consideration. As Calvin's student activities director Ken Heffner explained in the campus paper, "Cultural discernment" (as the administration likes to refer to the policy) means that "Calvin College finds a way for Christians to engage with culture without becoming of it. . . . It's a way out of the trap of liberalism, which leads to no more salt and light [referring to Jesus's words to the Apostles to be "salt of the earth" and "a light to the world"], and it's also a way out of the trap of fundamentalism, which leads to separatism."

Navigating the waters between the Scylla of fundamentalism and the Charybdis of liberalism is probably the single most important issue facing religious colleges today. And the traps of each are most evident in the responses of the administration to secular culture.

To begin with the issue of music, the wholehearted embrace by evangelicals of rock music is hardly surprising given the deep influence of contemporary music on their own church services. Chapel at Westmont or Calvin, for instance, often sounds just like a folk-rock concert, with a few hallelujahs added in. And Wheaton's decision to lift its ban on dancing to contemporary music (square dances were occasionally allowed) seems to be an acknowledgment not simply of the fact that dancing is not biblically prohibited but that modern music is an integral part of evangelical culture now. Mormon students listen regularly to secular rock music, but they seem a little more aware of the lyrics of some of the music out there and tend to stay away from the harsher songs.

The music rules at Bob Jones are entirely different from other religious colleges, mostly because they are not nearly as concerned with the lyrics as they are with the musical style. (The only school that is as strict is Magdalen, where students are not allowed any sort of radio or CD players in their rooms.) The ban on listening to Christian contemporary music even while students are able to go to operas that deal with themes like adultery puzzles many students when they first arrive. But the leaders of Bob Jones realize that lyrics are not necessarily the most influential part of music. As Allan Bloom argued in *The Closing of the American Mind*, "Young people know that rock has the beat of sexual intercourse."

Rick Pidcock, a Bob Jones student who eventually wants to run a music ministry, tells me he disagrees with the music rules at Bob Jones. He tries to explain the administration's position to me. "They believe that when a person becomes born again their old nature is passed away and they get a new nature and you need to forsake your sins, and I agree. What they believe, though, is that your music needs to change as well."

But Rick does not believe that rock music is inherently un-Christian.

When he plays guitar, sings, and write songs, Rick explains, he uses some biblical principles. "A lot of music out there is kind of just there to work up an emotional experience. It doesn't have that much real truth in it. The Bible says we need to communicate truth, but it also says we need to sing with grace in our hearts to the Lord. When you really have a grasp on all that Christ has done for you and you really ponder it, you're going to naturally sing about it in a passionate emotional way, but in a way that is rooted in the truth."

Bob Jones students are shielded from secular culture by an administration that discourages not just listening to certain kinds of music but also going to the movies and watching television. Like Bob Jones, Christendom, Thomas Aquinas, and Magdalen all ban televisions in the dorms and offer guidance to students regarding what movies are acceptable. At Christendom, for instance, students are not allowed to watch R-rated movies. PG-13 is acceptable if the rating is the result of language, but if it's the result of sexual content, the movie must be approved by the RA.

Mormons are not supposed to watch R-rated movies at all. (When I ask a professor at Southern Virginia University about Orrin Hatch's cameo appearance in the R-rated Traffic, he suggests that maybe Hatch didn't see the rest of the movie.) As Edwin Sexton, the vice president for academic affairs at SVU, notes,

> There is enough vulgarity that we are exposed to living in the world going through day to day life, that I would say that the typical person here at SVU is not seeking to expose themselves to additional things that would be offensive to them on a routine basis. Probably most of students here don't go to R-rated movies, I hope. Sexual innuendo and swearing and graphic violence—I don't believe those type of things are uplifting or ennobling.

Faculty members at SVU and some other schools find religious rules based on the rating system a little strange, if not silly, since the ratings can be changed at any time by people who have nothing to do with the Church, and have grown more and more lenient in recent years. Nonetheless, the administrators argue, they have to draw the line somewhere.

But there are so many ways for the messages and values of secular culture to seep into a religious college, it's hard for these communities not to become overprotective. At SVU, a faculty member was forced to write the word "whore" out of a student production of *Man of La Mancha* (even though, as one professor points out, the word actually appears in the Bible). And while one might be inclined to wonder about Magdalen College's forbidding students from reading popular magazines or novels, it's true that issues of *Cosmopolitan* or *Maxim* and even some chick-lit novels read like explicit sex manuals.

Nor do the messages of secular culture simply end at sexual hedonism, graphic violence, and drug and alcohol use. Administrators at religious colleges are also wary of the pervasive materialism in American culture. Magdalen makes all its students work in some job on campus even if they don't need it to pay for tuition. Most of the people running religious colleges feel a special duty to keep tuition down and provide plenty of financial aid since they see the education of these youngsters as a religious mission. But how do you demand tens of thousands of dollars from students and their families while at the same time telling them that money is not important?

The extent of the influence of secular culture cannot be understood completely until you think about filtering it out. Even something as simple as sports, a staple of university education (for the player and the spectator) has to be rethought in the context of religion. What does it mean to be playing alongside schools like the University of Colorado and Florida State, which were reported in recent years to be offering not only luxury accommodations for their recruits but also promises of sex from young women on campus?

At Notre Dame, of course, the school's athletic programs are an integral part of its identity, with thousands of alumni attending mass together after each home game. But the administrations there as well as at Baylor and BYU must somehow shield the players from the kind of financial, sexual, and drug-related scandals that have come to plague high-level athletics in America. Cultural discernment, that is, teaching students the best of what secular culture has to offer and providing them with the tools for examining it themselves, requires constant vigilance and a lot of forethought from religious college leaders, but the rewards for success are tremendous. Striking the right balance means producing graduates who are unafraid of the world, can participate in some aspects of it, change other parts of it, and all the while maintain their religious grounding.

CHAPTER TEN

THE UNDERDOG:
HOW MEMBERS OF MINORITY RELIGIOUS GROUPS
ARE TREATED ON CAMPUS

In February 2003, Soka University decided not to renew the teaching contract of Joe McGinniss. The best-selling author complained to the press that he was the victim of religious discrimination, that is, he claimed the school didn't want him anymore because he wasn't a member of Soka Gakkhai International (SGI), the Buddhist group that is the sponsoring order of the school. McGinniss was actually the fourth employee of the school to make this claim. The director of information and the registrar have filed suit against the school for terminating their contracts on the grounds of religious discrimination. Biology professor Anne Houtman, who resigned the month before McGinniss, explained to the *Orange County Register* that the administration and the religious group that runs it are "secretive, hierarchical, coercive, and deceitful."

In making his case to the local paper, McGinniss offered proof from an e-mail that the school's dean, Fred Balitzer, had sent out to the faculty. "Let us not indulge in language that suggests we are a nonsectarian institution or that the Soka Gakkai is so far in the background that we never think about it or it never comes to mind." Considering the weakness of the statement itself and the fact that it came from a Jewish dean, it does not sound as if McGinniss has much basis for complaint. (Indeed, the school maintained that he was only hired temporarily and was getting too expensive.) But after visiting the school, the claims seem almost outlandish.

Most administrators, faculty, and students refuse to call Soka a religious school at all because even though the values of the religion make up the foundation of the school, its mission is not ultimately the sustenance or propagation of the faith. Moreover, those values—"peace, human rights, and the sanctity of life"—are pretty universal. As literature professor and Buddhist Ken Saragosa explains, "SGI is not a very dogmatic thing. There really isn't an SGI perspective. What SGI holds are values a lot of people hold."

Even though 90 percent of the school's entering class are SGI members,

Daniel Habuki, the president of Soka, predicts that in the future, "Many students from different religious backgrounds will come here." He says most people at the school want religious diversity. "SGI is a very open-minded organization and they are willing to interact with people of other religious backgrounds." Indeed, the school is eventually aiming for 60:40 ratio of Buddhist to non-Buddhist students.

Pilipino Navarro, Soka's student body president, is a Roman Catholic from the Philippines. It took some time for him to get adjusted at the university due in part to the fact that he believes he is among the more sexually conservative students. He also remembers being jarred by the Buddhist chanting. But now, he thinks of it as if his fellow students were reciting the "Our Father" and has concluded, "For someone who wants to change the world, Soka is a perfect place."

Samantha Hawkins, Soka's sole Mormon student, didn't expect the school to be so overwhelmingly SGI. But she tells me, "it doesn't bother me that much." She finds the chanting relaxing to listen to. And as for the more theological differences, Samantha offers this explanation:

> It's not that strange for me because in my religion we believe that everybody has truth. It's just that we believe that we have more of it. It's not like you're wrong and I'm right. It's not necessarily that [the other students] are leading a life that's not proper. It's just that they could have more. So even though people here think I don't have all the answers, I think the same of them so we're sort of on equal ground on that basis.

But there is another reason that Pilipino and Samantha feel so comfortable at Soka. As Balitzer observes, "The Buddhist students have become so sensitized to not overwhelm the non-Buddhist students that they bend over backward, sometimes too much." Cassie, an SGI student from Washington State, explains, "We try not to gather in large groups on campus. And we try really hard not to bring our religious beliefs into the classroom." Cassie acknowledges that it's a little strange. "I have several professors here who are SGI members and it's really weird to see them at meetings and sit with them and do our chanting and then go back to school, and remember to separate those things so that it's comfortable for everyone . . . so it's not dominated by one culture." Saragosa also wants to keep faith out of the classroom: "I like to remain ignorant of my students' religious backgrounds."

The irony of a religious school where students and professors go out of their way not to talk about or practice their religion publicly, but which is then sued on grounds of religious discrimination, is only understandable within the current legal climate. The most common and serious legal challenges faced by religious colleges are in the area of employment. From the most strictly religious schools like Bob Jones to the most open religious environments like Fordham, sectarian colleges and universities obviously give some preference to academics who share the school's faith, but they have to tiptoe around a good deal of regulation in order to do this.

The simplest case of this sort arises when a college receives a publicly funded research grant. According to Doug Laycock, law professor at the University of Texas, if a job is funded directly by a government grant, the school cannot discriminate in its hiring decision for the job. Laycock cites the recently publicized case of a woman fired by the Salvation Army because of her association with the Wiccan religion. Because a federal grant was used to fund her position, the plaintiff was able to convince the judge that it would be unconstitutional for the group to discriminate against her.

Religious colleges must also be vigilant about their legal standing while hiring for permanent positions. Under Title VII of the 1964 Civil Rights Act, employers of more than fifteen people are forbidden to discriminate on the basis of race, religion, or gender. The law contains an exemption for institutions sponsored by, controlled by, or affiliated with a religious denomination, which are allowed to discriminate on the basis of religion. Laycock thinks that even colleges without sponsoring churches can earn this exemption, as long as they "can easily demonstrate that they are seriously religious." This may pose a problem for schools like Soka, for instance, should they want to offer preference to members of their own faith.

But even if they jump the hurdles of Title VII, educational institutions have to contend with more restrictive state nondiscrimination laws, some of which don't provide an exemption for religious institutions at all. One approach taken by many religious colleges is to require employees to sign a profession of faith. While these professions can function as mission statements for the college, informing prospective students and their parents what the school is about, they can also serve an important legal purpose. Faculty who sign these documents agree as part of their employment contract to place restrictions on their teaching and publishing. Professors who run afoul of them will probably find themselves out of luck as most courts will side with the colleges in cases where such a document exists.

Though Boston lawyer Harvey Silverglate and his organization, the Foundation for Individual Rights in Education, have defended the religious freedom of many professors and students at secular universities across the country, he does not support professions of faith at religious colleges. From a legal standpoint, Silverglate believes the professions are acceptable only "if the religious profession is relevant to the course." But he thinks "it's questionable for an institution to insist on a profession of faith by a math professor, where the issue of faith is not relevant."

Calvin professor Ed Ericson believes this view is too narrow, explaining that it "doesn't wash in the evangelical world, where all truth is God's truth . . . [even in a discipline] as far away from religion as math." And Ericson may have the law on his side. Laycock understands the Title VII exemption to mean that religious colleges can "prefer members of their own faith in hiring everyone, including the janitor."

But what does it say about an institution that its faculty members are required to share the faith? That the institution is hostile to outsiders? That it does not trust nonbelievers to give a good education to its students? What if all of the students also have to belong to the institution's denomination? Is there a problem with the kind of isolation that results from such homogeneity among students and faculty? And, most importantly, what kind of effect will the school's attitude toward religious diversity have on students once they graduate?

In August of 2001, a few months after I published an article in *American Enterprise* on two religious schools that had recently opened their doors, I received a call from Rich Jefferson, the man in charge of media relations at one of the schools, the evangelical Patrick Henry College. Jefferson told me that he and many others at the college were very upset with the article and that after discussions with certain faculty members and administrators, he concluded that my assessment of Patrick Henry must have something to do with my "personal bias against evangelicals." When I asked him to explain why he thought I had such a bias, he responded as if the answer were obvious.

"You must have written these things because you are Roman Catholic."

After a brief pause, I told him that though I didn't think my religion was relevant, I was not Catholic but Jewish.

"Jewish?" he asked confusedly. When I questioned Jefferson on where he got the idea that I was Catholic, he told me it was because I had praised Ave Maria Law School in the same article and also because my father teaches at Holy Cross College. After this initial exchange, which gave him some pause, he brought up specific criticisms I had made in the article about the school's faculty. (Though I had been impressed with the caliber of the students, who were almost entirely drawn from the homeschooled population, and the mission of the school, its faculty had struck me as largely unimpressive.) Our conversation went on for almost an hour, at the end of which I mentioned that I hoped to come back and visit the school after it had more time to work out some of the kinks that inevitably accompany the founding of any new educational institution. Jefferson recommended that I speak with the dean, Paul Bonnicelli, when the time came for me to put in my request.

Shortly thereafter, I began making inquiries about visiting Liberty University—another evangelical school in Virginia, famous for its president, Jerry Falwell. My initial conversation with their director of public relations, Kim Parker, seemed very promising. But about a week later she called back to say that after speaking with Paul Bonicelli at Patrick Henry, she was not inclined to let me come.

I go through the details of this incident for a couple of reasons. First, the criticisms of my coverage of Patrick Henry have been leveled several times now. For example, Donald Hodel, president of Focus on the Family, who sits on Patrick Henry's board of trustees, sent me a letter reiterating the charges that the Patrick Henry administration made against me. He suggested that I did not attend a sufficient number of classes to make a judgment about faculty quality (I sat in on classes taught by four of the nine faculty members at the time), and that I did not have sufficient expertise in the subjects to assess the curriculum. (I wonder whether the parents of these homeschooled students would agree that one needs a PhD to form a judgment about the worth of a college-level political science class.)

Hodel asked me to "refrain from repeating [my] criticisms of the faculty or accusations about the alleged actions of anyone, Dr. Bonnicelli or others, causing other colleges to shut their doors to you." He concluded: "The more this controversy continues, the more likely it is that other colleges will hear of it and respond as did Liberty University."

The second, more important, reason that I relate this story is that it was a wakeup call for me, as I suspect it may be for some readers of this book. When I began this project, I thought of Catholics and evangelicals as Christians in some generic sense. Though I was aware of some obvious theological differences—that Catholics believe in the authority of the Pope—I could not pinpoint any cultural differences and, apart from Ireland, I was hard pressed to think of any instances of Christian intrareligious animosity being expressed today. My outlook, I think, was partly the result of being an outsider and partly the result of being young.

Of all of the cultural changes brought about by the baby boomer generation, perhaps the least mentioned is religious assimilation. Young people today take for granted this climate of religious diversity and toleration. Of all the ways that they still separate themselves from one another—gender, ethnicity, race, sexual orientation, geographical region—religion is often among the least of their concerns. Climbing rates of "religion-switching" (from 4 percent of adults who did not adhere to the faith of their upbringing in 1955 to more than 30 percent in the mid 1980s) and intermarriage are two signs of this trend.

The cause of this new level of religious tolerance is at least partly intellectual, that is, information about religious beliefs and practices has become more accessible to nonmembers. In recent years, national media coverage of religion has doubled, according to John Schmalzbauer, author of *People of Faith: Religious Conviction in American Journalism and Higher Education*. The number of members in the Religion Newswriters Association also doubled during that period and several major metropolitan newspapers have recently added religion sections.

Web sites like Beliefnet, which run articles and discussion groups on a variety of different faiths, are enormously popular, both among the devoutly religious and the spiritual seekers. According to a Pew Research Center study in 2001, over 20 percent of all U.S. adults using the Internet are searching online for spiritual or religious information. Readers of such Web sites and newspapers sections are not simply faithful people who want to know more about their own community. They are Catholics who want to find out about Buddhists, Jews who want to learn about Methodists, Unitarians who want to learn about Muslims.

There is also a certain ecumenical spirit that has come out of this era that would have been hard to imagine fifty years ago. As Diana Eck documents in her book, *A New Religious America: How a "Christian" Country Has Become the World's Most Religiously Diverse Nation*, religious minorities in the U.S. have been growing at a breakneck pace due to immigration, conversion, and high birth rates—and the result is an America that is diverse like never before. For the last dozen or so years, Eck, a professor of religion at Harvard, has headed the Ford Foundation–supported Pluralism Project, which has sent numerous researchers, including Eck herself, to cities and towns from Baltimore to Boise to learn how the millions of non-Judeo-Christians in this country live and worship. Though she offers a few incidents of bigotry here and there, the sum of her reporting points to a country where even the smallest, most isolated towns welcome the most exotic religious minorities with open arms.

But not everyone sees this religious harmony Eck describes as a positive development. Baby-boomer rebellion against traditional religion may mean that religious conflicts seem more trivial, but it also means that religion itself does. The idea of religion as just another choice people make does not sit well with the seriously religious.[14] In his book *The Naked Public Square*, Richard John Neuhaus, the director of the Institute on Religion and Public Life, describes a television commercial produced during the abortion wars of the early eighties by People for the American Way as a response to their adversaries in the Moral Majority. It portrayed a series of actors expressing how they liked their eggs cooked. Each person offered a different answer and the commercial ended with the mantra, "That's the American way!" As Neuhaus notes, religious tolerance today is extended to everyone except to those who would never compare their religious beliefs to their breakfast choices.

Ironically, this intolerance of strong religious belief has caused a new era of interfaith cooperation among the most staunchly religious communities. In the early eighties, faced with court decisions like *Roe v. Wade* and a ban on prayer in public schools, various conservative religious communities began to band together. The resulting religious right, as some still refer to it, now encompasses evangelicals, Catholics, Mormons, Orthodox Jews, and some Muslims as well.

Some of those who signed on to these political coalitions made clear their distaste for the kind of ecumenism that was expected to follow. But for other members of the coalition, a certain intellectual, theological, and cultural exchange began to occur. In 1992, as a result of growing conflicts between Catholics and evangelical Protestants in Latin America, some leaders of various denominations convened a conference and began a project called Evangelicals and Catholics Together. The idea behind it was to explain why it is necessary for these two groups to work together against the moral and cultural threats of secular society. The statement that emerged from the project is largely focused on theological agreements between evangelicals and Catholics because, "in the face of a society marked by unbelieving ideologies and the culture of death, we deem it all the more important to affirm those foundational truths of historic Christian orthodoxy that we do share in common."

A dozen years after the publication of *Evangelicals and Catholics Together*, the political affinities between these two groups are well established. Much

---

[14] Even those scholars, like Alan Wolfe, who are sympathetic to traditionally religious groups often present the situation this way. See Wolfe's *The Transformation of American Religion: How We Actually Live Our Faith.*

was made of the evangelical George W. Bush's efforts to reach out to Catholics in 2000 campaign (and it would be hard to imagine after the criticism Bush received from the Catholic community for speaking at Bob Jones University that any Republican frontrunner would ever go back). Similarly, when Joe Lieberman emphasizes in his speeches the importance of faith, he is speaking to a clearly defined group of traditional Christians, Jews, and Muslims. But the effects of this political ecumenism have only in recent years begun to reach the world of religious education. Indeed, though the suspicion of Catholics at Patrick Henry is probably more explicit than at most schools, the attitude at other evangelical colleges toward them, as well as toward Mormons, is only gradually thawing.

Perhaps the most interesting evidence of this lingering distance among religious groups is at the recently founded colleges. Given that the logistical problems of setting up a school are common to all, and the legal issues involved in founding a religious school are similar regardless of the denomination, it is surprising that very few representatives of these institutions had ever heard of each other. On the occasions when I mentioned some of these startup schools at other ones, my statements were answered with bewilderment and then, often, an attempt on the part of administrators and faculty to dissociate their school from the others. On the one hand, this is a natural reaction: People who have devoted enormous amounts of time and effort to starting a college would obviously want to insist that it is entirely different from anything else out there today. On the other hand, the result has been some reinventing of the wheel. When it comes to things like fund-raising, building permits, employment regulations, and even extracurricular activities, each school insists on starting from scratch.

Organizations like the American Academy of Liberal Education[15] are starting to bridge these gaps by sponsoring meetings of some of the schools they work with. But many organizations for institutions of higher education are restricted to particular denominations. Thus the Council for Christian Colleges and Universities admits only evangelical schools, and the American Council for Catholic Colleges and Universities excludes Protestant institutions. Though these restrictions make some sense—they have to draw the line somewhere—there is an argument to be made that colleges of different faiths that are equally serious about their faith have more in common than colleges of the same faith that have experienced many different levels of secularization. So, for example, a representative of Thomas Aquinas

---

[15] See Chapter 11 for more information on the AALE.

College would probably find his conversation less productive with an administrator from Fordham than with one at the Mormon Southern Virginia University.

But how does this distance among religious groups filter down to the college experience? Students at Wheaton, Westmont, and Gordon Colleges (the triumvirate of competitive small evangelical liberal arts schools) do not encounter any Catholic professors. According to Mark Sargent, Gordon's provost, "There are no Catholics on the faculty because we have a statement of faith that underscores the importance of salvation by faith [as opposed to works] which Catholics can't sign." The school's president, Jud Carlberg, believes that having Catholics on the faculty would "water down Gordon's religious character." The school is so serious about this policy that a few years ago a Gordon professor who converted to Catholicism was fired.

What are the theological justifications behind this policy? Alan Jacobs, a professor at Wheaton, offers succinctly:

> *What it comes down to is the issue of the Bible. For Catholics, the Bible has as much authority as it does for Protestants, but Catholics have the Magisterium—the teachings of the Church—that is the officially designated interpreter of scripture. Historically, for this community, that's the rub. It is deeply ingrained in Protestant tradition the idea that every prayerful, thoughtful Christian is a fit interpreter of scripture. When you have a Magisterium, that looks (to someone from our tradition) like a weakening of the authority of scripture, or, at the very best, an imposition of another authority between us and scripture.*

Like many faculty members at the three schools, Westmont chemistry professor Niva Tro would personally be supportive of bringing Catholic faculty on board. He believes that for the administration, "It's not a question of whether they think Catholics are Christians—almost everyone would say that's not the issue. They would say that we have a Protestant heritage and that's something we have to maintain because there is a distinctiveness to that which is valuable." But, Tro concludes, "I think there might be more to gain by crossing that boundary."

"I view a lot of these debates as discussions around a family table," says Robert Wennberg, who teaches theology at Westmont. "My feeling is that you have 'evangelical Catholics' who are similar in spirit [to evangelicals]." Wennberg offers the example of a Catholic visiting professor who taught at Westmont briefly.

"He was a rich person to have here. He understood us. He was not trying to undermine what we were doing." Though Wennberg understands the concern on the part of trustees—"that we are a Protestant institution and we're evangelical, and that is our theological core"—he believes, "You could still maintain that core and add some Roman Catholics." As many of the professors interviewed pointed out, there is probably more of a range among the evangelicals (from Pentecostal to Episcopalian, say) than there would be between some of the high-church denominations and Catholicism.

Some students, like Westmont senior Kevin Lewis, are unaware that their schools do not allow Catholic professors. When I inform him of the policy, he says he feels that Catholics are "my brothers and sisters in Christ and I don't dwell on the ways I differ from them." He adds that he had a visiting professor who was a former Jesuit priest. "It was a very interesting dynamic in terms of his faith. It was interesting to hear his reflections on what he did in monasteries."

Many faculty members at evangelical colleges believe that hiring Catholics will not only broaden students' religious experience but also their intellectual one. There is a strong feeling that evangelicals have neglected a large part of the Christian intellectual tradition by steering clear of Catholic thinkers for so long, and that those first 1500 years of Christian thought need to be reintroduced into Protestant education. Alan Jacobs describes the history:

> In the fifties and sixties, there was an attempt to create our own intellectual tradition and it didn't work. It was too hard and it is not necessary. There are these great traditions out there. We just have to recognize that evangelicalism as such does not have an intellectual tradition. That's not what we've been about. We've [been about bringing] people into the church. Now that we have them, what do we do with them and how do we nourish them intellectually?

This is a particularly pressing issue for Joseph Clair, a Wheaton senior, who takes me to his evangelical Episcopal church for a Sunday morning service. Clair says he is attracted to the Episcopal church's extensive liturgy, and jokes about himself and a friend who accompanies us, "I guess we're not bold enough to become Catholic and this is the next best thing." Clair is part of a growing population of evangelical college students who are searching for a deeper intellectual tradition in their worship service and their religious study.

Students in individual disciplines, from business to philosophy, complain about the hollowness of the evangelical intellectual tradition. But the problem goes much deeper, according to some. "Evangelical ethics? What is that?" asks Robert Wennberg, who thinks there "is so much richness in the Roman Catholic tradition that [evangelicals] can appropriate and shape." For example, Wennberg offers: "Thomas Aquinas is the greatest of Christian philosophers. [At Westmont], we're not thomistic. Our philosophy comes out of the analytic tradition, which is a certain advantage because it doesn't come with a lot of commitments. But it can also become irrelevant and narrow. Our students don't always see how philosophy fits in with theology, but if you teach Aquinas, it provides a foundation."

"Now you are getting a more ecumenical approach," says Jacobs. "A lot of my own scholarly work has drawn heavily on Catholic tradition and I think there is almost universal recognition on the part of the administration that that is not only okay, it's a good thing." Jacobs, who was asked to be the director of the Faith and Learning Program at Wheaton, tells me that ten or fifteen years ago, "Anyone who worked in the Catholic intellectual tradition would not have been given that position."

If evangelical schools are starting to allow more of the Catholic intellectual tradition into their classroom, is it only a matter of time before they start to hire Catholic faculty? For most of these schools, the answer is no. If faculty hiring shapes the identity of a school, as many religious college observers and administrators have rightly come to believe, then changing the hiring policy, however minutely, could be ultimately detrimental to that identity. At Calvin College, for instance, professors must not only subscribe to an evangelical Protestant faith, they must more specifically belong to the Reformed Church of America, the Christian Reformed Church, or one of their affiliates, like the Korean Christian Church of America. The administration assures me that the hiring policy will not change.

What distinguishes Reformed theology? John Witvliet, the dean of the chapel at Calvin, explains, "There is a longstanding debate in evangelicalism about the relationship of God's action and human action in faith. It goes back to the doctrine of election. Did God choose us? Did we choose God?" Witvliet notes that at evangelical schools with Baptist or Methodist groundings, "Students would be asked all the time, 'Have you made a decision for Christ?' Your main salvation depends on your decision for Christ, you choosing to become a part of his community." In the Reformed tradition, Witvliet explains, "We live out of a commitment to Christ, but even that commitment is a gift that God has given you. God has acted prior to your action."

So how do these seemingly minor theological differences affect day-to-day life at Calvin? The worship service, according to Witvliet, is unlike that at other evangelical schools, "where everything leads up to that moment of decision and people coming forward" to offer testimony.

"The Calvinist impulse," he observes, "is to say people's commitment is great, but even that is a gift. We live out of the context of God's prior work in our life so our worship service . . . expresses gratitude in prayer." This difference is ultimately evident in that "there's going to be less of that kind of evangelistic zeal around here, less of a 'winning souls for Christ' kind of language."

But why do these distinctions preclude hiring non-Reformed evangelicals or Catholics? The school's president, Gaylen Byker, maintains, "We are not mere Christians," referring to C. S. Lewis's *Mere Christianity,* which describes the basic beliefs and moral mandates that all Christians share. Byker continues, "Christian universities, like Christian individuals, are not Christians in general. At least not for very long."

"Christianity in general is a weigh station on the road to secularity," he says. Byker even doubts that the nondenominational evangelical churches that have sprouted up in Grand Rapids (where Calvin is located) will be around for long. Many of them, he points out with a certain amount of ridicule, "are now Unitarian."

Some religious college leaders argue that the issue is not simply holding on to an identity for its own sake. There is an educational benefit to be gained in an environment where people are coming from a similar intellectual and spiritual standpoint. Of course, this idea runs contrary to what most experts say about higher education today, that is, education can only happen when students encounter viewpoints opposed to their own. But there is a problem with this educational theory, and anyone who has ever conducted an argument with someone who has a completely different set of assumptions will be able to recognize it. When there is no common ground in a conversation to begin with, the conversation tends to go nowhere.

And common ground is an aspect of the intellectual life that many religious college students appreciate. At Ave Maria, for instance, most of the students agree with the idea that a fetus is a human life, but many disagree about how the law should address abortion. As more than one student pointed out, it would be impossible for them to ever get beyond the former idea with many of their classmates at secular schools. The conversation at

Ave Maria is more productive for them because it can move beyond first principles.

This theory, that religious colleges must remain denominationally specific in order to stay educationally interesting and religiously strong, was put forth originally by James Tunstead Burtchaell and more recently echoed by Robert Benne. In Burtchaell's seminal work, *The Dying of the Light,* he offers accounts of how over time, religious colleges tend to widen their boundaries—in terms of faculty hiring, student admissions, campus rules, and curricular issues—until those boundaries disappear and the school is left with little to distinguish itself from its secular neighbors. In an effort to compete with their secular rivals, many religious institutions had built expensive campus facilities and dangled high salaries to attract big names to their academic departments. Burtchaell describes the road toward secularization: "As the colleges gained in sophistication and financially, they naturally suffered church fools less gladly."

Calvin is one of the six schools profiled in Robert Benne's book *Quality with Soul,* which presents what he believes are the exceptions to Burtchaell's rule—institutions that have "kept faith with their religious traditions." Benne identifies several key administrative policies that can make or break a school's religious identity, for instance, that it is supported by a network of "tightly knit and highly disciplined churches and a system of elementary and secondary schools." The backing of the founding church and a ready supply of faculty and students who strongly identify with the faith are important components in the fight against secularism, not least because they help to guarantee financial security (the lack of which was a factor in the widespread secularization of the past).

Others believe that ship has sailed, that is, most religious colleges could no longer depend on their founding churches for the kind of money necessary to fund a college even if they wanted to. (There are exceptions, like Brigham Young, but the tithing rates among Mormons are extremely high and the percentage of funds that the Church is willing to give to the school is unusually large.) Moreover, among evangelical churches, there is so much jumping around that it would be hard to guarantee the kind of loyalty that Calvin has had over the years. Indeed, even at Calvin, the percentage of students who identify themselves with a Reformed Church has dropped forty points in the last thirty years. Though some of those who come from a non-Reformed church background have parents or grandparents in the denomination, the connection will probably grow more tenuous over time. Indeed, one wonders whether in a few decades there will be a sufficient pool of academics that identify explicitly with the Reformed churches to make up Calvin's faculty.

Given the practical difficulties of maintaining denominational boundaries over time, the question remains whether there are other lines a college can draw without slipping into secularity? Is it possible to have a "mere Christian" university? Or a Judeo-Christian university? Would there be enough common ground for "productive conversations"? Would there be enough of an identity to bind a community together?

Baylor University is trying to find out. In 2001, the school partially severed ties with the Baptist General Convention of Texas because the administration was worried about certain fundamentalist elements within the Southern Baptist convention that were trying to take over the Texas branch. The Baylor board of regents used to be elected by the Texas Convention; now the convention elects only 25 percent of the regents, with the majority picked by the regents themselves. Some students and faculty share with me their suspicion that the Baptist affiliation may soon be dropped entirely.

With 1,500 Catholic students on a campus of 14,000, and a smattering of Jews, Muslims, Mormons, Jehovah's Witnesses, Pentecostals, etc., Baylor is easily the most religiously diverse of the evangelical colleges I visited. And its faculty members come from a wide range of denominational backgrounds. The president, Robert Sloan, speaks about a Christian tradition, not just a Baptist one. And when I ask him how Baylor plans to keep its religious identity over time, he offers this response: "I think you have to know who you are, and what is nonnegotiable. I think Baylor's identity as an institution of faith is nonnegotiable."

Whatever Baylor's prospects for maintaining its identity over time, and I think they are good, it is clear that religious diversity is working there now. Aside from the large Catholic population, the members of which hardly count themselves as religious minorities and are surprised to hear that Catholics are treated differently at other evangelical schools, there are a significant number of non-Christian students. Dharmpal Vansadia, who is Hindu, tells me that his freshman hall had Catholics, Muslims, Baptists, and Methodists and that they got along very well.

But why do students want to attend a school with a religious mission that is not their own? Dharmpal tells me that he was attracted to Baylor's strong premed program, and it turned out to be much less expensive for him than Tulane, the other school he was considering. Many non-Mormon students report similar reasons for attending BYU: strong academics at a low price.

Others are a little less savvy. When Mike Hurwitz chose to attend Thomas Aquinas, he barely considered the Catholic identity of the school, let alone the behavioral codes. He was attracted to the Great Books education offered at TAC, and he had never heard of any secular schools with similar curricula. Mormon Samantha Hawkins was attracted to Soka for nonreligious reasons as well. Visiting a friend (who is a Buddhist) during her senior year in high school, Samantha accompanied her to an introductory meeting about Soka. "I really liked the way it sounded," she recalls. "It was all about learning clusters and being really close with teachers. It seemed like the exact type of education that I wanted."

But professors and administrators at religious colleges believe they have something more than good academics and cheaper tuition to offer students. Indeed, many want to help students of other religious traditions explore their own. Jeff Brauch, the dean of Regent University's law school, tells me about a Jewish recent alumna. "She wasn't just tolerating the religious context here. She was saying 'I want to get everything I can out of this.'"

Dharmpal notes that he has gotten "a much deeper understanding of Christianity" at Baylor and the experience of "defending my religion [has made me] understand my own religion now better than my parents do. Baylor puts a lot of emphasis on finding out spiritually who you are. It rubs off on you. I am much more conscious of my spiritual side than before. My faith has become more personal and stronger."

It is not always comfortable for students of one faith to be at a college of another. The Catholic-Protestant crossovers constitute the most difficult interactions because those groups share the most religious common ground as well as the most cultural friction. Given that these two denominations have historically defined themselves against one another, it is tricky for a college of one to welcome a member of the other without blurring the lines of its own community.

Jeremy Chisholm, an evangelical first-year law student at Ave Maria, was raised in a "Catholic friendly" environment. His father, a Methodist pastor, used to co-officiate weddings with a Catholic priest "so I've attended mass many times. I'm familiar with the liturgy." Though he was initially worried that he wouldn't be fully accepted into the Ave Maria community, he happily reports that the school's chaplain had him pass out the rosary beads at the last mass. Jeremy acknowledges that he has friends at home who, since finding out where he chose to go to law school, have been worried about his soul. Indeed some of the Ave Maria students figured Jeremy would have problems with them.

"A lot of my Catholic friends here at this school have said, 'So don't you have issues with the Catholic church?' And I have said, 'Well, there are several questions I have but I think you probably have the same sort of questions about my faith and background as well.'"

The only Protestant I found during my visit to Christendom College was Emily Meeks, a cute girl wearing several bracelets and pink nail polish. On a rainy afternoon, we sit in the small wood-paneled conference room. Emily tells me that she grew up belonging to the Assemblies of God, but is now a member of the Charismatic Episcopal Church (CEC) (yet another religious group in the U.S. I had not heard of until I began this research). Emily explains, as she has had to do many times before, "It's Catholic doctrine with a liturgy of modern praise songs, but we're not under the authority of the Pope. The mission of the CEC, basically, is to bridge the gap between the Protestant and Catholic churches." But Emily is not necessarily standing in the middle of the two. When I ask her whether she considered attending a Protestant college, she tells me, "It would basically be taking a step back for me because I would be going back to what I formerly believed."

Emily says the Christendom community has been pretty open toward her and her beliefs, asking a lot of questions. Though some have asked her if she wants to become Catholic, she thinks they've all been very supportive. Admissions director Paul Heisler tells me Emily is dating his brother's nephew, adding with a smile, "I mean, we've got lots of girls here and he chooses the one who is not Catholic."

Ultimately, there seems to be little tension for the few evangelicals who choose to attend Catholic schools. But treatment of Catholics at evangelical schools is more problematic. In addition to the lack of Catholic professors, students often feel singled out by their fellow students and even the college administrations sometimes.

Laurie Tomczyck seems like a senior very much at home in her environment at Gordon College. She comes to our meeting in flip-flops with her long blond hair falling over her sweatshirt. Both her parents were born in Poland. "Our lineage," she explains, "is very much Polish and very much Catholic." She notes, for instance, that her parents attend only Latin masses and don't eat meat on Friday. Laurie's faith and ethnic background hardly make her unusual in the greater Boston area, but they certainly make her stick out at Gordon. So why is she there? Mostly it's the college's strong education major, but Laurie also had aspirations to be a singer and Gordon had a respectable music program.

"Freshman year," Laurie recalls, "I didn't fit in so well. . . . Some people don't look at you as Christian in any way. So many people come up to me and say, 'Can I talk to you about Jesus?' It's as if they are trying to lead me to be a Christian." There are about forty Catholic students out of 1,700 on the Gordon campus now, more than when Laurie first started, and she has been instrumental in organizing a Catholic student group. "You find out quickly who the Catholics are on campus and who are the Catholic sympathizers." But Laurie's efforts to make her fellow students more tolerant of her religious beliefs have sometimes been thwarted by the school's administration.

For instance, she describes Gordon's springtime symposium, an annual event with lectures and exhibitions organized around a particular theme. During her freshman year, the theme was "Who is your neighbor?" and the school brought in a panel of people "outside of the Gordon community." Laurie recalls a student from Kenya, a lesbian minister, and a Catholic priest. Though I learn from a number of administrators on campus that the event turned into something of a fiasco because students from a Christian high school were visiting that day and many were shocked to find a lesbian speaking in chapel, Laurie was horrified to find that the administration seemed to be saying that both lesbians and Catholics are considered equally distant from the Gordon community.[16]

Despite the difficulties, Laurie thinks that her experience at Gordon has made her faith stronger. "It has made me think more about Catholicism. It has forced me to learn more about my faith and why we believe what we believe, so that I can explain it to other people." Though Laurie used to be frustrated trying to explain to Protestants that she is in fact a Christian, she is comforted now "because I know what's in my heart and I know what's true." Still, she can't help but note to me sadly that she would never be allowed to teach at her alma mater.

In a May 2003 *Atlantic Monthly* article, journalist Jonathan Rauch tried to put a name on what he perceived as the common attitude toward religion among his friends and acquaintances. "Apatheism," he announced, is "a disinclination

---

[16] This issue is one that goes back to the principles of *Evangelicals and Catholics Together,* that is, whatever the disagreements between the two groups, theologically, they can at least agree on certain social evils.

to care all that much about one's own religion and an even stronger disinclination to care about other people's." It's an attitude that can be shared, according to Rauch, by Jews, Christians, Buddhists, agnostics, etc. Though he distinguishes it from staunch secularism, "an ACLU-style disapproval of any profession of religion in public life—a disapproval that seems puritanical and quaint to apatheists," he acknowledges that apatheists do not take well to religious fanatics either.

The religious tolerance of the last fifty years or so is premised in part on people not feeling strongly enough about their religion to proselytize. Religious diversity is fine, so the apatheists would say, as long as one keeps one's religious beliefs, if not completely private, then at least mostly so. The question remains: How does a Christian, who believes he is called upon by God to spread the Gospel and to help others find eternal salvation, do so in twenty-first-century America? Is it possible to proselytize without causing offense?

First, I should say that during my visits to these schools, only two people suggested I might personally consider another faith. One was the dean at Bob Jones, and the other was a young woman at Brigham Young who gave me a copy of the Book of Mormon.

The efforts of Bob Jones students and graduates to evangelize are fairly straightforward. Many plan careers as pastors and most students are involved in some sort of mission work either locally during the school year or elsewhere on mission trips during school vacations. Students at Brigham Young, however, take a different approach. They spend at least eighteen months working as missionaries in different parts of the country and the world, but few are involved in missionary work while they are enrolled in school. Indeed, at Southern Virginia University as well as at BYU, there is little talk of trying to convert people. An older couple at SVU, for instance, has been sent by the church to aid in some of the religious education but they tell me they don't have any "proselytizing duties here." In other words, the Mormon Church tries to separate the explicitly evangelizing roles from the rest of the lives of its members.

The effect of this in the secular world is fascinating. People see Mormons in two different ways—first, as the people who come to the doorstep in groups of two, dressed in suits, and carrying the Book of Mormon, and second, as highly successful and well-adjusted coworkers, neighbors, and friends. The fact that Mormons never do their mission work in the community where they're from means that they don't have to alienate the other members of the community by trying to explicitly convert them.

The situation for Catholics and evangelicals is more delicate. In the case of the former, there is very little explicit proselytizing, though this varies somewhat depending on the school. Thomas Aquinas president Thomas Dillon notes that there are probably some among the students at TAC "who may not have appropriate prudence and who may put pressure on others. Would I like the non-Catholic students to convert? Sure. I think the Catholic faith is true. But I also hold as a matter of faith that faith is a gift from God. It's not something someone else can impose. All I can do is dispose them well to it and draw them to it and the rest is in God's hands. I'm very much opposed to pushing people into it."

Many students and faculty are careful to note that there is no point in trying to force someone into conversion. Lauren Whitnah, a student at Gordon, tells me,

> I want to evangelize because I believe that Christianity is right . . . My friend Mark who is Mormon, I want him to be an orthodox Bible-believing Christian because I think he's got stuff a little messed up. However, I am not going to force that down his throat. I want him to respect me. I feel like mature dialogue back and forth is the way to do that. The same goes for my Muslim friend. I think evangelism would be the eventual goal. . . . I'm not going to run up to people and say, "You should be more Christian right now because otherwise you're going to hell." I think that would be doing Christianity a great disservice.

Some evangelical students take a similar approach to Mormons, separating their school lives from their missionary lives. They spend their summers or vacations in missionary activities abroad, for example, but don't explicitly proselytize during the school year. Christine Lindner, a student at Gordon, tells me she is a counselor at a camp over the summer and she does evangelize there, but not at the local homeless shelter where she works.

Indeed, this idea of evangelizing by living a particular kind of life and waiting for people to ask you about your faith (sometimes known as "lifestyle evangelism") rather than proclaiming the faith aggressively is prevalent at evangelical schools. Brent Van Norman, an alumnus of Regent University's law school, tries to draw the distinction between going to a colleague and saying, "If you die tonight, do you know where you're going?" and waiting for people to approach him when they observe how he lives his life and conducts his business.

But Alan Jacobs finds it difficult sometimes to get across to evangelical students that they can evangelize in ways other than through being a minister or missionary. "The apostle Paul makes it clear when he talks about many members of one body, all of whom have different roles. One of the things that's really hard to get young Christians to understand is that one role is not better or worse than another." Many times, Jacobs says, "I have to deal with students who want to go to grad school. They say, 'That's what I most enjoy and that's what I'd be best at, but I wonder [whether I] shouldn't be going into Christian ministry or service. What you have to tell them is that being a college professor can be Christian service just as much as being a pastor. It's not as direct but you can still make an enormous impact on people's lives." Even at a secular university "where you wouldn't be allowed to be explicitly Christian," Jacobs tells them, "you can still be effective and compassionate and fair-minded and show people the Christlike virtues in such a way that others find that attractive. And," he notes, "you never say a word of evangelizing."

CHAPTER ELEVEN

THE CLASSROOM AS CHAPEL:
CAN THE INTEGRATION OF FAITH
AND LEARNING WORK?

The first thing you notice about Noel Jabbour is his serious face. His build is still a teenager's, but Noel's face—determined dark eyes, bushy eyebrows, the beginnings of a five o'clock shadow all set on olive skin—makes him seem like a young man with direction. Noel is the student government president at Wheaton College, and though he tells me he just fell into the position (never having been involved in student government before, he was recruited by a friend to run on an "outsider" platform), his campaign and tenure have by no means been haphazard.

Noel might also claim that, like his election to office, his coming to Wheaton in the first place was something of a fluke. He attended Christian schools through eighth grade, but, as a senior at a public high school in West Virginia, he did not want to attend any Christian colleges because he had doubts about their academic rigor. A family friend, however, recommended Wheaton, and so along with the applications he sent to ten secular schools, Noel mailed one there. It was only after visiting the college that, he recalls, "I really appreciated the environment here on campus and the commitment to excellence." Noel, who plans to go into medicine, and maybe later politics, is tremendously satisfied with the education he has received at Wheaton and his prospects after graduation.

But Noel's initial doubts about religious schools are hardly unique, and his skepticism is understandable. In an era when students and parents are intensely aware of the *U.S. News & World Report* ranking of the schools they are considering, when paying college tuition can require a second mortgage, when jobs for recent grads are scarce, and graduate-school admissions more competitive than ever, it is only logical to scrutinize every option. But with well over seven hundred religious colleges and universities in the United States, it is difficult to generalize about the academic rigor of such schools. Indeed, it is most useful to think about religious and secular higher education as having parallel spectra, which range from the highly competitive liberal arts colleges and universities to the less demanding vocationally oriented schools.

The sample of twenty institutions examined in this book tend more toward the more academically rigorous end because it is the graduates of these institutions who are most likely to influence the wider culture through their careers. But even of these more competitive schools, the high school student must ask what kind of education he is getting for his (parents') money and whether he will be in a good position to pursue his professional goals upon graduation.

Are academically rigorous religious colleges a serious option for students like Noel who would otherwise be bound for the Ivy League? The first way to answer that question would be to find out where religious college students come from. Religious high schools? Homeschooling environments? Public schools? Independent secular schools? All of the above.

Having no system of primary or secondary schools, the Mormon Church has long depended on students who have matriculated from public schools and secular private schools choosing to attend BYU over other top schools. Students attending Yeshiva University and Touro College, on the other hand, generally come out of religious high schools. The academic programs at both schools assume a substantial background in Jewish texts and Hebrew language. But a growing number of *ba'alei teshuva*—men and women who come to the faith on their own later in life rather than having been brought up with it[17]—has caused a small but not insignificant rise in applicants from nonreligious high schools, and Yeshiva has recently added a religious program for these beginners.

Evangelical college admissions officers are also finding a greater interest from public high school students. In the fall of 2002, at a college fair outside of Philadelphia sponsored by the National Association of Christian College Admissions Personnel, the afternoon session, which consists mostly of students on field trips from their Christian high schools, is sparsely attended, and many of the students seem nonplussed by the experience. But during the evening session, public school students pour excitedly out of vans sponsored by their church youth groups. Sometimes these public-school teenagers are accompanied by parents, but the admissions officers manning tables at the fair tell me that, by and large, applications at their colleges seem to be fueled in the last few years more by student than parent interest. (This also

---

[17] Many of these students are immigrants from Eastern European countries who rediscovered their Jewish roots after decades of religious suppression under Communist rule.

seems to be true among the Mormon students, and even some of the Catholic students who are more conservative in their religious beliefs than their parents are.) Many of the students I interview at the college fair plan to apply to religious schools as well as secular ones.

Another relatively new addition to the pool of applicants interested in religious colleges and universities are homeschooled kids. Evangelical schools like Wheaton, which as recently as fifteen years ago had no homeschooled students at all, now averages about 10 percent. Close to the entire population at Patrick Henry College had some years of homeschooling. This trend has also affected admissions at fundamentalist schools like Bob Jones, where such students make up 10 percent of the population. (Bob Jones has even created a homeschooling curriculum for fundamentalist families.)

In the case of the conservative Catholic colleges, the numbers are even larger: roughly 20 percent of Thomas Aquinas and 30 percent of Christendom incoming freshmen are homeschooled. The rest are drawn from a combination of Catholic and public high schools. Among the former, there are a growing number of smaller orthodox high schools (St. Gregory's Academy in Scranton and Trivium in Central Massachusetts, for instance) that, like Christendom College and Thomas Aquinas College, emphasize the Great Books of Western Civilization as well as the classic texts of Catholicism.

Looking across the "parallel spectra" of religious and secular colleges, it is fair to say that at each level, the religious college is generally the lesser known (Harvard versus Brigham Young, Williams versus Wheaton, Claremont versus Thomas Aquinas). Some employers and graduate school admissions officers are especially skeptical of religious colleges, even ones they have heard of. These are disadvantages that must be considered when students are thinking about their options after graduation.

But in trying to decide between secular and religious colleges whose students report comparable SAT scores and GPAs, there is at least one academic (not just religious) advantage that colleges of faith seem to offer—a more motivated environment. The students I have observed and interviewed tend to approach their studies with a sense of mission. When asked how teaching at a religious college differs from their previous experience teaching at secular ones, dozens of professors have offered me the same answer: The students here do the work and they come to class.

More specifically, faculty members explain that where they might have a small number of students at any school who are innately intelligent and very devoted to their studies, at the religious institution, the *average* student tends to give greater time and effort to his academics than at a secular institution. These average students make all the difference to professors. Susan Bratton, the chair of the environmental studies department at Baylor, who has taught at several Christian and secular universities, puts it bluntly, "One thing I like about schools like Baylor, and Christian institutions generally, is that I don't have kids coming to class stoned at eleven in the morning."

But motivation can only make up for so much. Many religious college professors observe that their schools accept a greater range of students. This is the result of what some call mission-based admissions, where a school, like Bob Jones for example, might see it as their duty to take in any young person with a high school degree who has demonstrated a commitment to the faith (though the students are separated into more and less demanding majors once they arrive). Calvin College also boasts a fairly open admissions policy but its academic standards remain high in all disciplines, resulting in a somewhat low retention rate of 65 percent over four years.

A missions-based admissions policy is most problematic, though, at the graduate level. Administrators at Regent University's law school have recently been forced to raise the minimum LSAT score required for admission because too many of their graduates were not passing the bar exam. (Though students are not required to sign a profession of faith, they must agree to be taught in accordance with the school's religious mission.) The school's dean, Jeff Brauch, acknowledges that mission-based admissions led to this trouble, but now he maintains that higher standards are necessary even if they result in some of the faithful being rejected. "Regent graduates should be excellent at what they do. We would have blown it if we sent out half-baked lawyers. That's also part of the religious duty. We ought to send out the best."

In this regard, Regent has begun to model itself on the more recently founded Ave Maria School of Law, which rejected missions-based admissions at its founding. Thanks in large part to the generous scholarships of founder Tom Monaghan (former CEO and founder of Domino's Pizza), Ave Maria was able to attract quality students from the beginning. Monaghan's theory, that it would be extremely difficult to gain a good reputation once the school started admitting mediocre students, certainly rings true with the admissions and development officers at various colleges I have visited. Indeed, this policy has enabled the school to rise through the ranks quickly, landing it (in terms of LSATs and GPAs) around twenty-fifth in the nation.

* * *

That smart and motivated students are choosing religious colleges and universities certainly says something about the quality of the institutions, but it is not a sufficient basis for judging their academic rigor. It may seem counterintuitive, but there are instances in which religious schools attract better students than they should. Students and families become so devoted to the idea of a particular school—as a religious cause in and of itself—that they ignore the quality of the education provided.

A number of the courses at Soka University, for instance, are taught at a very basic level. The biology experiments seemed straight out of high school and the literature class I visited rarely rose above identifying the basic plot of a novel. The faculty seem much more concerned with cooperative teaching methods and faculty governance than with instilling any real knowledge in students. But parents and students, who were so taken with the idea of a school founded on Buddhist principles, rushed to sign up their sons and daughters. New schools also tend to attract a very motivated "pioneering" first class, but when the novelty wears off, the school will often experience a drop in applications, as Soka did during its second year of operation.

The case of Patrick Henry College, the very existence of which was the result of student and parent effort, is also instructive. Mike Farris, the school's founder, recalls that as president of the Home School Legal Defense Fund (HSLDF) he would travel the country meeting parents engaged in homeschooling. Inevitably, they would ask where they could send their kids for college that would serve to strengthen, rather than undermine, the Christian principles they had been trying to teach at home.

Farris says, "Secular schools are at war with people of faith." Politically correct teaching, he explains, is often "an attack on the Christian system of belief" and parents ask, "Why should I pay a hundred thousand dollars to have someone attack me and my child for four years?" (Though it is not a hard and fast rule, this kind of rhetoric is often a clue to an institution's being more focused on fighting the culture wars than on giving students an adequate education.) Farris, who has homeschooled ten children of his own, began what he calls "baby steps" to remedy this problem. First, HSLDF acquired some land in Purcellville, Virginia. Then they hired their first staff members to begin planning, hiring, and raising funds.

Patrick Henry has a traditional curriculum with an emphasis on political science, combining a Great Books education with lessons in practical government. Currently, government, classical liberal arts, history and literature are the school's only majors, but they are planning to add others like journalism. Because the school is only about an hour from Washington, students have opportunities in their junior and senior years for apprenticeships at think tanks and congressional offices.

When Brandon Wilhoite heard about Patrick Henry, he was well into the equivalent of his senior year of high school. Living with his mother and three siblings in Arizona, Wilhoite had been homeschooled his entire life (with the exception of a few classes at the local community college). But having done well on his SATs and his school work, while playing a little baseball on the side, Wilhoite thought about applying to Harvard, Yale, and Georgetown, though he was past the deadline for all three. Then he received an e-mail about Patrick Henry from a friend.

He admits to being skeptical. "The school didn't have a name. It wasn't accredited. I didn't expect it to have a good curriculum." So he applied to Georgetown after the deadline. The admissions office there agreed to consider his application, but he decided to apply to Patrick Henry as well. In the meantime, Wilhoite says, "I prayed. The Lord opens doors and closes doors." Within a week, he was admitted to Patrick Henry and accepted.

Wilhoite says he wasn't quite sure what to expect. "Other homeschooled kids I met over the years were generally smart, but the students here far exceeded my expectations." Indeed the students at Patrick Henry are an impressive bunch academically, having turned down Harvard, William and Mary, and other top schools to be there. Echoing his counterparts at other religious colleges, political scientist Robert Stacey says his students at Patrick Henry are "every bit as good as his best students" at the University of Virginia and the University of Richmond, where he taught previously. "I can hold these students to a higher standard than I have ever done in my life." They always come to class prepared, Stacey claims, and they show few problems adjusting to being in a classroom.

But if the students at Patrick Henry are first-rate, the faculty seems to have a ways to go. In the class on the Old Testament, the professor simply reads passages and then repeats them in plainer English. What discussion takes place seems to center merely on what "we" (those who believe that scripture is a God-given text) say in answer to "them" (secularists). In a state government class, the lecture is largely a screed against government overregulation. The students seem to know more about the subject than the professor, who talks only about his home state of Alabama, where he worked in a libertarian-leaning think tank.

With schools that have been in existence for a substantial length of time, it is fairly easy to find out about the quality of the academic program, but with the recent proliferation of newer religious colleges, students and parents may be in more of a bind. Patrick Henry, for instance, received glowing praise from various media outlets. Among conservatives, the school seemed a prime example of the success of homeschooling and the growing strength of a new strain in higher education. A recent *Washington Post* article finds Patrick Henry students working for the White House, the coalition authority in Iraq, various political campaigns, and conservative think tanks. In the mainstream press, reporters who spent a couple of hours on campus were simply impressed that the students were not the socially awkward introverts they imagined to be products of homeschooling.

The useful measure of a school's academic reputation is not a human-interest story in the *Washington Post* or the cheerleading of politically moti-vated groups, but the school's accreditation. Unfortunately, the six major regional accreditation agencies for institutions of higher education have been uneven, at best, in their assessments of smaller new religious colleges. The focus of these organizations—on, for instance, the size of a school's endowments, the number of books in the library, and the number of majors offered—are of less concern to parents and students than the quality of pro-fessors and the strength of the curriculum.

More significantly, the agendas of the regional accreditation groups are often at odds with the values of religious colleges, sanctioning schools that are unwilling to hire a homosexual, for instance. The administration at Thomas Aquinas College fought a long battle with the Western Association of Schools and Colleges when the organization demanded that the school of-fer a more culturally diverse curriculum. The struggle of Regent University (then called CBN University) to gain accreditation from the American Bar Association was resolved only when the fifty-four members of the 1989 grad-uating class sued the ABA, charging that it violated their rights and jeopard-ized their futures by not accrediting the school, simply because the professors were required to sign statements of faith. The Association granted provi-sional accreditation in June 1989, but didn't offer its full stamp of approval until 1996.

Recently, the Department of Education authorized another accrediting organization, the American Academy of Liberal Education (AALE). The AALE offers liberal arts schools (or universities with traditional liberal-arts programs) an extensive examination of their curriculum and faculty. Since its founding in 1992, the AALE has granted accreditation to more than fifty schools, more than twenty with strong religious identities, and, fortunately for parents and students interested in its findings, the organization's representatives do not seem inclined to allow a school's religious tenets to mitigate the group's high standards.

In 2003, the AALE announced that it was going to deny provisional accreditation to Patrick Henry College because the school had not complied with two essential criteria. By insisting that its faculty teach only a strict creationist doctrine and sign a statement to that effect, the school had failed to ensure that "liberty of thought and freedom of speech are supported and protected." Relatedly, the school was not providing a "basic knowledge" of the biological sciences.

In light of the fact that the AALE did offer its stamp of approval to the nearby Mormon school Southern Virgina University, PHC president Mike Farris released a statement reading in part: "We simply cannot understand why the AALE has singled out our evangelical Christian viewpoint for particularized discrimination." Of course, the reason that the AALE chose to accredit SVU and not PHC was not religious but educational. No one at SVU is required to sign a profession of faith, though most of its faculty and 98 percent of its students are Mormon. Rather, SVU looks for faculty and students who can support its mission, which includes studying the liberal arts to "enrich the spiritual lives of its students."

Mormons consider the Old Testament to be God-given and true, but as I discovered on a visit to SVU, many students and professors there view the pursuit of scientific knowledge as a way of using the brain God gave us to explore the world He created. Others see scientific understanding as itself a form of revelation. One student explained to his Sunday-school audience that, in the nineteenth century, when God spoke to Joseph Smith, "The light of God was restored to the human race," leading to "great advances in medicine and modern technology." The differences between SVU and Patrick Henry are striking, but not based on doctrinal distinctions between Mormons and evangelicals (as evidenced by the strong academic records of the other evangelical colleges examined in this book).

Ultimately, the AALE convened a panel of three representatives from other Christian colleges, who found the AALE's assessment to be legitimate, but who suggested that the school should be given another opportunity to comply with the biology requirement. According to Jeff Wallin, president of the AALE, Patrick Henry changed the statement faculty were required to sign (though the school's administration claimed they only clarified it), and proposed using a biology textbook that the academy found acceptable. In the spring of 2005, as a provision of preaccreditation, a committee will return to

PHC to make sure they have complied. "That's exactly how accreditation works," Wallin explains. "If someone doesn't meet a standard, you tell them and then they can meet it or not. But we have the freedom to uphold our standards."

With regard to academic quality, Patrick Henry seems to be the exception. Professors at religious colleges are rarely less and often more qualified than their counterparts at secular schools. In addition to their academic qualifications, they provide students with another dimension of learning. Religious belief does not simply motivate students and faculty to work harder, it also deeply informs the way faculty approach their discipline and the way they convey it to students. This idea, known as the "integration of faith and learning," which has become enormously popular at evangelical schools and has spread to the Mormon and fundamentalist institutions, is not new in its entirety.

Catholics taught for centuries that faith and reason were not only ultimately compatible but that the further one delved into one, the more developed one could become in the other. Indeed, Catholic schools have historically been responsible for ensuring the survival of the liberal arts in higher education. There are definite philosophical differences between the Catholic and evangelical approaches to the integration of faith and learning, but for the purposes of how each affects the college curriculum, they are quite similar.

There is also a Jewish understanding of the integration of faith and learning, Torah Umadda, a concept that is taken up more fully in the chapter on Yeshiva University. Touro dean Devorah Ehrlich explains Maimonides' philosophy in this light: "I don't think he saw a dichotomy between his science knowledge and Talmudic law, between his religious learning and secular learning. I think he saw secular learning as a path to religious learning." Again, there are important distinctions between the Jewish understanding of the relationship between religious and secular knowledge and the Christian understanding of it, but at the heart of these is the idea that a liberal arts education does not run contrary to religious teachings.

Though the underlying philosophy of these colleges is of great importance, the question of how these concepts play out in the classroom is of most interest. There are some general themes that recur in religious professors' discussions of their research and teaching. First, whether you are studying science or history, you are "studying the world God created," and that in and of itself is a religious activity. Second, as a person of faith, you have a certain responsibility to understand to the best of your ability the world around you in order to act a certain way in it. Finally, as a religious individual you can view your particular discipline through the lens of faith.

It is this last area where one needs concrete examples to understand just how the integration of faith and learning works. Mathematics and the natural sciences are the subjects in which people are most skeptical that a religious perspective can be brought to bear without detracting from the knowledge of the discipline. "Science is a particular way of looking at things," says Ben Pierce, associate dean of sciences at Baylor, "and has a fairly specific methodology and that methodology is not tied to any faith. If science works right, you should reach the same conclusion about a set of observations regardless of whether you are a Christian or a Muslim or a Buddhist or an atheist."

So where does religion come in? Harold Heie, who has taught math at Gordon and is now the director of the Center for Christian Studies there, tells me that he only began to see the connections when he started teaching at a religious college. He recalls one of his colleagues asking him, "'Harold, these numbers you work with, are they created or discovered?' I thought, 'Oh my goodness, what a dumb question.'" But now, he believes:

> *At a deep level, there are value assumptions that underline the doing of mathematics. People use terms like "elegant" to describe a proof. If you dig beneath the surface of what mathematicians do, it's an aesthetic enterprise. Math is art. At that level, I can ask my students whether there are some values that underlie mathematical activity. Do those comport with your Christian commitment? What about aesthetic values? Are Christians called to appreciate and foster beauty? I happen to think they are.*

Shmuel Auman, a senior at Touro, displays a similar excitement when describing these connections. He tells me about a great eighteenth century rabbi, the Vilna Gaon, who, though he never attended a formal school, wrote a math book that included theories of geometry and trigonometry. His knowledge of logic and argument carried through from his study of biblical commentaries into the realm of mathematics. It is a connection that is evident to the tutors at Thomas Aquinas College, where Euclid is discussed in theology seminars and St. Augustine in geometry classes.

From bioethics and the current debate over the morality of cloning to space exploration and environmental science, it is difficult to find an area that professors at these colleges do not have a religious take on. At West-mont, chemistry professor Niva Tro tries to offer a history lesson on the rela-tion between religion and science. He explains that he wants his students "to understand the sort of Christian worldview that science grew out of. Science developed primarily because people thought God created the world and that the world was orderly and that you can understand it." Tro emphasizes that "even though science and Christian faith have been seen historically to be enemies, there is a whole other story that isn't told as often. People like Isaac Newton and Pascal were very committed Christian men and their science grew out of their conviction that the world is orderly and understandable."

Despite such reassurances, it is hard to downplay the religion-science de-bate, particularly the creation question, at religious colleges. Patrick Henry may be rare among evangelical schools in its refusal to engage the idea of evolution, but it is hardly alone in facing the problem. Even though almost every school I have visited does teach evolution, problems always tend to arise over the context. Should it be taught as one theory among many? Should professors teach that it is incorrect? Or incomplete? Should they simply leave it up to students to come to their own conclusion?

The nuances turned out to be quite important for a professor of anthro-pology at Wheaton, who was dismissed, he told the *Chronicle of Higher Ed-ucation,* for discussing evolution in the wrong way in his classes. Christopher Kearney, who has taught biology at Baylor for several years, treads lightly when it comes to the issue of creation. "When we get to evolution in class, I read a statement trying to make it easier for students from a creationist background to ease into evolution. And I give them some ideas of how to combine the ideas of evolution and Genesis." (The evolution controversy at Baylor is discussed in detail in the chapter profiling the school.) Kearney com-pares science to history. "We look at history as individuals who have free choice and God is not pleased with most of the choices they make. There may be an individual sense of randomness, but God has an overarching purpose."

If faith can be integrated into the teaching of the natural sciences, perhaps the biggest hurdle has been overcome. The points of contact between reli-gion and other disciplines seem on the surface, at least, much more obvious and perhaps less fraught with conflict. At Gordon College, Tim Sherratt's class, Power and Justice, for instance, explores the roles that Christians play in American and European politics. He tackles the religious foundations of labor unions and political parties. In another segment, Sherratt, citing H. L.

Mencken's writings on William Jennings Bryan, asks his students to think about how evangelical Christians are considered "country hicks" by much of the American political structure.

Susan Penska, a former student of Sherratt's who has gone on to teach political science at Westmont College, credits her old professor with helping her think about what it means to be a Christian living in a multicultural world and how to think about political issues not just from the perspective of her own discipline but from a religious one as well.

Indeed, religious college classes do not simply involve a professor substituting his or her religious views for a rigorous curriculum. Rather, these professors often feel as though something is lacking from their discipline's perspective and they want to add it back in. Ed Feasel incorporates this moral perspective into his economics classes at Soka. Lamenting the fact that "in economics, there is a trend where you try to remove yourself from the normative or value aspect of things when you analyze an issue or problem, a trend which makes values a topic for discussion after class," he tells me that he tries to bring the issues confronting society into his classroom (even at the introductory levels) and discuss some possible solutions. Improving the standard of living in developing countries is one issue that particularly resonates with Soka's international student population.

Even after asking dozens of professors to talk about how religion affects their particular discipline, I was still surprised by Gordon artist in residence Mia Chung's response. "Learning-faith integration is not just concerned with the academic information that gets plugged into the person," Chung tries to remind her students. She tells me, "I feel very blessed because I feel music is one of those disciplines that requires a holistic approach. It parallels one's spiritual walk very closely." She believes the process of personal development in music and faith is similar. "Old things pass away. We talk about that musically. Once students have been enlightened about a certain concept then I expect them to no longer go back to old ways in how they treat musical phrases." Similarly, once people achieve a kind of spiritual enlightenment, their lives can no longer be the same.

In both music and life, Chung says, "You are always being tested to your limits and doing your best, but ultimately knowing that when you go out on stage it's a kind of act of faith. You have to let go. You are exercising elements of control in the process of preparing for a concert but when you go out on concert stage you have to let go." In life, she tells me, "We're asked to do our best absolutely, but there are many elements of life over which we have no control."

But for other professors, faith serves as a reminder that people can have a great deal of control over their circumstances and their environment, as well as the extent to which they have a responsibility to exercise that control. Religion for these students is both a very private matter—as in the case of the musician, able to depend only on herself to remember the next note and how to play it—and a very public one in which religion helps students to form a critique of the larger culture and to improve society.

Quentin Schultze, who calls himself "a fan of Alexis de Tocqueville," tells me that many of the potential problems with democracy that Tocqueville wrote about "are being exacerbated in this country by new communications." Describing the thesis of his recent book *Habits of the High-Tech Heart,* Schultze warns:

> *There have to be certain social morals that offset the instrumentalism of communication technology or else you don't have enough moral fabric for democracy to work. Tocqueville's big concern was what makes democracy work in a land that's so indifferent to tradition, and that doesn't have a state church. And he concluded that there are certain "habits of the heart"—that's his term—that exist. And he saw as the principle source of those [habits], volunteer involvement in a religious community. So that got me thinking about the Internet and the kind of rugged individualism that comes with these new technologies. And all this rhetoric about cyber-democracy and cyber-communities may be badly misguided.*

Schultze tells me he examined different theories of virtue from the Christian and Jewish traditions, and tried to learn how modern technologies helped or hindered the development of those virtues.

Philosophy and literature are the easiest and hardest disciplines to teach at a religious college: easy because the points of intersection between religion and those topics are numerous, there are plenty of religious philosophers and writers, and the habits of thought required to study philosophy and theology are similar; hard because many of the great modern philosophers and writers believe that God is dead and that religion is only an obstacle to serious intellectual engagement.

Scott Moore, who offers a Philosophy of Religion class at Baylor, laughingly tells me that his course provokes a lot of discussion. With Nietzsche, Moore acknowledges that students are being confronted with ideas that are antithetical to their religious beliefs. But, he tells me, "The great thing about Nietzsche is that a lot of eighteen-year-olds think no one has ever felt what they feel and no one is misunderstood the way they are and that just means they are grist for his mill."

"I had a similar experience when I was young," he says.

At Christendom College, Timothy O'Donnell, the school's president, says philosophy is a means to achieving the college's mission "to restore all things in Christ. When they're studying classical philosophy—you know, they're doing Plato, they're doing Aristotle—they're recognizing the great achievement that these men have made," he says. "But there would also be a Christian critique or a Catholic critique that would be brought there. That slavery is inappropriate, that their assessment of women is not fully accurate, not in keeping with the fuller [Catholic] vision."

O'Donnell argues, "Even when you come into modern philosophy, where there are people such as Nietzsche and others who are very hostile to a religious faith, there still needs to be an appreciation. You still have to know who those men are, and recognize the power in their ideas. I mean Nietzsche writes powerfully and beautifully. You can see why there would be a real attraction. So students need to be exposed to those things."

Some religious college professors report that their superiors do not want students to be exposed to certain philosophers,[18] but most seem to believe that they are more likely to encounter this kind of treatment at secular universities. Camille Lewis, who teaches rhetoric and public address at Bob Jones, tells me about her experience as a graduate student teaching at Indiana University. "In the classes I taught at IU, I had to be careful. I was a religious studies minor. Religious topics are of academic interest to me and so I would bring them up." She laments, "Students would get frustrated with me, thinking I was talking about something not appropriate for classroom." At Bob Jones, by contrast, she tells me, "The administration trusts me and I can do what I do." She also notes that she has "never had a complaint from a student and never heard of one either. They appreciate the fact that there can be differences [of opinion] and we have these friendly debates."

Alan Jacobs, who teaches English at Wheaton, describes his graduate student experience at UVA and the constraints placed upon him when he taught literature there. He recalls being one of three graduate students teaching a particular course. The second was a feminist, who, Jacobs says, made feminism the central theme of his course, and the third was a committed

---

[18] See the example of Damon Linker at Brigham Young in Chapter 1.

Marxist. Jacobs explains, "They had complete freedom to explore their convictions in the classroom, but I did not. And it was at that point that I began wondering what Christian higher education was like."

Twenty years later, Jacobs says the difference between teaching at UVA and teaching at Wheaton "is the experience of academic freedom. It was being able to explore my convictions and my concerns in the classroom and have people in the classroom willing to explore with me. That's what I found attractive from an early stage in my time here and it, more than anything else, keeps me here."

As an example of the contrast between these two positions, Jacobs discusses his experience teaching Dante:

> When I was at UVA, if I were talking about Dante, it was perfectly acceptable for me to fill in some historical context. Here is what he believed. But I was supposed to treat them as matters of historical record not available for evaluation. Here at Wheaton, one of the most interesting books for me to teach is Dante's Purgatory. My students don't believe in purgatory since they're Protestant. I don't believe in it myself. But Purgatory is not about purgatory. It's an allegory about the process of sanctification, about becoming holy, and when you're talking with Wheaton students about a book that discusses how one struggles against sin and how one grows spiritually, and how one can think about becoming more holy and Christlike, it's not an academic exercise. It's something they're thinking about and struggling with, and Dante then gets measured against experience of students. They're evaluating him not just in aesthetic terms but [asking whether] he is a reliable guide to the spiritual life. And generally they love that poem.

It works across religious lines as well. Arthur Budick, who teaches literature at Touro College, notices a similar reaction in his students when they are studying texts with religious themes. He assures me, "We don't foist Judaic notions on the writers we read—Joyce will not [turn] into an Orthodox Jew, no matter how you read him." But, he believes:

> In our attempt to understand writers, on the writers' own terms, we can approach the writers' point of view and background differently. We would try to understand Dubliners and Portrait of the Artist as a Young Man and later texts in light of Joyce's Catholic background. We try to see him as the general critical world sees him and enter into that other perspective,

but at the same time bring it back home, which means inevitably, as we discuss Joyce's Catholicism, we think about how it might relate to our own notions of what is Judaic.

When the students get to section three of Portrait *and study Stephen Daedalus's mortification of the senses, they're shocked because it's so fundamentally anti-Judaic, this rejection of the physical world. At the same time students will say there are elements of asceticism in Jewish tradition, as in the situation of the Nazirite who denies himself certain [material] things. It's kind of wonderful that the Judaic cultural background then becomes a means of entering into the cultural background of writers. It makes what is unfamiliar more familiar.*

What these descriptions of the integration of faith into the study of literature and philosophy have in common is that they tend to depend on trying to further understand the author's intent. But as anyone familiar with the modern academy will quickly note, this form of literary interpretation is not very popular now. To make matters more complicated for those attempting the integration of faith and learning, there has been a move within religious higher education, parallel to that in secular colleges and universities, toward a different, postmodern approach to the study of literature, politics, philosophy, and the social sciences.

My first hint of this drift came during a visit to Westmont College. Teaching at Westmont, an evangelical Christian school in Santa Barbara, California—the third wealthiest city in the U.S.—presents some obvious problems: How do you open the eyes of students to the problems of poverty when they never have to see it? How do you get them to free themselves from the competition to own the most expensive car when their environment seems to demand it? How do you induce them to attend church regularly when their lives are so comfortable? To Westmont's credit, its students are much involved in mission and service work, and most seem serious about their faith. But there is one difficulty that some of Westmont's professors don't know how to confront—theodicy. How do you explain to students, as one professor put it to me, "why I was born where I was and why I got what I got"? This question—why did God put me in California instead of Kabul?— is not an easy one to tackle. And, as Westmont's academic dean told me, some members of the Westmont community have decided that the problem is best addressed by viewing "reality as socially constructed."

There is a debate playing out at Westmont and other religious colleges around the country on the question of whether such a postmodern view of the world is compatible with true Christianity. (Until recently the conflict has been restricted to those religious colleges that are not as committed to their respective faiths, but now the trend seems to be moving into the more strongly religious schools.) Those who believe it is compatible justify their position by noting the Christian view that God's ways are unknowable to man, citing (for instance) the apostle Paul's remark that we humans only "see through a glass darkly." But one might well wonder whether, on the contrary, the historicist denial that we have *any* access to a reality that transcends our particular perspectives does not undermine the notion of religious truth itself.

So how has the very group that many believed would serve as a traditionalist bulwark against the disintegration of classical college education been coopted by the dogmas of postmodernism, radical feminism, historicism, and Marxism? And if this trend continues, will religious college faculty really have anything distinctive to pass on to their students?

Peer pressure is largely to blame for the move toward postmodernism. As other observers have pointed out, academia is a club, and professors at religious colleges want to join, too. Not only are they often coming out of the same graduate programs as their counterparts at secular schools, but once they obtain faculty appointments, they want to publish in the prominent academic journals and speak at the well-attended conferences.

But in recent years, as the popularity of the postmodern view grew and its scope expanded, religious scholars began to see it as a great point of entry for their own work: If all knowledge is essentially "perspectival" (as Nietzsche maintained) so that every subject needs to be addressed from, say, a woman's perspective and an African-American perspective, isn't a Christian perspective equally valid?

Many of the participants in the Lilly Seminar on Religion and Higher Education who produced the essays in *Religion, Scholarship, and Higher Education* would support John McGreevey, a history professor at Notre Dame, who notes in his essay, "I'm not convinced that framing religious perspectives as yet another assault on universal reason is the best strategy." But the contributors to the collection *Professing in the Postmodern Academy* are so thoroughly persuaded of the compatibility of Christianity and postmodernism that they jump through all sorts of rhetorical hoops to make latest academic trends fit their Christian worldview (or vice versa).

When it comes to faculty hiring, Margaret Falls-Corbitt, a professor of philosophy at Hendrix College in Arkansas, explains (in her contribution to the same book) how liberal Protestant colleges (like her own) are upholding the Christian virtue of tolerance by hiring non-Christian professors. Search committees at these schools, she observes, "work from an assumption of their own majority status. . . . From such a perspective, requiring candidates for faculty positions to be Christian feels like a prejudicial act, one that contributes to an unfair distribution of the scarce benefit of acceptance into the power structures that be." (One might question, of course, whether requiring professors at a religious college to be professing Christians is truly "prejudicial" in the sense that racial exclusions, having no relevance to any proper educational mission, do. And perhaps there's something a bit humorous about the belief that acquiring a teaching position at Hendrix College makes one part of the "power structure.")

Though there is an odd but growing concern among administrators and faculty at the more liberal religious schools that professors will be too biased when teaching about Christianity, professors of other world religions hired by the schools to instill diversity in the student body do not have any qualms about proclaiming the truth of their religions. Here is the situation at one Lutheran college as described in *Religion on Campus*: While Karen Cassidy, who teaches the History of Christianity, calls herself "a historian whose topic happens to be religion," Sinad Banik tells his classes that he is a "Hindu scholar rather than simply a scholar of Hinduism." It seems from this account that it is often regarded as more acceptable to teach non-Christian religions with less of a commitment to objectivity than Christian ones.

Although the very pursuit of higher learning undoubtedly requires ensuring that instruction at religious colleges seriously considers the perspectives of other religions and of the nonreligious, to ground the mission of a religious college in the postmodern notion of valuing "the other" or "the stranger" quickly raises some substantial problems. Does not a religious college by its very nature make what postmodernists call "truth claims"? May not its mission necessarily entail privileging some viewpoints over others?

Villanova economics professor Charles Zech's essay in *Religion, Education and the American Experience* serves as a reminder that the form of "tolerance" favored by professors at some of these colleges has its costs. Surveying the faculties and presidents of Catholic colleges and universities nationwide, Zech notes, "Some faculty were openly hostile to the notion that the Catholic identity of the school should be important. One respondent said, 'To introduce the bias of any religion into education, as this survey suggests, is totally counterproductive to the higher educational process. You should be ashamed of yourself for even suggesting it.'" Ironically, a policy of mere "tolerance" (understood as neutrality) can engender an intolerance of the religious perspective itself. And the college is left with nothing but an aggressively secular perspective.

Teachers at some of the less strongly religious colleges strive for the "separation of faith and learning," rather than its integration. Elizabeth Newman, who teaches at St. Mary's, Notre Dame, cites the example of a colleague who teaches economics and tries to keep his own religious beliefs out of the classroom. While properly emphasizing that teaching should not be a form of "indoctrination," he added that the very use of "'values language often serves as a cloak for one's political bias.'" Newman rightly observes that this "privatization of values" does not result in a classroom free of bias—religious, political, or otherwise—but instead simply enhances the likelihood that students will unthinkingly adopt the views of the surrounding culture.

Presumably, one reason students choose to attend a religious institution was the expectation that the claims of faith would be addressed in the classroom, rather than merely bracketed. In fact, by simply submitting to the postmodern method of studying the humanities and social sciences, professors may be depriving students of the very things they long for at secular schools.

In the collection *Religion, Scholarship, and Higher Education,* Jean Bethke Elshtain, a professor of social and political ethics at the University of Chicago, describes this longing in her education: "Let me take the reader back to graduate school in the mid 1960s. This was not a calm time, culturally and politically speaking. . . . Many of us were struggling to understand what was going on and to sort out just where we 'fit' in the midst of all this. Who were we anyway—as a people, as singular persons? But with a rare few exceptions, none of my graduate courses in political science addressed any of these matters." That movements such as behaviorism and then rational choice theory stripped political science and many other disciplines of any of the important questions is echoed by Alan Wolfe, another contributor to the book, who "confess[es] to being flabbergasted by the popularity" of these "reductionist" models.

Contributor Susan Handelman, a professor of English at Bar-Ilan University in Israel, cites the consequences of this shift in a number of letters her students in a Literature and Religion class wrote to one another when she was teaching at the University of Maryland. Student Caleb laments, "Nothing in my studies has ever given me sufficient reason for pause. Nothing in my life has 'arrested the senses.'" Nat, a philosophy major, writes, "I hope you all find the answers you are looking for. And if you do, please e-mail me because I am so tired of asking paradoxically unanswerable questions that at this point I'm pretty much open to anything you got."

Besides leaving students with nothing but "paradoxically unanswerable questions," it is true that removing the religious perspective from the classroom simply leaves a different irreligious and sometimes antireligious perspective remaining. To the claim that scholars of religion in particular must keep their views out of a secular classroom, Warren Nord plausibly responds (in *Religion, Education and the American Experience*):

> *If a neo-Darwinian biologist can argue that evolution and ultimate reality are purposeless, surely a scholar in religious studies can argue that reality is purposeful; if a Freudian can argue that God is nothing more than the neurotic projection of our unconscious minds, surely a scholar in religious studies can argue that some religious experiences are veridical experiences of God; if a philosopher can argue that the existentialists had it right and that reality is absurd, surely a scholar of religious studies can argue that the religious thinkers have it right and that God gives meaning to reality.*

Despite this sound observation, in the end, Nord's essay, like many others in these books, still represents the central function of education as assisting each student to develop and express his particular "identity," rather than transmitting a common core of religiously grounded knowledge to students with a view to making them both educated and thoughtfully religious human beings.

Even if they can avoid the trap of the postmodern approach to truth, many professors still adopt the perspectivalism inherent in the theory. The contributors' focus is typically on what Elizabeth Newman calls "the personal coefficient," and what another author calls "relatedness." Numerous contributors seem to see their schools' religious identity as best expressed in service learning projects or in small seminars devoted to encouraging each student to describe his personal experiences and discuss how his identity was shaped: Education is seen more as a focus of self-expression rather than a vehicle for properly shaping young people's "selves." Judging from these volumes, postmodernism, and the radical individualism that it encourages, has too often served as a vehicle for evading fundamental questions arising from the interaction between faith and learning. What's left is just a lot of individuals sharing their perspectives with other individuals who have their own idiosyncratic perspectives.

These postmodern tendencies are certainly beginning to eat away at the identities of a few of the colleges that I visited. But another conflicting trend—one that arises from the more practical, vocational spheres of study—is acting as a bulwark against them. Though it is true that a disproportionate number of students at some religious colleges go on to academic careers (in a 1994 study by Franklin and Marshall College, Wheaton ranked eleventh out of 925 liberal arts colleges in terms of the number of its graduates who go on to receive PhDs), most religious college graduates enter other professions. And many of those nonacademic professions are increasingly demanding college graduates with answers to some of those "paradoxically unanswerable questions." In the fields of law, business, medicine, and government, for example, employers are looking for candidates who have given some thought to the ethical issues they will face in their professional lives and how they will respond to them.

Tom Monaghan is counting on this. When this founder of Domino's Pizza sold his holdings for about $4 billion, he set out to create a number of new Catholic educational enterprises. Most recently, he broke ground on a new Catholic university covering 750 acres near Naples, Florida. The school, to which Monaghan has committed $200 million, "is for students whose faith is central to their lives," he told *The New York Times*. Expressing concern that "at some Catholic universities, students graduate with their religious faith more shaky than when they arrive"—a finding confirmed by a recent study from the Cardinal Newman Society—Monaghan's new school will have no coed dorms or gay support groups. And, most importantly, faith will be an integral part of the curriculum.

But before Monaghan headed to the Sunshine State, he conceived the idea for the Ave Maria School of Law. When Monaghan called his friend Bernard Dobranski, then dean of Catholic University's law school, and said, "I'm thinking about starting a new law school," Dobranski recalls laughing, "What? Do you think we have too few lawyers, Tom?" But Dobranski seems to have already known what Monaghan was getting at.

He tells me, "I think you have to ask a different question. Do we have enough good lawyers? If your answer is no, then another law school devoted to doing things differently would be appropriate." At the end of the conversation, Monaghan asked Dobranski if he was ready to come up to Ann Arbor, Michigan, and start Ave Maria.

Less than two years later, the school opened its doors—in a former laboratory building that Monaghan purchased from the University of Michigan—to an inaugural class of seventy-five. Its mission, according to Dobranski, was to "offer an outstanding legal education in fidelity to the Catholic faith." Stephen Safranek explains that rather than substituting religious education for legal education, the professors are committed to making students more well-rounded lawyers: "When they come out of here, they will understand the fundamental principles more than other law students would."

Christopher McGowan, who proudly announces that he "was the first person to say yes to Ave Maria," had never intended to go to law school. After stints working on political campaigns in his home state of Iowa, going to flight school, and working for the Honeywell Corporation, McGowan, thirty-three, says when he read about Ave Maria, he thought, "If that's what they're teaching, then it's worth going to law school."

Indeed, McGowan's story is hardly unique at Ave Maria. The school has enrolled many older students in the middle of other careers, who once considered law, but were turned off by the reputation of the profession. At the age of thirty-one, David Krause left his job as a mechanical engineer in Louisiana and moved with his wife and three kids to Michigan in order to attend Ave Maria. He learned about the school from an article in USA Today. "It was about lawyers who were interested in justice over winning," he remarks with some lingering amazement.

In the fall of 2002, two years after my first visit and just as job searches were gearing up for the first class of graduates, I asked these students whether the experiment has worked, whether it is possible to include classical philosophy and Catholic social teaching in a legal education without the former taking away from the latter. Monica Secord, who has become the editor of the school's fledgling law review, offers me what she thinks is "the most notable example [of this integration]. In my labor law class, we worked on some of the papal encyclicals on labor and unions. And I guess it was a little bit surprising to me that the Pope has treatises on unions and labor that really speak to modern problems in a very real way. And so that was probably the most successful integration for me personally as sort of a wakeup. I thought, 'That's really a neat way to approach the issues.'"

Generally speaking, she tells me, "I think where religion does come up, it's a natural fit and it doesn't take much of a stretch when you're not thinking about law in isolation. When you start looking at the whole person involved in these legal problems, it's really easy to integrate that into the curriculum and to add something to the discussion, and not just some tangent."

In his constitutional law classes, Richard Myers continues to develop ways of including a faith perspective. "We cover a range of different things, but in particular we focus on a lot of the privacy issues: abortion, assisted suicide, and things like that. And there we've read some of the papal encyclicals. But I think it's an area where what the Catholic Church has said about the nature of freedom, the value of human life, provides a real perspective on those cases." Myers also discusses some of the less obvious connections between law and the Church, as in the principle of subsidiarity. Even though it is not explicitly in the U.S. Constitution, Myers believes that the learning about the Church's support of this doctrine can give people "an appreciation for some of the benefits of federalism and the benefit of focusing on intermediate communities or mediating institutions, like the family and churches and neighborhoods."

In a First Amendment class discussion of a case involving abortion protesters, there is one student who tries to steer things off track into a simply religious realm, but the professor cuts him off quickly. The Ave Maria faculty does not for a moment let students believe that their education is a purely academic exercise. And contrary to my initial suspicions about the group of students who would come to an unknown law school for which they had to pay very little, these students are not looking at the school as a way to continue their liberal arts education. Seventy percent of the first graduating class (2003) already have taken jobs making use of their degree. Out of the sixty-five graduates, nineteen are working at law firms around the country, ten have federal or state clerkships, another four are working in state government, four are in the Judge Advocate's General (JAG) program, two are working for public policy groups, two are at corporations, and three have taken positions at their alma mater.

As much as Americans may suspect the members of the legal profession of having few scruples, nowhere has the divorce between a profession and its ethics been more evident recently than in the world of business. And those who believe the corporate scandals that have plagued the country over the last couple of years are over would be well advised to look at a recent National Association of Scholars survey of how the current crop of college graduates view their responsibilities in business. Zogby International, which conducted the poll of 401 randomly selected college seniors, found that 73 percent of students agreed with the proposition that "what is right and wrong depends on differences in individual values and cultural diversity," as opposed to only 25 percent who believed "there are clear and uniform standards of right and wrong by which everyone should be judged." This translated directly into business practices, according to the NAS:

> When the students were asked to prioritize the importance of various business practices, based on what they had been taught at college, "recruiting a diverse workforce in which women and minorities are advanced and promoted" outpolled "providing clear and accurate business statements to stockholders and creditors" as most important, the former being supported by 38 percent of the respondents and the latter 23 percent. Another 18 percent ranked "minimizing environmental pollution by adopting the latest anti-pollution technology and complying with government regulations" as most important, while still another 18 percent gave first place to "avoiding layoffs by not exporting jobs or moving plants from one area to another."

> Among business and accounting majors, a plurality (43 percent) reported being taught that "providing clear and accurate business statements" was the most important business practice. But even within this group a majority (56 percent) preferred one of the other three alternatives.

The question of how to combat current and future corporate irresponsibility has begun to grab the attention of religious communities. Faith-based investment funds, for instance, have been expanding rapidly (over a dozen were founded in 2002). The Ave Maria Fund favors companies that adhere to Catholic values by refusing, for example, to produce or sell contraceptives. The Azzad/Dow Jones Ethical Market Fund, a Muslim group, buys only shares of companies that do not charge or pay interest. And the Noah Fund shuns corporations that produce or distribute alcohol, tobacco, and pornography. Bill Van Allen, the chief executive of Noah, told the *Washington Post*: "If Jesus were doing the investing, he would invest the way we do."

But wouldn't it be better if Jesus were running the companies? After all, these funds don't look any more closely than secular ones at accounting methods, an aspect of business where vice has been rampant of late. Indeed, within days of the Enron scandal, corporations were scrambling to institute business ethics programs to stave off both the practical effects of cheating employees and the resulting lack of consumer confidence they had created.

But the students who have studied business at religious colleges and graduate institutions already offer employers that expertise. Ralph Miller, a professor at Regent, tells me he integrates faith into the classroom by emphasizing the biblical concept of "stewardship"—the idea that businessmen are entrusted with protecting the interests of many groups. "We often forget about the stakeholders" in a company, he says, other than customers and employers. "How about your banker? Your supplier?" Miller says, "Being a Christian businessman is not all about being a nice guy. It's about being righteous and godly in relationships."

At Touro College, Meyer Peikes, a professor of finance, explains to his student that "the difference between Jewish business ethics and secular ethics is basically that the former is *halachah*—law." There are ways to be a businessman that go above and beyond what Jewish law requires, but the *shulchan aroch* (a sixteenth-century concordance to Jewish law) is extensive in its prescriptions. He notes: "We do have a principle not to help those who are propagating sin." For Jews, this might include tobacco companies, Peikes explains, "because Judaism forbids the purposeful infliction of harm on the body."

Of course, with business there is always a bottom line. Why would a company hire students from religious institutions? Todd Brotherson, a professor of business at Southern Virginia University, citing the Mormon missionary experience, suggests that his students have excelled at personal finance services because they have a background in talking to people, and he adds, half jokingly, "They are not dissuaded by a high failure rate." Kenneth Bigel, a Touro professor, says his students are instilled with the belief that they "need to be 'a light unto the nations,' as the Bible says." In short, "They must always be aware that the world is looking at them and they need to be doing the right thing, even to the small mundane everyday matters." But the sentiment that may most comfort employers and investors is expressed by Jordi Arimany, a Regent student. "It is the boss who promotes me," but ultimately, "I'm accountable to God."

Given the pervasiveness of this sentiment among religious college graduates in all walks of life, it was hardly surprising when *Time* named Coleen Rowley, the FBI whistleblower and a graduate of the evangelical Wartburg College in Iowa, as one of its people of the year for 2002. Though she rarely mentions her faith explicitly, Rowley's statements do belie the sense of purpose that she and her husband found at an evangelical college. Speaking to a constitutional law class at her alma mater, she explained how she was able to write the memo that sparked a major investigation into the FBI after September 11. "Everyone says, 'I can't change the world,' and people have a sense of futility. On the other side, you have to live with yourself and you have to try."

Religious college graduates are also trying to change the political world (a subject taken up in detail in the chapter on political activism). Massachusetts governor Mitt Romney (Brigham Young '71) and House Speaker Dennis Hastert (Wheaton '64) are showing their younger counterparts that it's possible to bring religious values into mainstream politics. And the medical world's need for professionals well versed in the problems presented by modern science can be filled increasingly by religious college graduates. Baylor, with its minor in medical humanities and medical mission programs (see the chapter on Baylor), and Notre Dame, with its bioethics lectures for students and recent graduates, are leading this charge.

Ultimately, religious colleges and universities have a tremendous opportunity to provide hospitals, law firms, businesses, and political organizations with the kind of ethically aware professionals that they desperately need today. If administrators and professors at these schools follow their impulses to teach their students the ways in which faith can inform students' vocations, they will be doing a tremendous service. If they leave students with only a series of unanswerable questions and instill in them the principle that one's personal "perspective" counts for more than religious truth, it is unlikely that graduates of religious colleges will add anything distinctive to American life.

CHAPTER TWELVE

WHERE ARE THE PROTESTS?
POLITICAL ACTIVISM AT RELIGIOUS COLLEGES

The 10 million college students in the United States under the age of twenty-five may be a key swing group in the 2004 presidential election, according to a recent study conducted by Harvard University's Institute of Politics. Fifty-nine percent of those surveyed say they "will definitely vote" and another 27 percent say they "will probably vote." But such a high level of participation would barely approach that of the fevered political pitch of the 1960s, when sit-ins and walk-outs became college rites of passage.[19] Though American universities were never very far removed from the political debates of the day (a recent book called *The Campus and Nation in Crisis* by historian Willis Rudy argues that political activity has been a vital part of university life in the U.S. from the time of the Revolutionary War), the nature of campus political activity changed considerably during that decade.

In an essay called "What Happened at Berkeley," Nathan Glazer, who taught at the school during the free speech movement, describes the cultural shift that took place then. The protests began when students demanded that the university administration remove restrictions on bringing speakers to campus. Glazer explains that those restrictions "go back to a time when no political activity of any kind was allowed on campus. Under this earlier situation, even candidates for the presidency were not allowed to speak at Berkeley: to have permitted such a thing would presumably have involved the university in 'politics' and as a state university it was not supposed to be involved in politics." Campus political discourse quickly turned from one that was intellectually based to one that was advocacy-based.

What did they advocate? From pulling out of Vietnam and pushing for civil rights in the sixties and seventies, to rallying against U.S. involvement in Central America in the eighties and building shantytowns on campus quad-

---

[19] Voting turnout among young people aged 18 to 24 declined by 13 percentage points between 1972 and 2000, according to the Youth Vote Coalition.

rangles to get universities to divest from companies doing business in South Africa, no political issue has escaped college student notice. The nineties brought Take Back the Night rallies by campus feminists to promote awareness of violence against women and a more radical agenda of female "empowerment." Gay and lesbian students began to demand university recognition and funding for their activities. As the economy slumped in the late eighties and early nineties, students protested tuition hikes and cuts in the number and amount of federal financial aid packages. (A nationwide boycott of Coors was organized because the beer manufacturer was said to be giving money to right-wing organizations like the Heritage Foundation, which advocated such cost-cutting measures.) Finally, the late nineties brought student protests over sweatshop conditions in Third-World countries and demands of "living wages" for university employees.

And today, foreign policy is back. Voices speaking against U.S. retaliation in Afghanistan were reported on campuses across the country. As U.S. presence there began to fade from the headlines, students at some larger and more liberal universities, like UCLA, took up the cause of the Palestinians. Retaliation by the Israeli government for a rash of suicide bombings in the spring of 2002, including the infamous Passover Seder massacre, prompted numerous anti-Semitic incidents on campuses and rallies supporting both sides of the conflict. Other students have been involved in the protests of globalization (though it's been somewhat harder to pinpoint the exact nature of their objections). The war in Iraq has brought an even greater response with tens of thousands of students participating in protests last spring.

The return to foreign policy as a subject of campus debate, though, has brought out a new group on college campuses—conservative activists. Indeed, those in favor of the war have also staged events—a spring 2003 survey found that hawks outnumbered doves two to one on campuses—demonstrating support for the military and U.S. policy.

A few years ago, college student activity on behalf of the American government would have been unheard of, but the campus conservative movement has been growing and students on the right, tired of being ridiculed by the monolith of liberal faculty and administrators, are adopting some of the same tactics as their baby boomer predecessors. A recent *Los Angeles Times* story documented the increasing number and influence of conservative newspapers on campus. And a *New York Times Magazine* cover story described the phenomenon of the "Hipublicans," a new generation of college conservatives who do not dress in Brooks Brothers and penny loafers, who are in touch with the sensibilities of their fellow students with regard to homosexuality and racial tolerance, but who protest administrative speech codes and university bans of ROTC on campus. Groups of conservative undergraduates at the University of Michigan and Columbia, among other places, won significant media attention in 2003 and 2004 by hosting bake sales where black students paid less for cookies than white students, sending the message that affirmative action holds people of different races to different standards.

Generally speaking, students at religious colleges have not entered the political fray to the extent of their secular counterparts, and certainly not in the same manner. In part, this is due to the conservative outlook that is widespread on these campuses—unlike those at secular colleges, conservatives at religious colleges have not faced much opposition—but other factors are also at work. First, religious college students are sometimes purposefully isolated from the political environment they live in, the result of administrators and parents who are trying to shelter them from the secular world. Second, the students are generally very committed to their studies, and are thus reluctant to become too caught up in political activities. Third, their religious beliefs provide a sense of purpose in their lives that secular students, who become involved in political causes, sometimes lack.

To assess how much these factors are at work, it is useful to look at political activism on religious campuses with regard not only to recent national debates but also in terms of student involvement in campus, local, and religious communities. THINK GLOBALLY, ACT LOCALLY, reads the bumper sticker, and it's true that the best way to understand the political worldview of religious college students is to examine how they behave on the smaller scale.

Almost every college in the country has a student government and a student newspaper, both constructed to imitate the structures of the world outside, with elected bodies in charge of the government and journalists assigned to educate their fellow students about current events. But as every thoughtful undergraduate finds out eventually, such arrangements are also illusions. After all, parents pay for their children to be part of the college community and students agree that the school's administration has the final say. Not to get overwrought, but going to college is like choosing to live under a dictatorship, the leaders of which allow some freedoms but are under no obligation to do so.

At religious colleges, the administrations are invested with even more authority than at secular schools. This is particularly true, for instance, at

Brigham Young where the leaders of the church make up the administration of the school and at some Catholic schools where a particular order of clergy is responsible for the university's governance. But there is an extent to which students at all strongly religious colleges afford administrators a degree of reverence not present at other schools.

A meeting with the BYUSA, Brigham Young's student association, reveals a close relationship with the university leadership. As Andrea Uale, the student vice president, explains, "We have a mission statement that is directly in line with BYU's." When asked whether they ever disagree with the administration, Andrea explains they might at first, but then, "You come to understand that the administration is working on a different part of [an issue] and maybe you didn't see it and maybe you didn't understand. A lot of the time you understand after the fact." Students seem to invest the administration with something approaching a sense of divine mystery.

Nor is it just the administrators who have this divine mandate. Many of the young men and women who get involved in student government, like Heath Lambert, president of the Gordon College Student Association (GCSA), tell me they feel as though there are religious duties that come with the office. Having come to Gordon with a desire to go into politics, Heath added Bible as a second major and then decided he wanted to be a pastor instead. It's clear from the way he describes his position that the two callings are deeply connected. "I told people last year that the goal of the GCSA was the advancement of the glory of God, and we would exist for His honor. I feel responsibility to obey the moral law in the student handbook and to be somebody who is sort of above reproach. I'm not on some kind of elitist kick but being a student government leader at a religious school is different in that you have to set an example and be more of a spiritual leader."

Student elections at religious college are, needless to say, rarely mudslinging events. Jeremy Chisholm, a first-year law student at Ave Maria, compares his experience running for class representative to the student bar association with his previous experiences in school politics. "When you're here with seventy students in your class, that's like an extended family. I mean you're friends with all these people, you can't demonize them." The combination of the common faith and the small student population at Ave Maria, explains Jeremy, make "you kind of feel bad if you beat [your opponent]."

Admittedly, this kind of sentiment among students can also lead to some pretty boring elections. When I ask the editor of the newspaper at Bob Jones about the platforms that various student candidates ran on last year, she tells me that one's goal was "unity and leading the student body toward

Christlikeness." Acknowledging that the other candidate's goal was basically the same, she adds, the newspaper "doesn't really bother to cover politics on campus since it's just a popularity issue." And at Christendom College, the campus community does not even pretend to have disagreements over how student government should be run. When Paul Jalsevac wanted to be president of the student council, he asked the administration, which, along with the previous year's council, chose the new leadership.

Aside from acting as spiritual guides for their fellow students and representing the university to alumni and donors, most of the religious college student governments are in charge of doling out a certain amount of money to other student groups and using the remainder to organize campus social events. Occasionally, though, student governments at religious colleges do weigh in on institutional conflicts. For instance, the Calvin student government recently issued a statement opposing the rule that faculty must send their children to a Christian school. Student government leader Betsy Cooper tells me, "We lose faculty because of the requirement." But she laments that other than "opening up the debate, there's not a whole lot we can do." Similarly, though Baylor's student body president Matthew Flanigan has concerns about his school's proposed increase in tuition, he does not think that students will be able to change the administration's position on the matter.

Some of the more recently founded schools have asked for greater input from their student governments in formulating school policy. Young men and women at Patrick Henry and Soka have been busily engaged in drafting their own student constitutions. Michael Daniels, the chairman of PHC's student government, tells me, "It's like a microcosm of the Constitutional Convention in 1787." His eyes light up as he notes, "We want to keep the government as limited as possible."

Since student governments rarely butt heads with administrators, it often falls to student journalists to serve as campus contrarians. But newspapers at religious schools are generally tightly regulated. On the most restrictive end of the spectrum, there is the Bob Jones *Collegian,* which doubles as a kind of alumni newsletter. As a result, it is completely uninteresting—filled with stories of people happily playing soccer or flattering interviews with administrators. *The Daily Universe,* BYU's paper, has a circulation of over 30,000 and does cover a wider range of topics, but by making the newspaper an academic class supervised by a teacher, and by paying many of the editors, the school's administration ensures that nothing controversial is printed in it.

Newspapers at other religious colleges have more freedom. Christian

Bell, the editor of *The Chimes* at Calvin, tells me that that his school is one of the few strongly Christian colleges that allows its student newspaper an independent voice. He thinks the newspaper has an influence on administrative decisions, and even on the Christian Reformed Church denomination. But with this influence comes a responsibility, says Beth Heinen, his coeditor. The day before I spoke with them, the editors rejected an ad for bartenders. Christian notes that most people wouldn't be offended by such an ad, but the paper tries to respect the administration's "dry-campus" rules. When I ask the editors of *The Chimes* whether they ever run anything controversial, they tell me about a piece that ran in the opinion section last year called "Were Jesus' Actions Really Without Sin?," which elicited many angry letters. And there are nontheological controversies as well. In one issue Beth and Christian published an article on "critical violations" of the Michigan state health code in two of the school's dining halls, which the administration was pretty unhappy with.

Some religious college newspapers, like Notre Dame's, Yeshiva's, and Baylor's, do tend to be regularly engaged in open criticism of their schools' policies. In the case of the first, coverage of the efforts by a gay and lesbian group to be recognized by the administration as well as criticism of the new *Ex Corde* standards have stirred some controversy. In the second, the newspaper has taken issue with the school's search process for a new president and its faculty hiring policies. At Baylor, the newspaper's editorials in favor of the legalization of gay marriage, greater faculty diversity, and tolerance for women ministers in the Baptist Church have sparked heated debate on campus.

Even on campuses bustling with extracurricular activities and campus controversies, the young men and women involved with student government and campus newspapers make up a small percentage of the population. Over the last few decades, as campus politics has been toned down, community service activities have come to replace it. This new "activism" has become a big draw for students at secular colleges (at Harvard for instance, the umbrella service group, Philips Brooks House, involves more undergraduates than any other organization), but its size and scope at religious schools is almost overwhelming.

At Gordon, about 25 percent of the students participate in one of the school's fourteen service programs, and an additional four or five groups go on service trips during school breaks. More than half of Westmont students are involved in some kind of service program, which include urban initiatives in San Francisco and Los Angeles, in addition to a yearly trip to Mexico, where over four hundred students camp out as they help build homes for the area's poor. At Wheaton, about four hundred students take part in weekly activities, serving in hospitals or correctional institutions. Another couple of hundred participate during the summer or spring break.

Service has become so popular and time consuming that many religious college administrators and faculty have become concerned it is overtaking academics as a priority for their students. At several evangelical colleges, faculty members expressed the worry that students see their faith calling them to devote their time to Habitat for Humanity–type programs instead of their academics. Coming out of activist evangelical youth groups, it is much easier for students to see their religious obligation to build homes for the poor than to study chemistry.

Even if religious faculty are able to get their charges to place service work in its proper context within a university education, there are other issues they must address. Like just how much the discussion of faith should be an element of service. Tim Sisk, director of Christian outreach at Wheaton, explains, "Some work in hospitals where technically you can't talk about religion, and so they don't. They just go there to serve. With other types of things, they have freedom to proclaim or preach the Bible. And students will fall into whatever category they're comfortable with." Sisk emphasizes that whatever the type of service, you don't want to intrude on someone's life in order to proselytize. "We see it as a much more comfortable building of relationships."

At almost all of the Christian schools I visit, some student or professor would describe the institution's evangelization efforts in the words of St. Francis of Assisi: "Everywhere you go, preach the Gospels. Use words if you must!" Serving in soup kitchens, tutoring, building homes, or volunteering in prisons are obvious ways that students can spiritually influence others without handing out pamphlets or proselytizing door to door. Indeed, for many students, service work has all but replaced their more explicit evangelization efforts.

As welcome as this change might seem for those on the receiving end of such efforts, there are those in religious communities who find it cause for consternation. In the recent debates over government funding of faith-based organizations, for instance, faith leaders wondered whether forcing such groups to limit their religious language in performing their service (as would be required by the government) would result in the dilution of their missions, and, moreover, whether they can be as effective if they are forced to make such changes. Even if the service itself proves no less helpful to the men and women at the homeless shelter or to the children learning to read, removing the religious mission from volunteer work will affect the volunteers.

Religious college students, of course, have obligations to a community beyond their immediate geographic one. Involvement in a faith community for some just means serving on a committee at a local church, but students at religious colleges tend to be more deeply concerned with the direction of a nationwide or even worldwide denomination. Calvin, for instance, has been drawn into debates over the role of women in the Reformed churches, and Baylor has been at the center of Baptist controversies on homosexuality and evolution.

But nowhere more than at the orthodox Catholic schools is there as much of a personal sense of the burden to save a worldwide church from forces that would corrupt it. Students regularly scrutinize Vatican documents for greater understanding of the church's direction. During my visit to Christendom, for instance, an announcement of a small change in the rosary prayer provokes heated debate. It is somewhat surprising, then, that students at these schools express only a hazy understanding of the sexual abuse scandals that have rocked the Church in the last few years.

Students at Thomas Aquinas College had not heard of the priests in their own Los Angeles area who had been dismissed on charges of sexual misconduct, and no one at the school would offer opinions about the Church cover-ups on a national level. A student at Christendom, who matriculated from St. Gregory's High School in Scranton (where members of the Society of St. John were accused of getting male students drunk and sleeping in the same beds with them) tells me, "The scandals don't concern me personally."

Students at Magdalen College, perhaps because of their location in southern New Hampshire, could not remain removed from the scandals for as long. It really came home to the student body recently, explains junior Kristen Sticha, more than a year after the first stories about how the Church had handled itself began to appear in the *Boston Globe*. "We really realized what was going on when we went down to the cathedral in Manchester because the bishop had asked us to come." But her reaction to the meeting is surprising. "It was the most incredible feeling of solidarity because here's the bishop and he was talking to his people. It was so awesome to be there, supporting him."

Sticha, who first came to Magdalen for a high school summer program, explains, "I totally believe in the authority of the Holy Father, and that the Catholic Church isn't a democracy. No matter how many people say Bishop [John] McCormack should leave because he has made mistakes, it doesn't matter as long as the Holy Father thinks he should be there. He's our father. It would be like kids saying we don't want him to be our dad." As tutor Mark Gillis puts it, "Our faith is not dependent on the vice or virtue of individuals."

Even at Thomas More College, by far the most liberal of this group of schools, theology and mathematics professor Karl Cooper does not believe there is a problem with the Church's decision-making structure. Rather, he tells me the most important factor in preventing sexual abuse by the clergy is for parents and children to spend time together. "If there are healthy relationships between parents and children, there will be fewer opportunities for them to become involved with adults outside the family in ways that their parents don't know about."

Such attitudes are a far cry from the Catholic mainstream in the Boston area near Magdalen and Thomas More, where outrage with the Church's cover-ups has reached a fevered pitch. According to a 2003 *Boston Globe* poll, clear majorities support allowing priests to marry and the ordination of women, and some 40 percent say they would support an American church independent of the Vatican.

There are two factors behind the disconnect of these colleges from the Catholic mainstream. The first is Vatican II. Though some at these colleges would reject the principles behind the Second Vatican Council entirely, most would simply say the document has been misinterpreted. Vatican II, Gillis tells me, calls on everyone to "be a saint," whether he is a doctor, a lawyer, or a garbageman, as he himself once was. As a layperson, Gillis says, "You can't know less than Father So-and-So, because you're just as accountable." At Magdalen, students and faculty alike say that a correct interpretation of Vatican II would elevate the role of the laity without bringing down the clergy. It is the misinterpretation of Vatican II that students and faculty believe is responsible for the tolerance of homosexual behavior at many seminaries in the country and, as a result, the current sexual scandals.

The second reason for the odd reaction (or lack of reaction) to the controversy is that these colleges are isolated from the outside world. Magdalen, for instance, bans TV and radio. While newspapers are permitted, few students pay attention to them. (As tutor Patrick Powers explains, "The whole education here encourages you to suspend interest in [contemporary] issues for several years.") Nancy Carlin admits that she never reads the newspaper, but doesn't think that she would get anything out of it anyway. She probably will read one when she graduates, but worries that some of the headlines are just regurgitations from the previous day, that the editors are more concerned with sales than with the enlargement of readers' minds, and finally, expresses concern that newspapers are all "too slanted."

Magdalen president Jeffrey Karls is somewhat worried about the potential isolation of his students. While he supports the school's restrictive policies on television and radio, he has invited local political candidates to speak on campus. The school's founding years, Karls says, "were more focused on making sure students were prevented from being swallowed up by the culture and its immorality." But now, he says, "We have to get beyond being fearful."

Most religious college students, though, are not fearful of the world outside. They find themselves deeply interested in politics, often more so than their secular counterparts. Outsiders to these institutions may think they already have a pretty good idea of where students stand on the political issues of the day. In short, they must be pro-life, pro–death penalty, anti–gay rights, pro–school prayer, anti-welfare, anti-divorce, etc. But are religious college graduates, as many people suspect, simply filling out the ranks of the armies of the religious right?

Ashley Woodiwiss, a political science professor at Wheaton College, cuts short his "Gandhi, King and Havel" seminar so that I can ask his upper level students some questions about their views on religion and politics. The twenty or so students hold a relatively wide range of political views but they all seem to agree with one student who tells me, "Christianity should never be reduced to politics. The Christian Coalition perverts the cause of the church and the cause of Christ."

It is a surprising sentiment to find at the nation's flagship evangelical college that counts Billy Graham among its graduates.

But the thoughts expressed in Woodiwiss's class are fairly common among evangelical and Catholic college students across the country, and they are confusing a certain set of liberal commentators. Former *New York Times* columnist Bill Keller recently noted, "As an independent political structure, the Christian right is dying. For one thing, the organizations that hit their stride in the 1980s have waned. The Moral Majority is long gone. The Christian Coalition is withering. Bombastic evangelical power brokers like Jerry Falwell and Pat Robertson have aged into irrelevance, and now exist mainly as ludicrous foils."

But where did the members of this once ubiquitous coalition go? Has evangelical Christianity simply died out as a force in politics? Keller thinks they have been somehow subsumed into the Republican Party base where they are occasionally "mollified" in the same way as other segments of the party. Keller's fellow *Times* columnist Nicholas Kristof suggests that the Moral Majority types are just softening, even liberalizing.

Neither Kristof nor Keller take any note of the fact that both Falwell and Robertson, rather than aging "into irrelevance," are pouring most of their time and money into religious colleges. Both Falwell's Liberty University and Robertson's Regent University have been growing at a fast clip, with the former adding a law school and the latter adding an undergraduate program in the fall of 2004. Both have also had some success in sending their graduates into politics upon graduation. But these universities are not simply forming clones of their founders, either. Their views are generally more interesting and thoughtful.

Understanding the political outlook of students matriculating from religious colleges today requires a look back to the time they were born—the mid eighties. It was the height of the culture wars and the abortion wars, the time of Margaret Atwood's hysterical antireligious satire and the founding of the staunchly secular People for the American Way. In 1984, Richard Neuhaus published *The Naked Public Square,* arguing that the Moral Majority and other groups like it had emerged as a reaction to a public sphere that was becoming increasingly devoid of religious voices, and the "secular reduction of moral discourse to a contest over interests."

On the surface, perhaps, it seems as though little has changed since 1984: *Roe v. Wade* is still the law of the land, there's a Republican president, and the ACLU is still suing over the slightest public mention of religion. But twenty years have wrought some interesting changes. The Supreme Court has approved public voucher programs for religious schools. Organizations like the Foundation for Individual Rights in Education are winning battles for religious students on college campuses. *Newsweek* is running cover stories on "Bush and God." Recent books like Colleen Carroll's *The New Faithful* chronicle how young Christians are bringing their faith into professions as varied as entertainment and medicine. And John Schmalzbauer's *People of Faith* chronicles the reemergence of religion in journalism and social science. In fact, the public square seems much less naked lately.

But now that religion is back, the young faithful must decide how it should influence their political views. Neuhaus argued that there are at least two problems with the marriage of Christianity and politics. First, the church becomes a servant to its political affiliations, a temptation, Neuhaus does not hesitate to point out, to which liberal churches are equally susceptible. The second is the tendency toward theocracy, "in which . . . religion claims to embody and authoritatively articulate absolute truth," a problem Neuhaus calls "idolatry."

It is clear that religious college students today recognize these twin dangers. So what do they think is the proper relationship between religion and politics? There are lively debates on the death penalty at many of the religious campuses I visit. It is certainly a dividing issue among students at Catholic schools. Ave Maria student Christopher McGowan explains, "On our faculty, we have deans that are on opposite sides of the issue, we have faculty members who are on opposite sides of this issue, and we have priests who are on opposite sides of this issue."

In terms of abortion, which once was, and, arguably still is, the national flashpoint in this question of the relation between religion and politics, the attitude of students at Ave Maria Law School is instructive. At the time of my visit, a few students have been regularly picketing the church of attorney general Jennifer Granholm, a pro-choice Catholic running for governor. According to professor Richard Myers, "Her husband actually passed out literature on the steps of their church, standing next to the pastor," expressing her views on abortion. The students have been trying to get the cardinal in Detroit to explain that her position is not an authentically Catholic one. In a First Amendment class at Ave Maria, professor Scott Gaylord discusses a recent Ninth Circuit decision regarding whether pro-life groups have a right to put up "Wanted" posters for abortion doctors even though similar publicity has resulted in other doctors being killed. The students do not bring in their personal views of abortion, but argue from both sides of the case.

Though religious college students are certainly more inclined to be pro-life than their secular counterparts, the desire to make abortion illegal is not universally felt. At Notre Dame, where several busloads of students travel each year to Washington, D.C. for a march on the anniversary of *Roe v. Wade,* I meet a number of students who are less than sure of their position on the issue. At Baylor, where most of the student body opposes abortion, there was a lot of disagreement last year, according to newspaper editor John Drake, over "a huge anti-abortion display on campus that showed some aborted fetuses." The paper, Drake reports, "was flooded with letters even from people who agreed with the views expressed but thought the display was offensive."

Despite what seems like a thoughtful approach on the part of students to the issue, James Bratt, who teaches political science at Calvin, worries that his students are casting their votes using abortion as the litmus test. He points out, "You would have to hunt high and low to find any kind of antiabortion statement in the Scripture." On the other hand, he notes, "You will find a lot of concern about money and about care for the poor. That doesn't mean that Jesus and the prophets are necessarily socialists, but for them, the [measure] of a righteous people, of a good society is how well are the poor and needy and defenseless taken care of. I find that a lot more compatible with the Democratic Party agenda than with the Republican Party agenda."

And Bratt is certainly part of a new liberal group of professors and students on evangelical campuses. Sarah Franklin, a member of Wheaton's student government, estimates that her classmates vote Republican by a 70 to 30 margin, compared with her parents' generation, which, she tells me, was probably closer to 90 to 10. But this only tells part of the story. As Calvin professors James Penning and Corwin Smidt document in *Evangelicalism: The Next Generation,* the percentage of students on these campuses identifying as Republicans dramatically increased between 1982 (when James Davison Hunter conducted his survey) and 1996 from 51 to 71 percent. The number of self-identified moderates fell from 49 to 18 percent and just about all of those moved into the conservative or "very conservative" categories.

But to reduce the change in evangelical attitudes toward politics to these numbers is too simplistic. Indeed, the change was not a push in one direction. While the percentage of students favoring a ban on all abortions decreased to 50 from 55 percent, the number that favored the death penalty for murderers increased to 59 from 47 percent. Support for an increase in defense spending fell, but support for "government social programs as a way to deal with social problems" rose in the same period.

The picture at other religious colleges is also in flux. Catholics, who have historically voted Democratic, have started to favor Republicans. A similar shift has taken place among many Orthodox Jews. Earlier Jewish generations of Jews who think of the Democratic Party as the one that rescued them from the Depression and the evils of Nazi-occupied Europe, have been replaced by their observant children and grandchildren who favor the Republican stance on school-voucher programs and a more cautious approach to stem-cell research, for instance.

All of this rethinking of party affiliations has provided for lively and thoughtful political debate on religious campuses. And faculty members are trying to encourage that. They note that religious students are not just trying to figure out how many of a political party's positions match up with biblical mandates, but believe there are other conceptions of how religion should influence politics. Mike Leroy, a political science professor who taught at William and Mary before landing at Wheaton, explains, "There are going to be multiple and highly contingent models of a Christian in politics." In his own classes, Leroy tells me, he is "trying to foster the model St. Augustine gives in *The City of God,* where Christians are pilgrims. . . . We're here. We're engaged in the world. There is work to be done and government can be used as a tool for the good of all, not just Christians."

But, as Leroy notes, "There are few specific biblical guidelines of what the good of all is. There are some, but they don't fit nicely into our political system. Those basic things would be, for example, the value of life and the care of and concern for the poor. How do we serve and minister to those needs?" But Leroy emphasizes, "It would never be the job of government to make more Christians. That's the job of the church and the job of believers. If we get into a kind of government-mandated faith, we have no faith."

But what about issues like same-sex marriage? If homosexuality is considered sinful no matter who practices it, then shouldn't Christians do everything in their power to discourage such behavior? Leroy acknowledges "that the scriptures are fairly clear on behavioral norms for sexuality and . . . that homosexuality is outside those boundaries." But, he continues:

> *What the Bible doesn't tell us is whether this is a rule of living that the government should enforce or a rule of life that Christians enforce. There are faithful evangelical Christians who would say that the laws of the land need to reflect that biblical norm and there are other Christians who say, "No, we can't confuse civil law with the law of God. What we need is to allow civil law to create its own laws but we need to preserve the integrity of Christian marriage. If the government wanted to allow gay marriage that's fine because it would create an important distinction between what it is to be married in the church and what it means to be married under governmental law. [Legalizing homosexual marriage] could strengthen the Christian conception of marriage."*

The Mormon understanding of the line between religious and civil law is not as defined, and there are few students at Brigham Young who would take up Leroy's position on gay marriage, but, like their counterparts at Wheaton, they would also hesitate to use the Bible as a checklist for political stances. Though BYU students are social conservatives, there is also a libertarian streak running through the community. Many Mormons, in other words, elect officials based not on what the government can do to shape the morality of citizens or to take care of them financially, but rather with a view to who will limit the government's power.

Though Utah is often seen as a kind of Mormon theocracy striving to be apart from the rest of the country—the Mormon Church sets up its own hospitals, farms, food-processing plants, charitable organizations, etc.—the students coming out of Brigham Young feel a strong sense of duty to the country as a whole. Alan Wilkins, the vice president for academic affairs, believes that Mormon students must be inculcated with this duty in order to prevent the disasters of their past from recurring. Teaching students about the conflicts between Mormons and other American settlers (which eventually led to the murder of their leader, Joseph Smith), Wilkins notes, "If you step back and look at it sociologically, here is a people who move to the frontiers of the U.S., who believe that they have the truth and look pretty insular, economically, politically, and socially." That kind of insularity, Wilkins argues, put Mormons in a dangerous position. "Boy, should we learn our lesson. For us not to be a part of the United States, not to mention the world, in terms of being good citizens . . . we have to be a part of that."

There are some BYU students, like Andrea Uale, who worry that politics can be a corrupting influence on the people who become involved in it, but she and many of her classmates seem determined to do it anyway. Andrea explains, "You need people to go into politics to raise the standards."

On September 11, 2001, BYU was already scheduled to have campuswide devotional. When news of the terrorist attacks reached Provo, the planned speaker was canceled and twenty thousand students filed into the Marriott Center to hear the school's leaders try to make sense of the tragedy. After the pledge of allegiance, an opening prayer, and a hymn, the school's president, Merrill Bateman, took to the stage. His brief speech emphasized "the eternal perspective. Even though we live in troubled times," he acknowledged, "it is possible for each of us to feel peace. One of the greatest things we can do is celebrate the message of the gospel. We have seen this morning how fleeting life can be." Finally, he emphasized to students, "The world depends on you young people. The world's peace is on your shoulders. You have the only message that gives hope."

At religious colleges, almost all students attended prayer services to honor those killed in the attacks and to ask for God's guidance for America's leaders. Lou Nanni, an administrator at Notre Dame, which held a mass for several thousand, explains, "When a tragedy like this occurs, we do the one thing we know how to do as a Catholic university—gather in prayer." In addition to their religious services, students at Bob Jones immediately organized a mission trip to New York City, bringing clothes and supplies, but also offering spiritual counsel to the survivors.

There were some visible effects of the attacks months after they occurred. At Wheaton, Mike Leroy tells me, the political science department quickly got another fifteen majors. Also, whereas there used to be twenty newspapers or so left in a stack in the department office at the end of the day, now Leroy tells me, it's more like five or six. When *Wall Street Journal* reporter Daniel Pearl was tortured and killed in Pakistan, the students at Soka University renamed the campus paper *The Pearl* in his memory. Literature professor Ken Saragosa tells me, "The students really feel they're a part of world events. They want to be people who can exert a positive influence in how humanity is responding to things at this moment."

The schools' religious missions provided spiritual solace, and though secular colleges certainly held a wide variety of religious services, there is a particular kind of solidarity and, perhaps, comfort, created when everyone on a campus is praying to the same God for the same thing. It is something that I noticed more as an outsider than even individuals within the community might have. Anyone who has sat in on the religious service of another group will know what I mean. It gives you not simply a sense of being excluded (which is surely not what they intended for me) but a longing to be in a group like that of your own.

The conversations about September 11 at religious colleges were also different. At schools like Ave Maria and Southern Virginia, the study of philosophers like Aristotle and theologians like St. Augustine and Thomas Aquinas gives students a ground for moral and political reflection considerably deeper than the cafeteria-style offerings of most secular schools. Students at religious schools thus seem more likely to react to current events not by indulging in antiestablishment feelings but by considering the "just war" doctrine developed by theologians and jurisprudential thinkers over a millennium.

But their conversations are not all hypothetical. Asked what he thinks about U.S. retaliation for the terrorist attacks, Christopher McGowan, an Ave Maria student, replies: "Tom Paine was pretty much on the money: 'Those who expect to reap the blessings of freedom must, like men, undergo the fatigue of supporting it.'" Chris speaks with some experience. Before coming to the Catholic school, he served five years in the National Guard.

Since the September 11 attacks, the divide between religious and secular colleges has become ever more evident. Harvard still bans ROTC from its campus; Wesleyan students have held teach-ins on "Cultures of Masculinity and Militarism in the U.S."; and some Berkeley students formed a "Stop the War" coalition. Meanwhile, at Bob Jones University three students have left to join the military; several students at Southern Virginia University are seriously considering enlisting; and ROTC students at Brigham Young University are wearing their uniforms even when not training. Many of these students have role models in the faculty and administration. Two days after the planes hit the World Trade Center, Joseph Falvey, a professor and administrator at Ave Maria, was called up for active duty as a lieutenant colonel in the U.S. Marine Corps.

Why the divide? According to Damon Linker, a former professor at Brigham Young, the students there have "tremendous respect for legitimate authority." Andrea Uale, Brigham Young's student vice president, explains: "The religious aspect of the school makes you channel your energies differently. Instead of starting a protest, you work to raise awareness of issues." But it is not just blind obedience that encourages patriotism at religious colleges. At Ave Maria, says Chris, "We talk about how this nation's history is rooted in a respect for religious freedom. You cannot separate the two." Students at religious colleges are obviously interested in politics, but they seem to possess a sense of purpose separate from it. Politics will never be the cause they sell themselves to.

The marches against the war in Iraq were much larger than those against American retaliation in Afghanistan. But again, students at strongly religious colleges did not join in any significant way. Even at Soka University, where many of the students count themselves pacifists, Dean Fred Balitzer tells me that September 11 was a sort of wakeup call for them, and many began to support American retaliation, if not "preemptive" action.

Some pacifist elements also popped up at Catholic universities. Pax Christi groups at both Notre Dame and Fordham organized rallies against the war. These students were following the lead of the Pope who himself opposed the U.S.-led invasion. Notre Dame professor Rev. Michael Baxter has been waging a campaign to get rid of ROTC on his university's campus.

At the two Jewish schools, Israel constitutes the primary reason for political activity. Students at Touro and Yeshiva recently participated in pro-Israel marches in New York City and Washington, D.C. They read Israeli newspapers, and the Israel group is the extracurricular club with the largest membership on Yeshiva's campus. In addition to the attachment these Orthodox youth share with other American Jews to the state of Israel, many of these students plan to move to Israel when they are done with school. And most have family members who are already there. Student interest in Israel often outweighs concern with domestic politics.

Shmuel Auman, a junior at Touro, tells me, "A lot of guys here, I think, couldn't care less about America one way or the other."

His classmate Ari Lasker notes, "Some people here feel they have more of a civic responsibility to Israel. I guess they feel it's their homeland." As for Lasker, he tells me, "I feel at home here in America. I'm treated fine here. I guess to an extent religious Jews are being treated here better than they're being treated in Israel."

In November 2002, with the governor's race in Massachusetts in a dead heat, candidate Mitt Romney, like many of his GOP predecessors, tried to eke out a victory by touting conservative fiscal policies and hoping no one would ask him about anything else. But Romney—a former chief executive of Bain Capital, a rescuer of the Salt Lake City Olympics and one of the country's most prominent Mormons—found it was not that simple. Just before the election, the *Boston Globe* asked how, as a graduate of Brigham Young University, he could reconcile his financial support of his alma mater with his statements opposing discrimination against homosexuals. BYU bans homosexual behavior by its students and faculty.

Romney replied: "BYU is a religiously oriented university. I just don't think religion should be part of a campaign." Not exactly a forceful response. Presumably Romney had been advised to make it clear to voters that, if elected, he would not run Massachusetts as a Mormon protectorate, rewriting the laws to reflect the rules of the Church of Jesus Christ of Latter-Day Saints.

But the pressure for Romney to condemn BYU didn't let up. Scott Abbot, a former BYU professor, rehashed (in the *Boston Globe*) charges brought against the school five years ago by the American Association of University Professors. Abbot cited, among other things, the denial of a tenure-track position to a professor who had spoken at pro-choice rally and the denial of tenure to another whose academic writings criticized the church's views on women. Abbot blamed Romney in part because his $1 million gift to BYU's business school, given just months after the AAUP report, "lessened the moral force of the AAUP's censure." BYU's trustees and administrators, Abbot lamented, "could easily read Romney's gift as a statement that women's reproductive rights, gay and lesbian issues, and academic freedom were not issues of consequence to donors like Romney."

BYU's honor code—which includes regulations for appropriate dress and a ban on all premarital sex (not just the homosexual variety)—is based on the rules of the Mormon Church, and BYU, a private university, is under no legal obligation to change them. The school seems to be on firm moral ground as well: It allows any qualified student to enroll, regardless of sexual orientation—or, for that matter, religious affiliation. It merely asks that students respect the divine laws of the Church. As for academic freedom, BYU is well within bounds. Religious colleges—particularly those sponsored directly by a church—have no legal duty to hire or grant tenure to professors who criticize the church or its policies. Nor is there any reason that a religious college should let its students engage in practices that violate the tenets of its sponsoring faith. The case was a simple one for Mr. Romney to make. But he kept silent.

It is no small concern at religious colleges that when their graduates enter the secular world—especially the world of politics—they will clam up. It's not just that, as was the case with Romney, they won't defend the practices of their alma maters, but that they won't defend the place of their religious beliefs in the public square. Since his election, though, Romney has been far from a disappointment to his community. For example, he said during the campaign that he favored some protections for gay couples, but that he would not support gay marriage. And sure enough when the Massachusetts Supreme Judicial Court ruled it was unconstitutional for the state not to allow homosexuals to marry, Romney balked. He announced he would accept a civil unions bill but would work hard to pass a constitutional amendment banning gay marriage. Even in the face of one of the most liberal legislatures and courts in the country, Romney seems steadfast.

Romney again took the media by surprise when he forced veteran politician William Bulger out of his post as president of the University of Massachusetts when it became clear that Bulger was withholding from the FBI information on the whereabouts of his gangster brother. Romney decided this was not acceptable behavior for a public figure, no matter how many decades he had been in state government. The *Boston Globe* recently assessed the governor's tenure in an article titled "Understanding the Gentleman Warrior." The author notes, "As Romney rounds the turn into his second year in office, this much is clear: The private-sector chief executive turned public-sector CEO is unlike anything Beacon Hill has seen before. He's an outsider who takes his campaign promises as his governing instructions, [and] a reformer who insists that the old days of the wink-and-nod deal are dead." Noting some of the controversies Romney has faced, the article concludes,

"Through it all, Romney, who early in the year seemed palpably skittish at times, has evolved into a happy political warrior, ready, willing, able, and eager to join a war of ideas."

Thanks to the example of Romney, as well as others like Wheaton graduate and U.S. House Speaker Dennis Hastert, religious college graduates in this younger generation do have personal models of how faith can influence a political career. They are much less likely to suggest, as Romney tried to do, that religion does not belong in a political debate. How and to what extent these young men and women believe faith should enter the public square will vary widely among them, but their educations, both inside and outside the classroom, have already given them much food for thought.

CONCLUSION

"Have you visited any Muslim colleges?"

Given the events of the last few years, it's not surprising that this is one of the questions I have been asked most often during the course of my research for this book. But the answer is surprising. Despite an estimated population of some four million Muslims in the U.S., Muslim higher education is virtually nonexistent. The only Muslim post-secondary schools are a radical seminary near Los Angeles, a couple of graduate programs in Virginia, and a school of twenty students focusing on computer science and Islam in Chicago. "You're not going to find anything like the model of Notre Dame or Yeshiva University," says Khaled abou El-Fadl, a professor of law at UCLA and a Muslim. "The reality is pretty abysmal."

What's the explanation for this? Some scholars cite the organizational difficulties that arise from the diversity of ethnicities and languages within Islam. Would Sunni Muslims from Pakistan unite in an educational enterprise with Shi'a Muslims from Morocco? Others say the reason for the moribund state of Muslim higher education in America is that as an immigrant group, Muslims are still relative newcomers lacking in the wealth needed to found a major college. But many deny that money is the issue. Nader Hashemi, who is writing a dissertation at the University of Toronto on secularism, democracy, and Islam, remarks: "The money is there. There are a lot of affluent doctors and engineers in the community. They are willing to spend money on lavish weddings . . . or fund-raisers to fight discrimination, but to transfer resources to and appreciate the value of a liberal education, that hasn't sunk in."

Perhaps the biggest obstacle to the creation of a Muslim college in America is the fact that Muslims are increasingly attending good secular schools. Many of the most prominent religious universities in this country were formed in response to discrimination against particular religious minorities (e.g., through old quota systems in college admissions which limited the number of Jews or Catholics who could enroll). What incentive do Muslims have to form their own college in the absence of such discrimination? What could such a college do for the community?

El-Fadl suggests one obvious benefit: Such an institution could help Muslims worldwide (whose own universities are typically overseen by authoritarian governments) to rediscover their ancient intellectual traditions. Fouad Ajami, the director of the Middle East Studies program at Johns Hopkins, agrees that there is much more to Islamic thought than today's fundamentalist imams would have one believe. "Do they know anything about Islamic thought in the Andalusian world? Do they know about the Islamic skeptics and philosophers who honored the life of the mind and knew life should be lived in harmony with your fellow man even if they are irreligious?"

Truth be told, though, almost every scholar that I spoke to immediately expressed concern that a Muslim university could be easily coopted by radicals. But there are other anxieties as well. Hashemi, who describes himself as "a strong believer in the public education system," worries that Muslims going to their own schools "might create a ghetto mentality." And Ajami is skeptical of the idea of a Muslim institution of higher education altogether. "The Muslims need to keep it simple. They need to focus on assimilation."

But total and immediate assimilation seems unlikely, and perhaps even un-American. As James Q. Wilson, professor of political science at Pepperdine University, wrote in a recent City Journal article titled "The Reform Islam Needs," "the West has mastered the problem of reconciling religion and freedom, while several Middle Eastern nations have not." In fact, this reconciliation is a continuing process even in the U.S. today, and one that religious colleges and universities help facilitate. "Having American institutions Americanizes people," explains Daniel Pipes, director of the Middle East Forum. Religious colleges can help to bring the values of open intellectual inquiry and democracy into faith communities that might otherwise have remained isolated. The colleges described in this book should provide models of what a Muslim college could look like and accomplish. And maybe it is not unreasonable to hope that a future generation of Muslims in the U.S. will see the benefits that religious colleges have provided other faith communities and take these lessons to heart.

What will they see? First, the students who attend religious colleges in America are not what outsiders imagine. Few of them had their college choices dictated for them by overprotective parents. Whether they come from public, private, or religious schools, or a homeschooling environment, these young men and women are choosing religious colleges for themselves. Indeed, at a few of these schools, like Notre Dame and Yeshiva, the students represent the most spiritually interested and morally serious element of the school. Once installed at religious universities, the administration and faculty devote enormous effort to forming the intellectual and moral character of students. Students are challenged intellectually to deepen their faith in an environment that values both the life of the spirit and the life of the mind. The education is formulated to help students develop a religious worldview that will hold up in their years after graduation.

It is easy to see the temptations pulling religious college students in a more secular, less distinctive direction. Some of these cultural influences, like feminism, have been successfully negotiated, with religious college graduates reaching a sort of sophisticated accommodation to modernity. But there are other areas of conflict between secular culture and religious beliefs where it is not clear that accommodation is possible or even desirable. The influence of postmodernism, for example, is slowly seeping into religious higher education, threatening to undermine the very idea that there is religious truth. Secular understandings of the purpose of community service combined with an era in which explicit proselytizing is seen as backward, if not offensive, tempt religious schools into covering over their greatest motivation for engaging in service. And contemporary ideas about solving problems of racial inequality threaten to render ineffectual the potential of religious colleges to use faith as a racial unifier.

Given these dangers, it is not surprising that some religious colleges try to insulate themselves and their students from the broader culture. What better way to hold off against these secularizing influences than to erect fences to keep them out? Banning movies, television, modern music, or contemporary fiction may seem effective means of shutting out morally debilitating influences in the broader secular society. But the fence doesn't just keep outsiders out; it keeps insiders in. The religious college graduates who will be most successful in influencing secular society are those that engage in "cultural discernment," helping their students to form judgments about what is worthwhile in the general culture. And the administrations that keep this principle in mind when monitoring students' behavior are also most likely to produce graduates who are comfortable interacting in the secular world. The most successful of these colleges set their moral standards high, discipline students in proportion to the infraction committed and with an eye to the principles of repentance and forgiveness, and conduct serious and open discussions about the religious basis for campus rules. Students cannot simply be taught to avoid the areas of conflict. They must be able to speak thoughtfully about issues like feminism, homosexuality, religious and racial diversity, and postmodernism, addressing the social, cultural, and political forces that have engendered enormous changes in American life over the past four decades.

If religious college leaders can navigate between the dangers of secularization and isolation, these schools can more effectively transmit their ideas to a larger American audience. Even if administrators at a school like Bob Jones may represent exposure to the broader culture as simply a means to more effective proselytization, the truth is that effective religious higher education can serve American society as a whole by contributing thoughtful and community-minded citizens, whose religious beliefs strengthen the causes of civic commitment, moral decency, and family stability.

As I hope the foregoing pages have demonstrated, the widely held notion that the members of strongly religious communities in America are somehow intellectually backward is a myth. Devotion to the idea that "the glory of God is intelligence" is ubiquitous among religious colleges, and the schools disproportionately require students to complete a rigorous traditional core curriculum, at the same time that the curricula of their secular rivals have often been watered down. High grades alone do not bring them satisfaction—they hunger for real knowledge, not a padded résumé—and low grades do not send them scurrying to renegotiate—they have too much respect for their professors. Not only are these intellectually curious students typically engaged at a high level of scholarship, faculty at religious colleges are being taken more seriously by their secular colleagues. While the intellectual rigor of many evangelical colleges has developed only in recent decades, other strongly religious institutions like Brigham Young and Thomas Aquinas are now gaining the recognition they deserve. After decades in which religious college grads have been matriculating to top graduate schools and taking positions at prominent universities, and in which their professors have been offering valuable contributions to their respective disciplines, the message is finally getting through.

In business, law, and medicine, religious college graduates are also bringing something distinctive—a sense of vocation. Though these students are not the only ones who work hard in school, it certainly seems that a disproportionate number of them do. And it's clear that they plan to carry that same sense of purpose to their professions. Spending time in college trying to figure out what God is calling them to accomplish means not only that these young men and women will be particularly devoted to their careers, but also have a particular sense of how that vocation should be carried out. Religious college graduates are more likely to have studied the specific ethi-

260

cal dilemmas they will face when they enter these professional fields and the answers they will offer. Alumni of religious colleges are exactly what businesses and graduate schools claim to be seeking—well-rounded, engaged young men and women who want to make a difference in their communities.

On a cultural level, there is no question that religious college graduates will be the vanguard of a more conservative generation. But it will not be the conservatism of their parents and grandparents. While religious students still focus highly on marriage and family, they have assimilated contemporary attitudes on the role of women in the society (while arguably taking better account of women's actual goals and desires than more doctrinaire feminist groups do). Similarly, today's religious college students are more tolerant of homosexuality than their past counterparts: While still regarding homosexual behavior as sinful, this does not entail personal contempt for gays. And religious colleges' efforts to redress historic racial inequalities and to overcome the racial tensions that characterized some of their campuses in the past are in earnest. Where some fundamentalists once found a mandate in the Bible for racist policies, today's religious college graduates see a mission to heal racial wounds. Their attitudes toward members of other faiths are similarly respectful and interested. Although evangelicals, Mormons, and some Catholics still hope to convert their neighbors, they have found that even that goal is better achieved by example than by public campaigns of proselytization.

And where will religious college graduates fall in politics? They have a more nuanced understanding of the relationship between church and state than either the religious right of the eighties, which sometimes seemed to want to merge the two, or militant secularists who have added so many bricks to the "wall of separation" that people standing on one side can't even see the other. Not only do they accept the inevitable gap between religious and secular law in a liberal, constitutional republic, they appreciate the religious freedom that our political system provides. Far from withdrawing from civic commitment, the graduates of today's religious college are often first in line to serve their country through everything from military service to providing for the poor. Contrary to the occasional claims of militant secularists that American religious traditionalists and fundamentalists somehow embody the same sort of danger to freedom and tolerance that Islamic radicalism does, the scores of young men and women I have presented in this book demonstrate by their example the truth of Tocqueville's observation that the spirit of religion harmonizes with the spirit of liberty in this country in a way that enhances both.

Although America's most seriously religious colleges have an evangelical mission, it is a broader one that that of spreading their faith. Today's "missionary generation" seeks to enhance the ethical core of American life, combating the tendencies toward individualism and materialism against which thoughtful observers since Tocqueville have warned. If the perpetuation of liberty depends on the continued propagation of virtues like integrity, loyalty, courage, charity, and self-restraint, then America's religious colleges will be a vital component in this country's future. Those schools that succeed best at integrating serious spiritual and intellectual education may even help bridge the recent divide between Red and Blue America.

The following is a list of schools I have visited that are discussed in *God on the Quad*.

Mormon
Brigham Young University
Southern Virginia University

Catholic
University of Notre Dame
Fordham University
Thomas Aquinas College
Christendom College
Ave Maria School of Law
Magdalen College
Thomas More College of Liberal Arts

Evangelical (nondenominational)
Gordon College
Westmont College
Wheaton College
Patrick Henry College
Regent University (law school, business school, education school)

Evangelical (Baptist)
Baylor University

Evangelical (Reformed)
Calvin College

Fundamentalist
Bob Jones University

Buddhist
Soka University

Jewish
Touro College (Lander College for Men, Lander College for Women)
Yeshiva University (Yeshiva College)

SUGGESTED READINGS

Bartlett, Robert, "Souls Without Longing," *The Public Interest,* Winter 2003

Benne, Robert, *Quality with Soul: How Six Premier Colleges and Universities Keep Faith with Their Religious Traditions*

Blumhofer, Edith, editor, *Religion, Education, and the American Experience*

Brooks, David, "One Nation, Slightly Divisible," *Atlantic Monthly,* December 2001

Buckley, William F., *God and Man at Yale*

James Burtchaell, *The Dying of the Light: The Disengagement of Colleges and Universities from Their Christian Churches*

Colleen Carroll, *The New Faithful: Why Young Adults Are Embracing Christian Orthodoxy*

Colson, Charles, and Richard John Neuhaus, editors, *Evangelicals and Catholics Together: Toward a Common Mission*

Cherry, Conrad, Betty A. DeBerg, and Amanda Porterfield, *Religion on Campus*

Dovre, Paul J., editor, *The Future of Religious Colleges*

Eck, Diana, *A New Religious America: How a "Christian Country" Has Become the World's Most Religiously Diverse Nation*

Gurock, Jeffrey S., *The Men and Women of Yeshiva: Higher Education, Orthodoxy, and American Judaism*

Helmreich, William B., *The World of Yeshiva: An Intimate Portrait of Orthodox Jewry*

Himmelfarb, Gertrude, *One Nation, Two Cultures*

Hunter, James Davison, *Evangelicalism: The Coming Generation*

Kors, Alan Charles, and Harvey A. Silverglate, *The Shadow University: The Betrayal of Liberty on America's Campuses*

Marsden, George M., *Understanding Fundamentalism and Evangelicalism*

Neuhaus, Richard John, *The Naked Public Square: Religion and Democracy in America*

Newman, John Henry, *The Idea of a University*

Noll, Mark, *The Scandal of the Evangelical Mind*

Ostling, Richard and Joan, *Mormon America: The Power and the Promise*

Penning, James M., and Corwin E. Smidt, *Evangelicalism: The Next Gerneration*

Schmalzbauer, John, *People of Faith: Religious Conviction in American Journalism and Higher Education*

Soloveitchik, Joseph B., *The Lonely Man of Faith*

Steinfels, Peter, *A People Adrift: The Crisis of the Roman Catholic Church in America*

Sterk, Andrea, editor, *Religion, Scholarship, and Higher Education: Perspectives, Models and Future Prospects*

Whitehead, Barbara Dafoe, *Why There Are No Good Men Left*

Wolfe, Alan, *The Transformation of American Religion*

Wolfe, Alan, "The Opening of the Evangelical Mind," *Atlantic Monthly*, October 2000

INDEX